Foreign Economic Policy of the United States

Outstanding Studies and Dissertations

Stuart Bruchey
University of Maine
General Editor

A GARLAND SERIES

DATE DUE

MAR 14 1994 FEB 13 2008	

FOREIGN ECONOMIC POLICY OF THE UNITED STATES

A Dollar to Poland Is a Dollar to Russia

U.S. Economic Policy Toward Poland 1945–1952

SHELDON R. ANDERSON

GARLAND PUBLISHING, INC.
NEW YORK & LONDON • 1993

Library of Congress Cataloging-in-Publication Data

Anderson, Sheldon R., 1951–
A dollar to Poland is a dollar to Russia : U.S. economic policy toward Poland, 1945–1952 / Sheldon R. Anderson.
p. cm. — (Foreign economic policy of the United States)
Originally presented as the author's thesis (Ph. D.).
ISBN 0-8153-1108-7 (alk. paper)
1. Economic assistance, American—Poland. 2. Poland—Economic conditions—1945–1980. 3. United States—Commercial policy.
I. Title. II. Series.
HC340.3.A66 1993
338.9'1730438—dc20 92-40971
CIP

Printed on acid-free, 250-year-life paper
Manufactured in the United States of America

FOR MY PARENTS, OSCAR AND LEE

Contents

Preface

Many historians of American postwar diplomacy and the Cold War have assumed that American policy toward Poland and the rest of Eastern Europe was formulated solely on the basis of Soviet-American relations, especially after the Truman administration promoted aid for Greece and Turkey and advanced the Marshall Plan in 1947.[1] Of course, American policy toward Poland cannot be divorced from overall superpower relations, but the United States had different policies for each country in Eastern Europe, and the Eastern European countries had varying degrees of political and economic freedom from the Soviet Union.

In order to better understand the nuances of American, Polish, and Soviet foreign policy in the early postwar period, as well as Poland's role in the development of the Cold War, the record of Polish-American economic relations during the Truman administration warrants closer examination. Although there are several excellent works on American foreign policy toward Eastern Europe after the Second World War, little research has been done on American economic policy in Eastern Europe during the Truman administration.[2] Furthermore, this research has been characteristically one-sided; Western historians have been unable to use the documents from Eastern European archives that are essential to reconstruct a truer account of postwar diplomatic relations. Geir Lundestad, the author of one of the most comprehensive works on postwar American foreign policy toward Eastern Europe, introduces his study by noting that "how American actions influenced those of Soviet and Eastern European leaders will . . . not be dealt with to any significant extent."[3] In this study of postwar Polish and American economic diplomacy, I consider the objectives and actions of Poland's diplomats as well, and how their policies influenced American foreign policy. Hopefully this will provide a more balanced historical account of the early Cold War period, and will also construct a clearer picture of Soviet economic policy toward Poland.

Based on Polish as well as American sources, I argue that although Poland's political future was clearly in Stalin's hands, American officials did not recognize that for the first few years after the war, Poland exercised relative freedom from the Soviet Union in economic matters.[4] Many U.S. government officials thought that the Soviets were running the Eastern European economies for the benefit of the Soviet Union, and that the Eastern European countries would not cooperate with Western Europe after the Soviets mandated that Poland and Czechoslovakia reject the Marshall Plan. For example, the U.S. ambassador to Poland in 1947, Stanton Griffis, declared that giving any further economic assistance to Poland was a mistake because "a dollar to Poland is a dollar to Russia."[5] State Department counselor George Kennan, author of the "containment" policy, also overemphasized Soviet control over the Eastern European economies, arguing that if the Marshall Plan were by chance accepted by Eastern Europe, it could be used to force Eastern Europe to "abandon [the] near-exclusive Soviet orientation of their economies."[6]

Historians have often reflected this view of Eastern European diplomacy; few histories of American policy toward Eastern Europe continue beyond 1947, as though the Soviet bloc's refusal to participate in the Marshall Plan signalled the end of meaningful economic relations with the West, and was a final indication that the Eastern European countries were fully integrated satellites of the Soviet Union.[7] Of course, the Polish government had to have Moscow's approval to make any major economic decisions that affected Poland's economic and political sovereignty (such as Poland's participation in the Marshall Plan), but with few exceptions the Polish government ran its own economy for its own benefit.

Unlike the Soviets, Poland sought to increase its commercial contacts with the West after the war. But by 1947, most U.S. government officials assumed that the Soviets had a full-fledged satellite relationship with Poland. I contend that the Truman administration lost any influence that it might have had on the development of the Polish economy by denying Poland any more economic assistance after 1946. There is also evidence that the administration's strategic embargo of Poland and the Soviet bloc countries expedited the integration of Poland's economy into the Soviet bloc economic community. On the other hand, the U.S. embargo was not very successful in undermining Poland's military buildup, because until the early fifties the Polish government was quite successful in using the profits from coal exports to buy many of the embargoed goods in Western Europe.

I would like to thank Dr. Richard Rudolph and Dr. Kinley Brauer of the University of Minnesota for their helpful criticisms of the initial drafts of the book. I owe special thanks to former State Department officer David L. Smith, who made invaluable suggestions for organizational revisions and stylistic improvements. Dr. Gary O. Larson inspired me to write the book and assisted my research in Washington, D.C. I could not have completed this project without the help of Dr. Wojciech Roszkowski, his colleagues at the Warsaw School of Economics, Basia and Macek Roszkowski, and my friends at ASZ Lublin, all of whom made my research in Poland possible. Last but not least, I am especially grateful to my wife Kristie for her sustained support and encouragement.

NOTES

1. See Hans J. Morganthau, "The Containment Policy and the Rationale of the Alliance System," in *American Diplomacy in a New Era*, ed. Stephen D. Kertesz (South Bend: University of Notre Dame Press, 1961), 66; and George H. Glinka-Janczewski, "American Policy Toward Poland Under the Truman Administration, 1945-1952" (Ph.D. dissertation, Georgetown University Press, 1966), 320. Both Morganthau and Glinka-Janczewski disregard the nuances of Polish foreign policy that were different from Soviet policy, and the way American policy toward Poland differed from U.S. policy toward the other countries in Eastern Europe.

2. Geir Lundestad's *American Non-Policy Towards Eastern Europe, 1943-1947: Universalism in an Area not of Essential Interest to the United States* (Oslo: Universitetsforlaget, 1975) is the most thorough work on American policy toward Eastern Europe in the postwar period. Lundestad relies primarily on memoirs and the State Department's published documents in its series *Foreign Relations of the United States (FRUS)*. Another excellent study of American diplomacy toward Eastern Europe is Lynn E. Davis's *The Cold War Begins: Soviet American Conflict over Eastern Europe* (Princeton: Princeton University Press, 1974), as well as Bennett Kovrig's *The Myth of Liberation: East-Central Europe in U.S. Diplomacy and Politics Since*

1941 (Baltimore: The Johns Hopkins University Press, 1973). Kovrig focusses on the public illusion created by the American officials that the U.S. government considered Eastern Europe to be of primary importance at the conference table during the war, and that the United States would aid Eastern European independence movements after the war. American economic policy toward Eastern Europe is beyond the scope of his work. There are several important articles in the edited volume by Stephen Kertesz, *The Fate of East Central Europe: Hope and Failures of American Foreign Policy* (Notre Dame, Indiana: University of Notre Dame Press, 1956). Two published monographs that deal specifically with Polish-American relations after the Second World War are Richard C. Lukas's *Bitter Legacy: Polish-American relations in the Wake of World War II* (Lexington: University of Kentucky Press, 1982), and Piotr Wandycz's *The United States and Poland* (Cambridge: Harvard University Press, 1980). Lukas includes political relations from 1945 to 1947 and employs *FRUS* sources. Wandycz surveys the two-hundred year history of U.S.-Polish relations and includes a small and general section on the postwar period. Michael Boll, *The Cold War in the Balkans: American Foreign Policy and the Emergence of Communist Bulgaria, 1943-1947* (Louisville: The University of Kentucky Press, 1984), concentrates specifically on American postwar policy toward Bulgaria.

3. See Lundestad, *The American Non-Policy Towards Eastern Europe 1943-1947*, 31; see also John Lewis Gaddis, "The Emerging Post-Revisionist Synthesis on the Origins of the Cold War," *Diplomatic History* 7 (Summer, 1983): 187, who comments that historians "need to begin to consider, more than we have, the impact of U.S. policies on foreign countries."

4. See Bronisław Wojciechowski, "Handel Zagraniczny Polski" [The foreign trade of Poland], in *Gospodarka Polski Ludowej, 1944-1955* [The economy of Peoples' Poland], eds. Janusz Kalinski and Zbigniew Landau (Warsaw: Książka i Wiedza, 1986), 371; Norman Davies, *God's Playground: A History of Poland*, vol. 2: *1795 to the Present* (New York: Columbia University Press, 1982), 556; John N. Cable, "The United States and the Polish Question, 1939-1948," (Ph.D. dissertation, Vanderbilt University, 1972), 339; John N. Cable, "Arthur Bliss Lane: Cold Warrior in Warsaw, 1945-1947," *Polish American Studies* 30 (Autumn, 1973): 75; and Mieczysław Sokolowski, *Obroty zagraniczne Polski w okresie 1945-1958* [Foreign commerce of Poland

in the period 1945 to 1958] (London: Szkoła Nauk Politycznych i Społecznych, 1960), 1. Wojciechowski and Davies agree that the Polish Workers Party (PPR) and the Polish Socialist Party (PPS) had considerable autonomy in economic affairs. This view contrasts with Cable and Sokolowski, who exaggerate Soviet control over the Polish economy.

5. Griffis to Marshall, 15 October 1947, General Records of the Department of State, Records Group 59, State Department Decimal File, 860c.51, File 6385, National Archives, Washington D.C. (hereafter RG 59 with filing information); see Sheldon Anderson, "'A Dollar to Poland is a Dollar to Russia': United States Economic Diplomacy toward Poland, 1945-1950," *East European Quarterly* 26 (Spring 1992): 77-108.

6. John L. Gaddis, *Strategies of Containment: A Critical Appraisal of Postwar American National Security Policy* (Oxford: Oxford University Press, 1982), 66.

7. See Sheldon Anderson, "Poland and the Marshall Plan," *Diplomatic History* 15 (Fall 1991): 473-494.

Introduction

One of the principal causes of the Cold War after the Second World War was the Soviet-American conflict over the political and economic future of Eastern Europe. The United States was consistently frustrated in meeting its goal of establishing independent governments and Open Door market economies in the region, and the Soviet Union's military presence in Eastern Europe severely limited U.S. policy options to achieve these objectives. The Soviet domination of postwar governments in Eastern Europe was not a direct threat to U.S. security, however, and Washington never seriously considered using force to push the Soviets out of Eastern Europe or to ensure that Stalin fulfilled the agreements made at Yalta for "free and unfettered" elections.[1] But American protests to the Soviet government, threats of ending allied cooperation, and appeals to world opinion proved ineffective in reducing the communist grip on political power in Eastern Europe.

Many U.S. government officials thought that economic assistance was the only effective diplomatic means to further American objectives in Eastern Europe. The U.S. ambassador to the Soviet Union, Averell Harriman, told Secretary of State Cordell Hull in 1944 that economic aid offered "one of the most effective weapons at our disposal to influence European political events in the direction we desire and to avoid the development of a sphere of influence of the Soviet Union over Eastern Europe and the Balkans."[2] Shortly after the war ended, Elbridge Durbrow of the State Department's East European Division also argued that economic assistance was "the only real lever . . . to bring about any semblance of economic and political stability in East Europe."[3] Because of Europe's devastating human and material losses from the war, and the emergence of the United States as the world's foremost economic power, American officials were understandably optimistic that the United States could use trade, loans, and direct economic aid to impose its political and economic will on Eastern as well as Western Europe.

Poland seemed to be the ideal test case for this policy. The destruction of Poland was so complete that State Department officials thought that the chances were good that the Polish communist-dominated government would agree to relatively free elections and to other American political demands in order to receive economic assistance.[4] In addition, Harriman contended that the United States could demand Polish political independence because the Soviets also desperately needed American aid.[5] President Harry S. Truman himself overestimated the power of American economic diplomacy to influence the political development of Eastern Europe. Shortly after taking office in April 1945, Truman declared that "the Russians need us more than we need them."[6]

Poland was a crucible of allied cooperation for several reasons. The Soviet Union, the United States, and Great Britain had more political and economic interest in the fate of Poland than in the rest of Soviet-occupied Eastern Europe.[7] Soviet actions in Eastern Europe contradicted Anglo-American principles of freedom and self-determination embodied in Wilson's Fourteen Points, the Atlantic Charter, and the U.N. Charter. Great Britain had entered the Second World War in 1939 because of its guarantee of Polish independence, and naturally London wanted to reestablish an independent Polish state. Poland and the United States had a long history of warm, friendly relations, from the participation of Polish generals Kazimierz Pułaski and Tadeusz Kościuszko in the American Revolution to President Woodrow Wilson's support for the resurrection and recognition of independent Poland in 1918. Finally, official American protests over breaches of the Yalta and Potsdam agreements on Poland were influenced in part by the Polish population in the United States, which was significantly larger than any other Eastern European emigrant group. The Polish-American community's vociferous opposition to the undemocratic methods of the Polish government kept the issue of a free Poland on the American political agenda.[8]

Poland was important to the West for economic reasons as well. Poland was the largest country in Eastern Europe, and had the potential to become one of Western Europe's most important trading partners through the export of Polish agricultural goods and raw materials.[9] The acquisition of Silesia from Germany doubled Poland's coal resources,[10] and before the war the Silesian coal field's output per worker had always surpassed output in either the Ruhr or the British fields.[11] This coal was indispensable for the rapid reconstruction of Western Europe.[12]

Although Poland's trade with the United States in the interwar period was insignificant, the chances for more trade between the two countries after the war seemed promising. Poland needed American reconstruction assistance, and the Polish leadership recognized that the United States, not the Soviet Union, would be the primary source of economic aid.[13] Furthermore, the United States was interested in the Polish economy because Poland could supply raw materials and foodstuffs to Western Europe.[14]

Poland was also Stalin's primary political, economic, and strategic interest in Eastern Europe. Poland presented special problems for the Soviets. In contrast to Czechoslovakia (another "liberated" ally), Stalin feared that a democratically-elected Polish government would conduct an anti Soviet foreign policy. The amicable interwar and immediate postwar relations between Moscow and Prague contrasted with the historic animosity that existed between Russia and Poland. The Soviet invasion of Poland in 1939, the Soviet massacre of Polish officers in the Katyn Forest in 1940, and Soviet reluctance to assist the Polish Home Army uprising against the Germans in 1944 added to the bad feelings between the two countries. Consequently, Soviet controls over the Polish government were tighter from the start, but not as tight as American officials thought.

Polish-American economic relations during the Truman administration, which includes American relief efforts, Poland's loan negotiations with the U.S. Export-Import Bank and the International Bank for Reconstruction and Development (IBRD), and the American embargo of strategic exports to Poland, was characterized by misperceptions and a lack of policy coordination on both sides. Certainly one of the major flaws in American policy toward Poland was the Truman administration's exaggeration of the power of economic diplomacy.[15] The Polish communists were always true to their word that they would not make any political concessions to obtain economic assistance. In addition, American officials overestimated the Soviet Union's exploitation of the Polish economy. Although the Soviet Union increased its economic isolation from the West after the war, Poland's trade with Western Europe grew until the end of the decade. The Poles were also members of international economic organizations that the Soviet Union rejected. Even after 1947, Poland cooperated in the

IBRD, the International Monetary Fund (IMF), and the Food and Agricultural Organization (FAO).

The turning point in Polish economic relations with the West did not come in 1947, but in 1950 when the Polish government withdrew from the IBRD, the IMF, and the FAO. But even after 1950, when the United States was trying to prevent the flow of Western European goods to Poland and Poland was maneuvering to circumvent the embargo, Poland maintained a brisk trade with Western Europe.

The Polish communists were also guilty of many misperceptions of American foreign policy. They underestimated the Truman administration's keen interest in a democratically-elected Polish government. As one of the countries that had suffered the most at the hands of the Germans, most Polish officials were convinced that Poland would receive economic assistance from the United States and the IBRD because they thought that Poland had a moral right to it. Even after the Polish communists rejected the Marshall Plan, they thought that if the Germans received reconstruction aid, the United States would surely extend Poland economic assistance as well.

In addition, the Polish communists failed to understand that Congress would be reluctant to offer foreign aid to Soviet-occupied areas,[16] or that American business had a natural mistrust of socialist economies, especially given the dismal record of past economic relations with the Soviet Union. The Polish communists also did not foresee that the United States would play politics in international economic institutions such as the IBRD.

Furthermore, some strict Polish Marxists believed that the United States would be forced to loan money to Poland to help develop the entire European market for American products. The Marxists argued that this would be the Truman administration's strategy to stave off overproduction and unemployment in the United States. They thought that as long as the Polish government maintained a good credit standing and abided by international economic agreements, the Truman administration would overlook the Polish political situation when it made decisions on economic assistance.[17] The Polish leadership was genuinely surprised when the United States did not grant Poland any more loans after the spring of 1946, when relief aid stopped in the summer of 1947, and when the IBRD stonewalled any loans for Poland.

American economic policy toward Poland after the Second World War is another example of what many historians have criticized as the general incoherence of U.S. foreign policy toward Eastern Europe in the early postwar period.[18] Vacillations and conflicts within and between various branches of the U.S. government certainly undermined the realization of American foreign policy objectives in Poland. Although Lundestad's characterization of U.S. policy in Eastern Europe as a "non-policy" may be an exaggeration, until 1947 the Truman administration had no clear, well-coordinated economic policy for Poland.

Diplomacy cannot be satisfactorily judged, however, without understanding the Polish policies to which American officials were reacting. Polish foreign policy also lacked coordination until the communists consolidated control over the Polish government in 1948. Until then Washington received contradictory signals from Polish diplomats that contributed to the indecisiveness of American policy.[19] For example, the Truman administration did not expect the Polish communists to do anything to jeopardize much-needed economic aid,[20] but the communists' own economic diplomacy was compromised by their undemocratic methods and by their dependence on Soviet support for the western boundary of Poland.[21]

Differences within the Polish government over foreign economic policy contributed to the government's inability to present a clear and consistent policy to American officials. For the first three years after the war, the ruling coalition of the Polish Workers' Party (PPR) and the Polish Socialist Party (PPS) allowed meaningful debate on trade and aid issues, and considerable friction developed between the positions of the Polish diplomats, economists, and the party bosses. For example, the diplomats negotiating trade and aid agreements in Washington were often upset over the criticism of the United States that frequently appeared in the Polish press. Ambassador Griffis complained that Warsaw "has its left hand extended for help and the right hand is a fist constantly attacking the United States."[22] Some Polish economic advisors recognized the futility of asking for aid while at the same time their government was chastising the American capitalist economy and American policy in Europe.[23] Toward the end of the decade these officials lost their influence in the Polish government.

For the first seven years after the end of the Second World War, American foreign economic policy was largely unsuccessful in achieving its primary objectives. American economic diplomacy had little impact on political developments in Poland. After American economic assistance had failed to achieve its political objectives and the

Polish communist government had eliminated any opposition parties by 1948, the Truman administration adopted a position that strict economic sanctions best served American interests.[24] The U.S. embargo of strategic exports to Poland and the Soviet bloc was also relatively unsuccessful in achieving U.S. political goals, and it did little to undermine the Poland's military capacity.

On the other hand, Polish economic diplomacy did not fare much better. Despite its ideological differences with the greatest capitalist power, the Polish communist government tried to balance close relations with Moscow, its own quest for political control of Poland, and the need for American economic assistance and commercial links with the West. Although Poland was able to acquire small amounts of American credits and loans in 1946, after 1947 Poland no longer received economic assistance of any kind from the United States.

NOTES

1. Norman Graebner, *America as a World Power* (Wilmington, Delaware: Scholarly Resources, Inc., 1984), 96; and Robert A. Pollard, *Economic Security and the Origins of the Cold War, 1945-1950* (New York: Columbia University Press, 1985), 244.

2. George C. Herring Jr., *Aid to Russia, 1941-1946: Strategy, Diplomacy, and the Origins of the Cold War* (New York: Columbia University Press, 1973), 140, 153-154.

3. Herring, *Aid to Russia, 1941-1946*, 259.

4. See Lundestad, *The American Non-Policy Towards Eastern Europe 1943-1947*, 205, 332, 386; Boll, *The Cold War in the Balkans*, 192; and Lloyd C. Gardner, "Will the Real Mr.'X' Please Stand Up?" in *Containment and the Cold War: American Foreign Policy Since 1945*, ed. Thomas G. Paterson (Reading, Massachusetts: Addison-Wesley Publishing Co., 1973), 89. The Soviets would not allow their protégés to bargain away communist control anyway, and thus risk the formation of governments hostile to the Soviet Union. Few officials in Washington predicted that the Soviet leadership and the communists in Eastern Europe would force their people to undergo severe hardships rather than agree to make political concessions for economic assistance.

5. Davis, *The Cold War Begins: Soviet-American Conflict over Eastern Europe*, 219.

6. Memorandum of conversation, Truman, Hull, Harriman, etal., 20 April 1945, U.S. Department of State, *Foreign Relations of the United States*, 1945: *Europe* (Washington, D.C.: United States Government Printing Office, 1967), 5:232 (hereafter *FRUS* with year, volume number, and page); and Stephen E. Ambrose, *Rise to Globalism: American Foreign Policy 1938-1976* (New York: Penguin Books, 1976), 112.

7. See Matthews minutes of 6 February 1945 meeting of Churchill, Roosevelt and Stalin, *FRUS, 1945* (Washington D.C.: United States Government Printing Office, 1960), 1:677-679. Greece and Yugoslavia were of greater strategic and economic significance to London, but they were not occupied by the Red Army. See also Davies, *God's Playground*, 59. Davies, one of the foremost English-speaking historians of Polish history, claims that for the first year and a half after the war the United States and Great Britain took little interest in the activities of the Polish Provisional Government. Although both countries had more important foreign policy priorities in this period, they actively worked for a democratic Poland.

8. The politics of the Polish-American community will be dealt with in this study only insofar as the community influenced the U.S. government's economic policy toward Poland. In only a few instances did this community have any significant input into American policy, usually through the Congress. Furthermore, the Polish-American community was split on whether or not to afford the Polish government economic assistance and favorable trade status.

9. See Barton J. Bernstein, "Commentary," in *The Truman Period as a Research Field: A Reappraisal, 1972*, ed. Richard S. Kirkendall (Columbia, Missouri: University of Missouri Press, 1974), 169.

10. Wandycz, *The United States and Poland*, 308.

11. United Nations Relief and Rehabilitation Agency (UNRRA), Operational Analysis Papers, No. 7: *Foreign Trade in Poland* (London: 1946), 15.

12. Lloyd C. Gardner, *Economic Aspects of New Deal Diplomacy* (Madison: University of Wisconsin Press, 1964), 310.

13. Cable, "The United States and the Polish Question, 1939-1948", 336.

14. Pollard, *Economic Security and the Origins of the Cold War*, 138; and Centralny Urząd Planowania [Central planning office], *Sytuacja Gospodarcza Polski* [The economic situation of Poland]

(Warsaw, 1947), 122. American products accounted for 17 percent of the total value of all Polish imports in 1930. This figure dropped to only 12 percent by 1938. Polish goods also made little headway into the American market, accounting for only 6.9 percent of the value of all Polish exports in 1938. American holdings in Polish companies in 1938 amounted to less than one fourth of the value of all foreign properties in Poland.

15. Pollard, *Economic Security and the Origins of the Cold War, 1945-1950*, 247; and H. Bradford Westerfield, *The Instruments of America's Foreign Policy* (New York: Thomas Crowell Co., 1963), 264.

16. Westerfield, *The Instruments of America's Foreign Policy*, 281; David A. Baldwin, *Economic Development and American Foreign Policy, 1943-1962* (Chicago: The University of Chicago Press, 1966), 258; and Thomas G. Paterson, *On Every Front: The Making of the Cold War* (New York: W.W. Norton and Co.), 133. Paterson points out that Congress and the American public did not wholeheartedly support a $1 billion loan to the British in 1946.

17. Mieczysław Rakowski, *The Foreign Policy of the Polish Peoples' Republic* (Warsaw: Interpress Publishers, 1975), 61.

18. See Lundestad, *The American Non-Policy Towards Europe 1943-1947*; and Davis, *The Cold War Begins: Soviet-American Conflict over Eastern Europe*. Both authors are critical of the lack of a coordinated U.S. policy toward Eastern Europe; see also Glinka-Janczewski, "American Policy Toward Poland Under the Truman Administration, 382; some historians, among them Zbigniew Brzezinski, "How the Cold War Was Played," *Foreign Affairs* 51 (October, 1972): 182, see American policy becoming crystallized in 1947.

19. Włodzimierz T. Kowalski, "Poland and the Western Powers 1945-1947," *Polish Western Affairs* 8:1 (1967): 51.

20. Lukas, *Bitter Legacy: Polish-American Relations in the Wake of World War II*, 43.

21. Arthur R. Rachwald, "Poland Between the Superpowers: Three Decades of Foreign Policy," *Orbis* 20 (Winter 1977): 1056.

22. Wandycz, *The United States and Poland*, 333.

23. Cable, "The United States and the Polish Question, 1939-1948," 338.

24. Pollard, *Economic Security and the Origins of the Cold War, 1945-1950*, 57.

A Dollar to Poland
Is a Dollar to Russia

Chapter One

Obstacles to Economic Cooperation, 1945-1946

I

At the Yalta Conference of the Big Three in February 1945, Soviet leader Josef Stalin made a general promise to hold "free and unfettered elections" in Eastern Europe.[1] In the case of Poland, however, Stalin knew that a democratically-elected government would probably have an anti-Soviet character. He had no intention of adhering to the Yalta agreement on free elections. On the issue of Poland's border with Germany, President Franklin D. Roosevelt and British Prime Minister Winston Churchill eventually agreed to Polish occupation and administration of Germany to the Oder and Western Neisse Rivers. The Big Three agreed, however, that the final Polish-German border would be decided in the peace treaty with Germany. In return for this concession on Poland's borders, Stalin promised to include elements of the Polish government-in-exile in London and non-communists in Poland to form a new reconstituted provisional government. This government was to replace the communist-dominated Polish Committee of National Liberation (the Lublin Committee).[2] Stalin did not keep his side of the bargain on this issue either, and shortly after Roosevelt's death President Truman admonished Soviet Foreign Minister Vyacheslaw Molotov about Stalin's broken promises. Truman sent Harry Hopkins to Moscow in May to mediate a compromise, and Stalin agreed to a new coalition government known as the Provisional Government of National Unity.

Nonetheless, power remained in the hands of the Moscow-loyal Polish communists and socialists from the Committee of National Liberation. Among those holding the most important cabinet positions in the new government were Bolesław Bierut, Hilary Minc, and Jakub Berman from the Polish Workers' Party (PPR), and Józef Cyrankiewicz, head of the Polish Socialist Party (PPS). These four were among the leaders who effectively controlled the Polish government until 1956.[3] Only seven of the twenty-one cabinet posts were held by Polish Peasant Party (PSL) members, the most popular opposition party. The PSL never had a chance to share real power in the coalition government that lasted until fraudulent elections were held in January 1947.

At the Potsdam Conference in July-August 1945, allied discussions of Poland focussed on Poland's western border. In return for Stalin's promises to limit the Soviet Union's role in administering Italy, and to reduce Soviet claims on reparations from occupied enemy territories, the United States and Britain confirmed Poland's right to administer German territories up to the Western Neisse River. The Allied leaders also agreed that the Polish provisional government would govern Poland until elections were held.[4] Although real power in the Polish government was still held by the communists, and communist repression of the opposition continued, the Polish political situation was not a major issue at Potsdam. No one knew at Potsdam that the war with Japan would be over within a few days; Truman thought that all he could do for Poland was to get Stalin's pledge to hold free Polish elections. In fact, until the summer of 1946 the Truman administration sought to achieve short-term humanitarian and economic objectives through its economic policy toward Poland. Only in the fall of 1946 did the administration begin to exert more pressure on the Polish government to make political concessions in return for economic assistance.

II

When the war ended in May 1945, both American and Polish government officials were optimistic about the prospects for close economic cooperation between the two countries. The Truman administration fully expected to provide Poland with relief assistance and substantial loans to facilitate Poland's recovery and integration into the European economy. There was little doubt among the Soviet and Eastern European experts in the State Department that most of Poland's early postwar trade would be with the Soviet Union and Eastern Europe, despite the fact that Poland had traded primarily with Western Europe and the United States before the war.[5] In early 1945, the U.S.

ambassador to the Soviet Union, Averell Harriman, reported to Washington that "the bulk of [Poland's] exports [are] likely to go to the Soviet Union."[6] During Hopkins' mission to Moscow in May, he told Stalin that the United States had no significant economic interests in Poland.[7] Some officials in the Truman administration understood that because of Poland's lack of hard currency and adequate communications, that country had to engage almost exclusively in barter trade with neighboring countries for the next few months.[8]

Because of the immense task of reconstructing the Polish economy, American diplomats were overly optimistic that dollars could buy political concessions from the Polish government.[9] Over one third of Poland's wealth had been lost in the war, most of Warsaw lay in ruins, and half of the port installations at Gdansk and Gdynia were unusable. In the German territories occupied by Poland after the war, 90 percent of the livestock, 60 percent of the industrial capacity, and 45 percent of the urban housing had been destroyed.[10] Two years after the war the United Nations still found that Poland was in desperate need of foreign economic assistance: "Unless Poland is able to obtain foreign help she will have to face a long and arduous struggle both to feed her people adequately and to rebuild her war shattered economy."[11]

During negotiations in Moscow in June over the composition of the new Polish provisional government, Harriman informed the State Department that Bierut and his associates "desire and need American moral and economic support and are ready to establish closer and more frank relations than Molotov appears at present to wish." Bierut told Harriman that Poland had urgent needs for water, rail, and road transport, and port equipment and machinery for industrial development. Bierut also wanted to increase exports to the United States in order to repay American loans. Harriman told Bierut that in addition to supplying U.N. relief for Poland, the United States was "sympathetically disposed to assist" Poland through the IBRD or the U.S. Export-Import Bank.[12] Later that month Acting Secretary of State Joseph Grew relayed Harriman's cables to Truman in two memoranda, but the administration made no immediate decision on a loan for Poland.[13]

The Truman administration was groping around for a well-defined foreign economic policy at this point. Harriman and many others in the State Department were optimistic about using economic aid to achieve American political objectives. He argued that economic assistance would have

> a far reaching and permanent effect on the influence of the US in the political scene in Poland and particularly on our influence in connection with the carrying out of the final step in the Crimea [Yalta] decision, namely the holding of truly free elections.

Harriman thought that some immediate gesture of good will, such as an unconditional shipment of a few hundred U.S. Army surplus trucks to Poland, would bolster the position of the new non-communist members of the Polish government.[14] The Office of Strategic Services (OSS) also reported in the spring of 1945 that the chances for democracy in Poland would be "considerably brighter" if its industrialization were financed with foreign loans.[15]

Many Republicans agreed with the U.S. ambassador to Poland, Arthur Bliss Lane, that any American economic aid should be linked to a promise from the Polish government to hold free elections. On 19 July the *New York Times* reported that some influential members of the Foreign Policy Association, such as former President Herbert Hoover, Alf Landon, and John Dewey, had urged the president to demand political concessions from the Poles at Potsdam.[16] To the disappointment of Lane and these Republicans, Poland's political situation was not the primary interest of the administration's economic policy toward that country in 1945.[17] Faced with many other more pressing domestic and foreign policy problems in 1945, Truman thought that the appearance of free elections in Poland was more important than who actually participated in the government. But the American public, having supported a war to liberate Europe from tyranny, had to be placated for the time being.[18] On 22 May Truman noted in his diary what he hoped Hopkins could accomplish during his mission to Moscow: "Poland ought to have 'free elections,' at least as free as [Frank] Hague, Tom Pendergast, Joe Martin or [Robert A.] Taft would allow in their respective bailiwicks."[19]

Truman and Secretary of State James Byrnes intended to tell Soviet and Polish leaders at Potsdam that they fully expected the new Polish provisional government to hold free elections, but Truman and Byrnes were equally concerned with the short-term objectives of American economic policy toward Poland. The administration wanted to rebuild the Polish economy quickly so that Poland could contribute to the reconstruction of Europe as a whole. Shortly before the Potsdam

Conference, Byrnes told Lane that the United States would entertain proposals of dollar payments for Polish exports, especially coal. He added that plans were being made to supply Poland with 1000 army surplus trucks.[20]

Polish Minister of Industry Hilary Minc developed economic policy for the Polish government. Minc planned to socialize the Polish economy, but not necessarily on the Soviet model. According to Czesław Bobrowski, the Socialist Party member who headed the Central Planning Office, Minc did not have a preconceived plan of economic development for the first few years after the war other than that the economy would be based on a combination of state, cooperative, and private enterprises.[21] Although he was a loyal Stalinist and confirmed Marxist, Minc was also a realist.[22] He hoped to maintain economic connections with the West and sought to normalize trade relations with the United States and Western Europe as well as with the Soviet Union.[23] On several occasions he expressed a desire to revise and expand the Polish-American Trade Treaty of 1931.

The Soviets closely monitored the political actions of the Polish government in the spring and summer of 1945, but Moscow did not give Minc orders to cut off economic relations with the United States and the rest of Europe.[24] Shortly after the war ended a Pole was elected governor of the IMF and another was appointed one of the governors of the IBRD. The Soviet Union never joined these institutions. Poland also cooperated in the U.N. Economic Committee for Europe (ECE) and the European Coal Commission (ECC); a Pole served as assistant chairman in the ECC.[25]

Poland's foreign economic policy was a serious topic of debate within the Polish provisional government in 1945, however. Minc recognized that Poland desperately needed Western economic aid, and he hoped to take advantage of all types of capital. But Minc planned to derive the bulk of investment capital from domestic sources in order to maintain Poland's economic independence.[26] Although both Polish communist and non-communist leaders frequently demonstrated their eagerness for economic aid, they were all wary about Poland becoming too dependent on foreign capital. Most of the political parties agreed that in the interwar period Poland's reliance on foreign capital had compromised the country's political independence.[27]

The Polish communists wanted and needed American aid, but preferably with no strings attached. By speaking out too loudly against an influx of foreign capital, however, they often undermined their own diplomatic efforts to obtain it.[28] Some communist ideologues in the PPR warned that it was a mistake to look to the United States for capital and to risk dependence on this source, especially because they thought that the West was simply hostile to the Slavic communist countries. The PPR press sharply criticized the PSL position that given Poland's desperate need for foreign aid, some economic concessions to the West would have to be made. The PPR argued that interwar Poland had compromised its economic and political sovereignty because of its dependence on foreign capital (much of it German) and its susceptibility to foreign trade discrimination. The PPR declared emphatically that the government would not make any political or economic concessions for foreign aid.[29] The Marxist theorists believed that the United States would be forced to grant foreign loans anyway in order to create overseas markets and prevent overproduction and unemployment.[30]

Despite the ongoing debate within the Polish government about the acceptable levels of foreign investment in Poland, the Polish communist leadership knew that they would not gain much popular support if they did not quickly provide the people with their basic needs. The communists simply needed American aid. The new Polish provisional government made its first official request for American economic assistance at the Potsdam Conference. The Polish delegation asked for American trade, direct aid, credits, and loans, and urged the American representatives to send an economic mission to Poland to determine the country's needs.[31] Specifically, the Poles requested a five-year loan of $190 million and a long-term reconstruction loan of $500 million.[32]

Rather than promise any loans at this time, the American delegation responded by making final plans for Poland's credit purchase of U.S. Army surplus trucks in Europe. Of utmost importance to the Americans was the transport of Polish coal to Western Europe. William Clayton, head of the State Department's Economic Affairs Division, repeatedly asked the Polish delegation how much coal they could export to Western Europe if the United States gave Poland a loan to buy transportation equipment. Minc answered that with a loan Poland could probably produce two and one half to three million tons monthly for export.[33] Although the U.S. government did not grant Poland a loan for the coal industry until the fall of 1946, the Poles were able to export about one and one half million tons monthly to Western Europe in 1946.[34]

Clayton told Polish officials to apply for immediate loans from the U.S. Export-Import Bank and to ask for longer-term loans from the IBRD. When the Poles asked for a loan to buy American cotton, Clayton replied that the Export-Import Bank had received loan requests from numerous sources and said that the bank did not have unlimited funds. On 28 July Polish Vice-President Stanisław Grabski, a non-communist who was sympathetic to the West, sent a note to the American delegation emphasizing that the economic cooperation of Poland with the West would be an important contribution to peace in Central Europe.[35] Both communist and non-communist leaders also argued that Poland, as the most devastated country in Europe, had a moral right to assistance, and that a healthy Polish economy was important to Western European recovery.[36]

The Polish delegation at Potsdam also made it clear that the Polish government wanted to become a reliable and trusted trading partner. Coal exports were critical to the Polish economy because the hard currency gained from these exports could be used to buy essential imports from Western Europe and the United States. As Minc told Clayton, "we say in Poland that coal is our foreign exchange."[37] Although some Polish economic officials stated that under no circumstances would Poland ship Silesian coal to the British, French, and American occupation zones in Germany (for the benefit of the Germans), the need for hard currency prompted the Poles to agree at Potsdam to ship 2,500 tons of coal to the American sector in Berlin.[38] Furthermore, in November the Polish government promised to send 250,000 tons of coal monthly to the western zones of Germany, if the western allies could provide the necessary coal cars and locomotives.[39]

Polish officials repeatedly emphasized that the Polish government wanted to expand economic relations with the United States and Western Europe. For example, when Polish Ambassador Oskar Lange presented his credentials to Truman in December 1945, he stated that

> in pursuit of reconstruction and peace Poland expects to establish extensive commercial relations with other countries, particularly with the United States. The acquisition by Poland of a large sea-coast will serve to promote Polish-American trade.[40]

The State Department warned Lange, however, that the undemocratic actions of the present Polish government toward the political opposition could hinder economic cooperation.[41]

Despite this warning, the Polish government hoped that the United States would not link its foreign economic policy to political issues. In order to qualify for loans from the West, the Polish leadership made sure that the socialization of the Polish economy would not contradict some of the terms of its previous trade agreements, such as the Polish-American Trade Treaty of 1931. In October 1945, Polish Minister of Shipping and Trade Stefan Jędrychowski posed this question to Minc:

> What changes would be necessary to adapt the treaty to the present structure of the Polish economy in order to safeguard us from eventual unfavorable pressure on our domestic economic relations?[42]

In November, the Polish government sent a note to the U.S. embassy in Warsaw inquiring about the possibility of advertising in American trade journals, and asked for a list of journals and the procedure for placing advertisements. Furthermore, Jędrychowski proposed to the Polish Council of Ministers that the government employ one of the Polish state trading firms to expand trade contacts with the United States and Great Britain.[43] Naturally the United States preferred to trade with private businesses, and the State Department tried to gather intelligence on whether the new Polish trading organizations were free from government control.[44] By the middle of 1946, however, most of Poland's foreign trade had been organized in state institutions, and at the end of 1948, only one percent of Polish trade was conducted by private firms.[45] Nonetheless, Poland aggressively sought trade connections with the United States and Western Europe.

Another indication of the Polish government's interest in trade with the United States was a proposal in March 1946 to establish a branch in New York City of the Washington-based Polish Reconstruction and Supply Commission. The Polish government now staffed these missions with permanent economic experts instead of temporary officials. The Polish leadership hoped that the responsibilities of the mission would go beyond the coordination of U.N. relief deliveries to facilitate the development of lasting trade contacts in the United States.[46]

Despite Minc's desire to expand trade with the West, he was careful not to alienate the Soviet Union or to betray his own socialist beliefs. At the PPR party congress in December 1945, Minc praised the Soviet Union for its crucial economic assistance before the U.N. relief shipments had arrived. He claimed that the economic agreements with the Soviet Union were not harming but helping Polish economic recovery. He pointed out that Poland had already received 19,000 tons of cotton from the Soviet Union but only 2,000 tons from the United States. Minc insisted that Soviet demand for "reparations coal" from Silesia was not "depriving the Poles of coal." This was true in the sense that Poland had enough coal to cover its own needs, but these exports to the Soviets cut into Poland's potential hard currency earnings.[47]

Poland's lack of hard currency and the disruption of communications from the war were the major barriers to closer trade relations with the West immediately after the war. Poland's large trade volume with the Soviet Union in 1945 seemed to be hard evidence to some American officials that the Soviets were establishing a quasi-colonial relationship with Poland. As early as April 1945 Secretary of State Edward R. Stettinius relayed a message to Truman from the French Foreign Office in which a French diplomat wrote that Poland was "already as Soviet as any of the sixteen Soviet republics."[48] Ignoring the realities of the Polish economic situation, in the fall the State Department began to pressure the Polish government to trade with the West on a non-barter basis. In December, the Polish daily *Życie Warszawy* complained that Poland had been forced to sell meat, butter, and concrete to Great Britain in order to settle a negative balance of payments account with the United States. The newspaper reported that this pressure to trade with the West would no longer work, because the Soviets were providing fair compensation for bartered goods. With its transportation system in shambles and lacking adequate hard currency reserves, it was natural for the Polish government to seek barter trade with its neighbor to the east.[49] Unfortunately for the Polish government, the Soviets could not meet all of Poland's import requirements.[50]

Poland's trade pattern in 1946 should have allayed the administration's fears that the Soviets were exploiting the Polish economy. The value of Poland's imports from the Soviet Union amounted to $31 million in 1945, and the value of exports $35 million.

Poland's trade with the Soviet Union in 1945 represented over 90 percent of Poland's imports and 93 percent of its exports. In 1946, the value of Poland's imports from the Soviet Union increased to $98 million, and the value of exports to $65 million, but the Soviet share of Poland's imports declined significantly to only 69.3 percent, and to just 46.3 percent of Poland's exports.[51] With the exception of the Silesian coal that the Soviets considered to be reparations from Germany, these statistics reveal that the Soviets did not force Poland to increase its trade with the Soviet Union. On the contrary, Moscow allowed and may have even encouraged Poland to expand its commercial relations with the West.

Truman learned from a personal source that trade with the Soviets was helping the Polish economy to rebound. Truman had asked Irving Brant, a *Chicago Sun* journalist, to send reports to the White House on economic and political affairs in Poland. In January 1946, the reporter wrote Truman that a gift of several thousand Soviet army trucks had initially revived communications in Poland, and that Soviet raw materials were fueling the reconstruction of the Polish textile industry and some heavy industries. In addition, Brant reported that the Soviets had helped Poland reopen its seaports and airports. Brant claimed that although the majority of Poland's trade was now with the Soviet Union and Sweden, the Polish government thought that the United States could become an equally important trade partner:

> Sentiment turns most Poles westward in foreign trade; ease of access draws them unwillingly eastward. Communists, who control the trade ministries, turn eastward in sentiment, but hard thinking sends them westward, to secure a wellrounded [sic] national economy.

Finally, Brant argued for giving Poland economic assistance because Poland could not trade on a barter basis with the United States (as it did with the Soviet Union):

> The bedrock fact is that liberal American credits offer the only assurance of genuine Polish independence. With them, the country can strike out on its own

> program of development. Without them, it will be absorbed into the Soviet economy.[52]

Based in part on Brant's assessment, Truman eventually supported a $90 million loan package for Poland in April 1946.

Despite Poland's predominant trade with the Soviet Union in 1945, the Polish government's formal economic plans called for an expansion of commercial relations with the United States, Western Europe, and Eastern Europe.[53] The first Three-Year Plan for 1946 to 1949 projected a balance in trade and foreign investment between East and West.[54] The U.N. Relief and Rehabilitation Administration (UNRRA) reported in 1946 that "ever since liberation, the Polish Government has adopted a positive attitude towards the development of international trade and has shown no desire to put obstacles in the way of its expansion in any direction."[55] Indeed, direct Polish-American trade remained small in the postwar period, but Poland's trade grew steadily with Western Europe, mainly with Sweden and Denmark.[56] Trade with Western Europe in 1938 accounted for approximately 64 percent of Poland's total trade, and 92.2 percent of its trade with capitalist countries worldwide.[57] Trade with capitalist countries jumped from 5.7 percent of Poland's trade in 1945 to 40.2 percent in 1946.[58] By 1947, Poland was conducting 56 percent of its trade with the developed capitalist countries.[59]

Friction in Soviet-American relations in 1945 had little impact on Polish economic policy toward the West. At the end of 1945 Poland signed the Bretton Woods agreements to join the IBRD and the IMF, and then made deposits in the IBRD in early 1946. The Poles hoped to gain long-term development loans from the IBRD and wanted to use the IMF to stabilize the zloty and expand Poland's trade relations.[60] The leading Polish economic journal, *Życie Gospodarcze*, expressed hope that the Soviet Union would also join the IBRD and the IMF in the near future.[61] Poland also became a member of the FAO; Stanisław Mikołajczyk, head of the PSL and the Polish Ministry of Agriculture, was elected to the FAO's executive committee.[62]

III

The fluctuations in American foreign economic policy in 1945 frequently confused and frustrated Polish government officials and the State Department's own ambassador in Warsaw, Arthur Bliss Lane. There was often a striking discrepancy between Lane's diplomacy and the State Department's instructions. Lane was one of the most vocal advocates of linking any American loans to the political policies of the Polish government. After Minc told Lane in the fall that he intended to ask the U.S. Export-Import Bank for a long-term reconstruction loan of $500 million, Lane was "determined to take advantage of the eagerness of the Polish Government for economic assistance and to use it as a lever by which we would obtain fulfillment of Polish commitments under Yalta and Potsdam decisions."[63]

Lane briefly softened his position in August when he intimated to the Polish leadership that a loan was possible without political concessions. Already Lane thought that the Polish leadership was taking most of its orders from Moscow anyway:

> I did not mention elections at this meeting believing it unwise to irritate an already sore spot. If I thought that the Poles were really masters in their own house, I would feel differently in proffering advice.

Lane told President Bierut that the United States could help Poland through the Export-Import Bank if the Poles would specify their requirements and provide the United States with information on the Polish government's finances. The Truman administration was particularly interested in the details of coal shipments to the Soviets.[64]

Lane and his embassy staff had to suffer through very spartan conditions in bombed-out Warsaw, and Lane became more and more frustrated with the Polish government's inequitable exchange rate, plans to nationalize the economy, and barter trade.[65] In several meetings with Polish leaders, Lane frequently exaggerated Byrnes's dissatisfaction with these economic developments. Lane told Premier Edward Osóbka-Morawski that the United States was "very much disturbed regarding the present economic and financial policy of the Polish Government which, if allowed to continue, would undermine confidence in Poland and would discourage investment of American capital in the reconstruction of Poland."[66]

The administration was more interested in the flow of Polish coal to Western Europe in 1945 than it was in Poland's domestic economic policy. Loans to Poland hinged on Polish assurances that coal would be shipped to Western Europe to help fuel economic recovery there.[67] The State Department feared, however, that a loan for the Polish coal industry would result in more exports to the Soviet Union rather than to Western Europe. These reservations were confirmed by Polish press reports indicating that the Soviets were indeed exploiting the Silesian coal fields. For example, in May 1945 *Życie Warszawy* reported that Polish miners in Katowice had placed a sign on the front of a trainload of coal that read, "To Mr. Stalin, from Polish miners, good luck."[68] Furthermore, Osóbka-Morawski admitted to Lane that Poland had agreed in July to ship five million metric tons of coal to the Soviet Union in exchange for various materials and manufactured goods.[69]

Reports circulating in Washington that the Soviets were carting away factories from the former German territories of Silesia and Posen also hurt Poland's chances for loans from the United States. Until the allies signed a peace treaty with Germany, the Soviets considered these areas to be a Polish zone of occupation and a legitimate source of reparations. When Władysław Gomułka, the vice premier and minister of recovered territories, demanded that Soviets stop the dismantling, one Polish official recalled that the Soviet general in charge of the operation "seized Gomułka by the lapels and threatened him." Gomułka did not back down, however, and ordered Polish law officers to shoot any Soviet soldiers caught looting.[70] In July, the Polish government obtained a restraining order from Moscow to halt the dismantling for the time being.

At Potsdam, Minc and Berman tried to convince Stalin and Molotov that Poland was facing an extremely difficult reconstruction task and could not afford to lose any more industries to the Soviet Union. According to Berman, the Soviets responded positively to this argument.[71] After Potsdam most of the dismantling stopped, and Poland received the rights to 144 factories in Lower Silesia that the Soviets had planned to transport to the Soviet Union.[72] The Polish government was also able to squelch Stalin's idea of joint Soviet-Polish ownership of the Silesian coal mines.

The Soviets still demanded Silesian coal at huge discounts, however. The Polish government agreed in August to ship eight million tons of coal to the Soviet zone of Germany in the next year, thirteen million tons the next year, and twelve million tons the year after that. The Soviets arbitrarily set the permanent price at $1.25 a ton, which was about one tenth of the world market price. In exchange, the Soviets promised Poland 15 percent of all reparations from the Soviet zone, and 1.5 percent of the reparations that the Soviets received from the western zones. Poland never received most of these promised reparations.[73]

There was little that the Polish government could do to stop the reparation coal shipments. The Soviets argued that because they had enabled Poland to occupy Silesia and had not dismantled any of the mining equipment, they had a right to a portion of the production.[74] According to Juliusz Kolipinski, an aide to Gomułka, the Soviets cheated Poland out of promised reparations from Germany by making Poland pay for them with coal shipments to the Soviet occupation zone.[75] The loss of hard currency revenue from the reparations coal shipments to the Soviets represented a significant reduction in Poland's ability to buy needed goods from the West. A Polish economic historian regards the impact of the reparation coal shipments on Poland's early postwar reconstruction as "inestimable."[76] Nonetheless, the Polish government was eager and able to increase coal exports to Western Europe. In 1945, only 3.7 percent of Poland's exported coal went to the developed capitalist countries, but this figure increased significantly to 30.3 percent in 1946.[77]

In addition to the reparations coal, the Soviets also had at least 30,000 Polish coal cars in its possession at the end of the war, transport that Poland desperately needed to increase its coal exports. Lavrenti Beria assured the Polish delegation at Potsdam that the his government would return the cars in the near future, but they remained in Soviet hands until March 1947.[78] The only way the Poles could replace them was to buy substitutes with U.S. loans. The Polish government eventually requested to use part of a U.S. Export-Import Bank loan to purchase coal cars.

Another issue that complicated Polish loan requests was the Polish nationalization law of 6 January 1946, which called for state ownership of private businesses with over fifty employees. Although the nationalization of private property contradicted American objectives for a free market economy in Poland, the Truman administration did not oppose nationalization if adequate compensation was provided for confiscated American property. Before the war ended, the principle of nationalization without compensation for Polish property owners had already drawn implicit support from the OSS in a report on land reform in Poland. The OSS concluded that land reform was essential to prevent a revolutionary situation in the countryside:

> For a number of political reasons the measures comprising the [land] reform are inevitable. Poland presents a glaring inequality in the contrast between the large estates belonging to prodigal absentee-owners and the dwarf holdings inadequate for the support of the large peasant families living on them. Such a situation cannot survive a period of revolutionary unrest and mass upheaval.[79]

And in a letter to Churchill in March 1945, Roosevelt had warned against giving the peasants

> the impression that we are proposing a halt in the land reforms. This would furnish the Lublin Poles with an opportunity to charge that they and they alone defend the interests of the peasants against the landlords.[80]

American acceptance of land reform in Poland set a precedent for the basic position that the Truman administration adopted toward nationalization. The State Department expected the Polish government to nationalize the economy, viewing it as a continuation of a prewar trend and an outcome of the chaotic economic conditions in postwar Poland. Many big industries of interwar Poland had been state monopolies or partially nationalized so that about one eighth of the total national wealth had been state-owned. Apart from compensation for American property, Byrnes viewed nationalization as an internal Polish affair.[81] The State Department also wanted to avoid antagonizing the PSL and its peasant supporters. The PSL had welcomed land reform without compensation and now advocated compensation for the property losses of foreign citizens only.

As long as the inspiration for the nationalization law was Polish and not Soviet, and if the law adequately compensated American property losses, the State Department was willing to accept the nationalization law without protest. When a French diplomat asked Elbridge Durbrow of the State Department's East European Division if the nationalization law was Soviet-inspired, Durbrow replied that there was no evidence that this was the case. He had no doubts, however, that the Soviets would approve of it. Durbrow thought that the State Department was only obligated to negotiate for full compensation of confiscated American property.[82]

In January 1946, Irving Brant assured Truman that the nationalization law was supported by the majority of the non-communist leaders in Poland. The reporter exaggerated the benefits of the law for the country's economic independence, however:

> One important effect of knocking out big industrial capitalism and landlordism is to eliminate the powerful core of anti-sovietism found, for example, in Hungary. This encourages a hands-off policy by Russia toward Poland's economic life, quite different from Russia's Hungarian attitude.[83]

Most of the Polish political parties agreed with Minc, who argued that some nationalization was essential for Poland to maintain control over its own economy. Minc informed the Polish National Council that before the war foreigners owned 52.5 percent of Poland's mining and metal industries, 87 percent of the oil fields, 66.1 percent of the electrical-technical industry, and 59.9 percent of the chemical industry. The PPR and PSL generally agreed that this preponderance of foreign ownership of Polish industry was now unacceptable, and both parties agreed to pay some compensation to foreigners.[84] PSL leader Stanisław Mikołajczyk knew that this compensation was likely to be symbolic, however, rather than an equitable payment of the value of the confiscated property.[85]

Minc also understood that the shortage of convertible currency would make it difficult to pay adequate compensation to foreign property owners. He realized, however, that the nationalization law could harm relations with the capitalist countries with whom he hoped to trade and from whom he hoped to acquire reconstruction loans. He feared that nationalization of the Soviet type, without compensation, would be a pretext for the West to isolate Poland economically.[86] In addition, Minc knew that nationalization without compensation would give the United States and Great Britain grounds to freeze Polish gold held in banks in those two countries.[87] In a speech to the National Council, Minc promised that nationalization in Poland would be different than it had been in the Soviet Union, and that Poland was not "conducting a socialist revolution and therefore would pay compensation."[88] Of course, Minc was conducting a socialist economic revolution, but between 1947 and 1949 Poland signed compensation agreements with most of the countries of Western Europe.

When the nationalization law went into effect in early 1946, the State Department briefly postponed the Export-Import Bank loan negotiations with Poland because the law was not clear on the principle of compensation for foreign property losses. On 17 January Byrnes told Zygmunt Modzelewski, the Polish deputy minister of foreign affairs and future foreign minister, that neither political considerations nor the State Department had anything to do with the delay in the loan negotiations. Byrnes maintained that the Export-Import Bank "dealt with applications on strictly business and financial grounds." Byrnes dodged direct responsibility for the delay by claiming that the State Department had no control over the directorate of the Export-Import Bank and that his department merely supplied the bank with economic information on foreign countries. Byrnes did not mention that these reports were often accompanied by a recommendation for or against a loan, or that these recommendations were often based on political considerations. Byrnes assured Modzelewski that Poland had the right to nationalize property (with equitable compensation), and stated that "the United States Government had no intention whatever of interfering with the internal affairs or policies of the Polish Government."[89] Byrnes was not completely truthful in this case either, because he was becoming increasingly concerned about political developments in Poland and wanted to do something it.

At first Ambassador Lane agreed with the State Department's position that the short delay in the loan negotiations was connected solely to a Polish commitment to compensate American property losses.[90] In an interview with Polish Foreign Minister Wincenty Rzymowski in January, Lane said that the United States did not oppose the nationalization law but objected to the refusal of the Polish government to allow American citizens into the country to inspect their property, as the Polish-American Trade Treaty of 1931 stipulated. Surprisingly, Rzymowski replied that the 1931 agreement did not apply to conditions in Poland at the time, although Minc and others in the government understood that adhering to the spirit of this treaty and other trade agreements would reap long-term benefits for Poland's economic development.[91] Rzymowski's position was not supported two months later when Stefan Litauer, an economic counselor in the Polish embassy in Washington, assured Acting Secretary of State Dean Acheson that "in all meritorious cases" U.S. owners of nationalized property could enter Poland to inspect it.[92]

Nonetheless, Lane exaggerated the importance of the compensation issue and warned the Polish leadership that without an agreement the United States would discontinue all loan negotiations. It was not the first or the last time that Lane's threats were not backed by his superiors in Washington. The State Department reopened the Export-Import Bank loan talks in March after the Polish government had tentatively agreed to establish a Polish-American commission to rule on American property claims and agreed to pay compensation in dollars. There were still significant outstanding issues, however. The State Department estimated that the value of American property losses was much higher than Polish estimates. In addition, the tentative agreement also included compensation for property nationalized in the territories acquired from Germany. Although this compensation benefitted American property owners in these territories, it proved to be a major legal obstacle to a final compensation agreement. American acceptance of compensation for property losses in these areas would have implied recognition of Poland's legal claim to this part of Germany.[93] No further serious negotiations on compensation for American property losses were held until 1957, and three years later an agreement was finally signed.[94] Over Lane's objections, the loan negotiations continued without a compensation agreement.

IV

Six months after the war ended in Europe, the U.S. government was still divided over its economic policy toward Poland. Truman, Byrnes, and the State Department's Economic Affairs Division determined that for the time being American economic policy would focus on short-term goals; loan negotiations continued despite protests from Lane and others over the Polish government's repressive political actions, socialization of Poland's economy, nationalization law, and preponderant bilateral barter trade with the Soviet Union. All of these policies of the Polish government were contradictions to general American objectives to establish independent democratic governments and free market economic systems in Europe. There was still an absence of a clear set of American goals for Poland, however, which resulted in a lack of economic policy coordination within the State Department. Short-term humanitarian and economic goals eventually informed U.S. loan and relief policy in the immediate postwar period; the U.S. government gave Poland $90 million in loans and credits in April 1946, but the lack of a consensus in the Truman administration over this economic policy was clearly evident during these long and drawn out loan negotiations.

NOTES

1. Lukas, *Bitter Legacy: Polish-American Relations in the Wake of World War II*, 4-5.

2. See *FRUS,1945 1*: 973-979. Stalin also agreed to pledge that the Polish Provisional Government of National Unity would hold free and unfettered elections.

3. Lukas, *Bitter-Legacy: Polish-American Relations in the Wake of World War II*, 5-8; Davies, *God's Playground*, 557-559. Other prominent communist figures in the Lublin Committee and the new provisional government were Premier Edward Osóbka-Morawski, Security Minister Stanisław Radkiewicz, Minister of the Recovered Territories Władysław Gomułka, and Defense Minister Michał Rola-Zymierski.

4. Davies, *God's Playground*, 559.

5. *Compendium Statystyczne Polskiego Handlu Zagranicznego w latach 1929-1938, 1945-1960* [Statistical compendium of Polish foreign trade, 1929-1938, 1945-1960] (Warsaw: Polska Izba Handlu Zagranicznego, 1961), 41-43. American goods accounted for only approximately 12 percent of the total value of Polish imports in 1938, and about 6.5 percent of Polish exports. This statistic on exports varies from 5.3 percent from this source to 6.9 percent in Central Planning Office, *Sytuacja Gospodarcza Polski*, 122. Trade with the Soviet Union comprised only 0.8 percent of the total value of Polish imports in 1938,

and only 0.1 percent of Polish exports; see also Frederick Pryor, "The Foreign Trade System of the European Communist Nations," (Ph.D. dissertation, Yale University, 1961), 176. The proportion of Polish trade with future Comecon members was only 13 percent of Poland's total trade in 1938.

6. Harriman to the secretary of state, 17 January 1945, RG 59, 860c.50, box 6381.

7. Memorandum of the fourth Hopkins-Stalin meeting in Moscow, 30 May 1945, *FRUS, 1945* 5:301-306.

8. Pollard, *Economic Security and the Origins of the Cold War, 1945-1950*, 42.

9. Protocols of the Proceedings of the Potsdam Conference, *FRUS, 1945* 2:1490-1492.

10. Richard Hiscocks, *Poland: Bridge for the Abyss? An Interpretation of Developments in Post-War Poland* (London: Oxford University Press, 1963), 119.

11. UNRRA, *Foreign Trade in Poland*, 45.

12. Harriman to Byrnes, 17 and 23 June 1945, *FRUS, 1945* 5:347, 360; and Harriman to Joseph Grew (acting secretary of state), 26 June 1945, *FRUS, 1945* 1:785.

13. Grew memoranda to Truman, 25 and 27 June 1945, Papers of Harry S. Truman, President's Secretary's File (PSF), Subject File, box 175, Truman Library, Independence, Missouri (hereafter Truman Papers, PSF, with filing information.

14. Harriman to Grew, 26 June 1945, *FRUS, 1945* 1:786.

15. Report by the Office of Strategic Services, "Postwar Poland: Economic and Political Outlook," 9 March 1945, RG 59, 860c.51, box 6366.

16. *New York Times*, 19 July 1945, 4-5.

17. Lundestad, *The American Non-Policy Towards Eastern Europe*, 321.

18. Glinka-Janczewski, "American Policy Toward Poland Under the Truman Administration, 1945-1952," 134.

19. Robert L. Messer, *The End of an Alliance: James F. Byrnes, Roosevelt, Truman, and the Origins of the Cold War* (Chapel Hill, Maryland: University of North Carolina Press, 1982), 82.

20. Byrnes to Lane, 12 July 1945, RG 59, 860c.50, box 6381.

21. Czesław Bobrowski, *Wspomnienia ze stulecia* [Memoirs from a century] (Lublin: Wydawnictwo Lubelskie, 1985), 147.

22. Hubert Ripka, *Czechoslovakia Enslaved: The Story of the Communist Coup d'Etat* (London: Victor Gollancz, Ltd., 1950), 52.

23. Polish Government, Krajowy Rada Narodowa, *Sprawozdanie Stenograficzne* [Polish national council, stenographic records], 23 July 1945, 211 (hereafter Polish National Council Records with date and page number).

24. Krystyna Kersten, *Narodziny Systemu Władzy Polska, 1943-1948* [The origins of the system of government in Poland, 1943-1948] (Warsaw: Wydawnictwo Krag, 1985), 127-128.

25. Cable, "The United States and the Polish Question, 1939-1948," 338.

26. Polish National Council Records, 21 July 1945, 27; ibid., 2 January 1946, 335-336; and ibid., 23 July 1946, 170.

27. Wiesław Dudek, *Międzynarodowe aspekty nacjonalizacji w Polsce* [International aspects of nationalization in Poland] (Warsaw: Państwowe Wydawnictwo Narodowe, 1976), 83. Of the foreign capital in Poland in 1933, 33.6 percent was American, 19.5 percent was French, and 5.8 percent was German.

28. See for example, *Życie Warszawy*, 4 December 1945, 1.

29. Polish National Council Records, 21 July 1945, 27; ibid., 2 January 1946, 335-336; and ibid., 23 July 1945, 170.

30. Lane to Byrnes, 11 December 1945, RG 59, 860c.51, box 6385.

31. Memorandum of conversation, Minc and Despres, 29 July 1945, *FRUS, 1945* 2:478-479.

32. Memorandum of conversation with the Polish delegation, 28 July 1945, *FRUS, 1945* 2:455-448.

33. Memorandum by Mikołajczyk of meeting at Potsdam, 28 July 1945, *FRUS, 1945* 2:1532-1538.

34. *Compendium Statystyczne Polskiego Handlu Zagranicznego w latach 1929-1938, 1945-1960*, 128.

35. Lubomir Zyblikiewicz, *Polityka Stanów Zjednoczonych i Wielkiej Brytanii wobec Polski, 1944-1949* [The policy of the United States and Great Britain toward Poland, 1944-1949] (Warsaw: Książka i Wiedza, 1984), 192.

36. Memorandum of meeting with the Polish delegation, 25 July 1945, *FRUS, 1945* 2:403-406.

37. Memorandum by Mikołajczyk of meeting with Clayton, 28 July 1945, *FRUS, 1945* 2:1532-1538.

38. Mikołajczyk papers on the Potsdam Conference, *FRUS, 1945* 2:1539; and *New York Times*, 13 July 1945, 5.

39. Memorandum of Allied Control Council, undated, Polish Government, Komitet Ekonomiczny Rady Ministrów, Podkomitet do Międzynarodowych Spraw Gospodarczych, Akty 1945-1946 [Economic committee of the council of ministers, subcommittee for international economic affairs], File 136, Archiwum Akt Nowych [Archive of new records], Warsaw (hereafter Economic Committee of the Council of Ministers Records with filing information). The price of the coal was set at $10 per ton, half of which was to be paid in dollars, and the other half in edible fats, meats, petrol, and lubricants.

40. Memorandum of conversation, Truman and Lange, 14 December 1945, Truman Papers, PSF, Official File, box 1297.

41. Cable, "The United States and the Polish Question, 1939-1948," 312.

42. Memorandum from the Ministry of Foreign Shipping and Trade to Minc, 8 October 1945, Ministerstwo Przemyslu i Handlu, Akty [Ministry of industry and trade, records], File 51, Archiwum Akt Nowych, Warsaw (hereafter Ministry of Industry and Trade Records with filing information).

43. Letter from the Polish Advertising Agency to the U.S. embassy in Warsaw, 15 November 1945, Department of State, Records of the Foreign Service Posts of the Department of State, Records Group 84, General Records, Poland, box 1, National Records Center, Suitland, Maryland (hereafter RG 84 with filing information); and "Proposal of the Minister of Foreign Shipping and Trade," 27 April 1946, Economic Committee of the Council of Ministers Records, Subcommittee of International Economic Affairs, File 136.

44. Lane to Byrnes, 13 November 1945, RG 84, General Records, box 1.

45. Pryor, "The Foreign Trade System of the European Communist Nations," Appendix C, 4.

46. Memorandum from Minc to Ruminski (vice minister of industry), 30 March 1946, Ministry of Industry and Trade Records, File 51.

47. *Rzeczpospolita*, 2 December 1945, 3; and Lane to Byrnes, 12 December 1945, RG 59, 860c.50, box 6381.

48. Memorandum from Stettinius to Truman, 23 April 1945, Truman Papers, PSF, Subject File, box 175.

49. Thad Paul Alton, *Polish Postwar Economy* (New York: Columbia University Press, 1955), 269.

50. *Zycie Warszawy*, 21 December 1945, 2.

51. Sokolowski, *Obroty zagraniczne Polski w okresie 1945-1958*, p. 5; *Compendium Statystyczne Polskiego Handlu Zagranicznego w latach 1929-1938, 1945-1960*, 208. These figures do not reflect the reparations coal shipments.

52. Irving Brant to Truman, 14 January 1946, Truman Papers, PSF, Subject File, box 186.

53. Lane to Byrnes, 2 January 1946, RG 59, 611.60c, box 2847.

54. Wojciechowski, "Handel Zagraniczny Polski," 371; and Eugeniusz Gajda, *Polska Polityka Zagraniczna, 1944-1971* [Polish foreign policy, 1944-1971] (Warsaw: Wydawnictwo Ministerstwa Obrony Narodowej, 1972), 49.

55. UNRRA, *Foreign Trade in Poland*, 17.

56. *Compendium Statystyczne Polskiego Handlu Zagranicznego w latach 1929-1938, 1945-1960*, 295. Imports from the United States amounted to 1.1 percent of Poland's total imports in 1946, and 0.3 percent of Polish exports. Sweden's share was 6.1 percent and 5.2 percent for 1945, and 15.9 percent and 19.4 percent in 1946. Denmark's share was 2.6 percent and 0.3 percent in 1945, and 2.4 percent and 6.0 percent in 1946. Of course, the increase in Polish exports was due to the export of Silesian coal.

57. John C. Campbell, *American Policy Toward Communist Eastern Europe: The Choices Ahead* (Minneapolis: University of Minnesota, 1965), 41-42; and *Compendium Statystyczne Polskiego Handlu Zagranicznego w latach 1929-1938, 1945-1960*, 57.

58. Henryk Różański, *Śladem wspomnień i dokumentów, 1943-1948* [Tracing remembrances and documents, 1943-1948] (Warsaw: Państwowe Wydawnictwo Naukowe, 1987), 277.

59. Stanisław Długosz and Wiesław Szczepaniec, *Stosunki handlowe Polski z rozwiniętymi krajami kapitalistycznymi* [Poland's trade relations with developed capitalist countries] (Warsaw: Państwowe Wydawnictwo Ekonomiczne, 1974), 109.

60. Polish National Council Records, 31 December 1945, 239-243.

61. *Życie Gospodarcze* 1 (15 February 1946): 98-99.

62. Proposal of Mikołajczyk (minister of agriculture), 30 April 1946, Economic Committee of the Council of Ministers Records,

Subcommittee of International Economic Affairs, File 136; and Różański, *Śladem wspomnień i dokumentów, 1943-1948*, 420.

63. Arthur Bliss Lane, *I Saw Poland Betrayed* (Indianapolis: The Bobbs-Merrill Co., 1948), 227.

64. Lane to Byrnes, 6 August 1945, RG 59, 860c.50, box 6381.

65. From the beginning of his tour in Warsaw Lane's relations with the Polish government were strained. Although it was not a major issue, controversy over an equitable exchange rate for the zloty contributed to this adversarial relationship. The embassy had the simple problem of purchasing needed supplies at a fair price. The Polish government was prepared to agree to a satisfactory exchange rate for American citizens visiting Poland, and was also willing to make arrangements for the U.S. embassy to receive credits in zlotys until an equitable exchange rate could be agreed upon. Unlike his own government, Lane was intransigent on this issue. He insisted on a new exchange rate to cover all transactions and a Polish currency that could be exchanged on the free market.

66. Lane to Byrnes, 22 August 1945, *FRUS, 1945* 5:364-365.

67. Poland had an advantage over Bulgaria, Rumania, and Hungary, which were given little consideration by the State Department for loans, because (as former Axis allies) they were paying reparations directly to the Soviet Union. The Truman administration was reluctant to grant any economic assistance to these countries if it did not directly benefit Western European recovery.

68. *Życie Warszawy*, 10 May 1945, 2.

69. Lane to Byrnes, 22 August 1945, *FRUS, 1945* 5:364-365.

70. Stefan Korbonski, *Warsaw in Exile* (New York: Frederick A. Praeger, 1966), 75.

71. Berman interview in Teresa Torańska, *Oni* [Them] (Cracow: Krakowskie Towarzystwo Wydawnicze, 1986), 268.

72. Różański, *Śladem wspomnień i dokumentów, 1943-1948*, 296, 316.

73. Różański, *Śladem wspomnień i dokumentów, 1943-1948*, 324-325; and UNRRA, *Foreign Trade in Poland*, 17.

74. Edward Ochab interview in Torańska, *Oni*, 29.

75. Juliusz Kolipinski interview with author, 15 March 1988, Warsaw.

76. Sokolowski, *Obroty zagraniczne Polski w okresie 1945-1958*, 7.

77. Długosz and Szczepaniec, *Stosunki handlowe Polski z rozwiniętymi krajami kapitalistycznymi*, 115.

78. Różański, *Śladem wspomnień i dokumentów, 1943-1948*, 292.

79. Office of Strategic Services, "Postwar Poland: Economic and Political Outlook," 31, RG 59, 860c.00, box 6366.

80. Telegram from Roosevelt to Churchill, 11 March 1945, *FRUS, 1945* 5:156.

81. Alton, *Polish Postwar Economy*, 14; and Byrnes to Lane, 9 November 1945, *FRUS, 1945* 5:412.

82. Memorandum of conversation, Armand Berand (counselor of the French embassy in Washington) and Durbrow, 11 October 1945, *FRUS, 1945* 5:386-388.

83. Brant to Truman, 14 January 1946, Truman Papers, PSF, Subject File, box 186; see Thomas G. Paterson, *Soviet-American Confrontation: Postwar Reconstruction and the Origins of the Cold War*, (Baltimore: Johns Hopkins University Press, 1973), 106. Paterson writes that the United States "overreacted" to nationalization as if the law was the result of Soviet pressure. Although loan negotiations were briefly halted after nationalization was announced, the Truman administration did not oppose it as long as Poland paid compensation for the loss of American-owned property. After it became clear that the Polish government intended to pay indemnities to American property owners, loan negotiations quickly resumed.

84. Polish National Council Records, 2 January 1946, 398, 436. One government-bloc party, the People's Party (SL), argued against any compensation for what they called "capitalist exploitation."

85. Polish National Council Records, 2 January 1946 417-419; Dudek, *Międzynarodowe aspekty nacjonalizacji w Polsce*, 91; There was disagreement between the PPR and the PSL, however, over the extent of nationalization and the compensation to be paid Polish citizens. The PSL proposed to raise the limit of nationalized industries from businesses with fifty employees to 100 employees. No compensation had been paid to Poles who lost land in the land reform of 1945, and the PSL opposed any compensation to Polish citizens under the new law. As a peasant party, the PSL was concerned that paying compensation would take away investment funds for agriculture; see also Joyce and Gabriel Kolko, *The Limits of Power: The World and United States Foreign Policy, 1945-1954* (New York: Harper and Row Publishers, 1972), 29. Because the United States was hoping for the

emergence of Mikołajczyk's PSL as the dominant party in Poland, the idea that the Truman administration was determined to reduce the influence of all socialist parties in postwar Europe cannot be supported.

86. Kolipinski interview with author, 15 March 1988; Polish National Council Records, 2 January 1946, 476; and Dudek, *Międzynarodowe aspekty nacjonalizacji w Polsce*, 91.

87. Polish National Council Records, 3 January 1946, 544.

88. Polish National Council Records, 2 January 1946, 404; and Davies, *God's Playground*, 569.

89. Memorandum of conversation, Modzelewski and Byrnes, etal., 17 January 1946, RG 59, 860c.51, box 6385.

90. Memorandum of conversation, Berard and Durbrow, 11 October 1945, *FRUS, 1945* 5:386-388; and Lane to Byrnes, 13 October 1945, ibid., 390.

91. Acheson to Byrnes in London, 22 January 1946, *FRUS, 1946: Eastern Europe and the Soviet Union* (Washington: Government Printing Office, 1969), 6:382-384.

92. Memorandum of conversation, Acheson and Litauer, 29 March 1946, *FRUS, 1946* 6:416.

93. Zyblikiewicz, *Polityka Stanów Zjednoczonych i Wielkiej Brytanii wobec Polski, 1944-1949*, 232; Stefan Rączkowski interview with author, 10 March 1988, Warsaw; and *New York Times*, 25 September 1948, 5. The United States wanted Poland to pay at least $100 million in compensation.

94. Różański, *Śladem wspomnień i dokumentów, 1943-1948*, 410; Zygmunt Karpinski, *Losy złota polskiego podczas drugiej wojny światowej* [The fate of Polish gold during the second world war] (Warsaw: Państwowe Wydawnictwo Naukowe, 1958), 50-51; and Mark Sekular, "Stosunki gospodarcze między Polska i Stanami Zjednoczonymy Ameryki po II wojnie światowej," [Economic relations between Poland and the United States after the second world war], Praca Magisterska (Warsaw: Central School of Planning and Statistics, 1977), 24-25.

Chapter Two

Negotiations for American Loans, 1945-1946

I

For the first year after the war, the primary goal of American economic policy in Europe was to reconstruct the European economy in order to create a reliable market for American goods. Above all the Truman administration wanted to avoid another depression. Truman laid out these objectives in his State of the Union Address in January 1946: "The foreign economic policy of the United States is designed to promote our own prosperity, and at the same time to aid in the restoration and expansion of world markets."[1] By early 1946, however, American and European economic recovery was not moving very fast. Unemployment in the United States had already risen from 500,000 to 2.7 million,[2] and at great expense the United States was providing two thirds of the U.N. relief to Europe. That aid alleviated widespread shortages of food, fuel, and other essential goods.

The import of Polish coal into Western Europe was so essential for the rapid economic recovery of Western Europe that in the fall of 1945 the State Department began serious negotiations with Poland for a loan to modernize the coal industry in Silesia. At this point many American officials were optimistic that reconstruction loans would also further U.S. political and economic interests in Poland. The loan negotiations not only reveal the ongoing disputes within the Truman administration over the objectives of American economic policy, but they expose the divisions within the Polish government over the wisdom of making economic concessions for American loans. The mixed signals that both sides gave the other fostered an atmosphere of distrust that severely strained relations between the two countries, even after they signed a loan agreement in April 1946.

II

Much of the confusion within the State Department over the objectives and implementation of U.S. loan policy toward Poland was the result of the distinction that Truman and Byrnes made between the criteria that Poland had to meet for short-term or long-term loans. When the Polish delegation at Potsdam asked the United States for a series of reconstruction loans, Byrnes concluded that granting a small, preliminary loan would be a sign to the Polish government that if it eventually agreed to American political demands, larger, long-term loans would follow. A small loan was targeted for the coal industry and was contingent on guarantees that Poland export more coal to Western Europe. Byrnes and most State Department officials agreed that the political situation in Poland would have to improve before any long-term loans were granted.[3]

Ambassador Lane often misrepresented Washington's position on this loan for the Polish coal industry. The Polish communists sharply rejected Lane's demand that they make significant political concessions in order to qualify for any loans. As a result, Lane's relationship with the Polish government became increasingly strained. For now State Department officials in Washington overlooked some of Poland's problems in adhering to the economic principles of the Open Door and simply pursued a gradual change in Poland's trade practices. Acting Secretary of State Dean Acheson wrote Lane in September that "the Department appreciates that Poland's present position is difficult and that for the next few months bilateral clearings, compensation agreements, and similar discriminating devices may be difficult to avoid." But Acheson counseled Lane to warn the Polish government that in the long run

> close economic relations . . . will not develop, and financial assistance to Poland will remain small, unless Poland is prepared to give assurances that it will, after a reasonable period of transition, abstain from discrimination in trade and investment.

Acheson also told Lane that the United States would not accept an exclusive position for any country in Poland's economy, which was an obvious reference to Poland's predominant trade with the Soviet Union in 1945.[4]

Rather than relay these messages to the Polish government, Lane pressed for immediate satisfaction on all American economic and political objectives. Bierut told Lane that he was concerned about the ambassador's negative attitude toward the Polish government's economic policies; Bierut claimed that Poland's economy would be closer in form to the American rather than to the Soviet system.[5] Of course, this was not the case, because Minc had a socialist plan for the Polish economy that relied heavily on the Soviet economic model. When Lane pressed Bierut on political matters, the Polish leader warned that the Polish people would not understand the refusal of reconstruction loans from an avowed friend, but that he himself fully understood the political advantages that the United States hoped to accrue from the loans. In subsequent conversations with Bierut, Lane continued to criticize the government's exchange rate, suppression of the press, and political arrests. Lane asked the State Department to reject any Polish loan requests on the grounds that the Polish government "is most desirous of obtaining a large credit to indicate to the Polish people its friendship with the United States Government and thereby to solidify its position politically within the country."[6]

At the beginning of September 1945, Dr. Ludwig Rajchman, head of the Polish delegation to the UNRRA in Washington, repeated the request that Minc had made at Potsdam for an initial loan of $190 million from the U.S. Export-Import Bank, followed by a long-term $500 million reconstruction loan.[7] One month later Rajchman revised that request by asking for an immediate loan of $380 million and another $320 million loan later. The $380 million loan was to be used to reconstruct port facilities and to purchase rolling stock for the transport of coal and other exports. Rajchman proposed that Poland repay $190 million of this loan with Polish exports.[8]

In addition to loans for the coal and transport industries, the Polish government asked for a credit to buy American cotton in order to supply the largely undamaged Polish textile industry. In October, the Export-Import Bank announced the establishment of a $100,000 credit fund to finance the export of 800,000 bales of cotton to Europe. The president of the bank, Wayne C. Taylor, listed Belgium, Czechoslovakia, Denmark, France, Italy, Holland, Norway and Poland as possible benefactors of the credit fund, but East European desk chief Elbridge Durbrow sent a note to the Office of Economic Development

(OED) recommending against credits for Poland. The OED then told Acheson that "we have accordingly asked the Eximbank to defer any action on cotton or other credits to Poland."[9]

In spite of the widespread destruction and poverty in Poland after the war, many Polish non-communists, like Lane, counseled against any American loans to the present Polish government. They feared that American financial assistance would only serve to consolidate power in the hands of the PPR and the PPS. Their thinking was that if the United States granted loans, the PPR would use them to show the Polish people that the present government was a legitimate government and had the economic support of the United States. Minc tactfully disassociated himself from the loan negotiations, however, so that if Poland did not receive any loans, the PPR would not have to take sole blame.[10] In October 1945, Lane raised the question of American loans to Poland with Stefan Sapieha, the archbishop of Cracow, former Premier Wincenty Witos, Zygmunt Zulawski, president of the old Polish Socialist Party, and Stanisław Kutrzeba, president of the Polish Academy of Science and Letters. All were opposed to a loan at this time, arguing that the Polish communists and the Polish people would interpret a loan as American indifference to the Polish government's repression of the political opposition. Sapieha said that at most only 10 percent of the population supported the present government.[11]

Lane again discussed American loans with Vice-President Grabski in October, who also argued against a loan at that time. Lane asked whether the present Polish government would become even more dependent on the Soviet Union if Poland did not receive American loans, but Grabski thought that the Soviet Union was in no position to help Poland's reconstruction anyway. If Poland received American loans, however, Grabski warned that the Soviets "would force Poland to give the benefit thereof to the Soviet Union."[12]

Some State Department officials viewed the reparations coal shipments, the rapacious behavior of the Red Army in Poland, and the attempts by the Soviets to form joint companies in Silesia as tangible evidence of an overall Soviet plan to exploit the Polish economy. This perception was also rapidly gaining adherents in the American press and in Congress. In November, the *New York Times* described the dilemma for the State Department as either "leaving Poland distressed and a hospitable vacuum for communism, or, in effect, fattening a cow that the Russians are in a position to milk." The newspaper reported that some U.S. government officials still thought that loans could be used to extract political concessions.[13] That fall a bill passed through the House of Representatives that prohibited the use of American funds in areas controlled by the Soviet Union. The bill eventually died in the Senate, but House and Senate Republicans kept the pressure on the White House by issuing a joint statement in December criticizing the administration's soft policy in Eastern Europe. Fortunately for Truman, Chairman of the Senate Foreign Relations Committee Arthur Vandenberg made public statements in support of the Yalta and Potsdam agreements on free elections, but he interfered little with the administration's economic policy toward Poland.[14]

Another letter from journalist Irving Brant to Truman in October encouraged the president to grant Poland economic assistance, either in the form of a loan or increased relief through the UNRRA. Brant wrote that

> Poland has an immense, critical need for transport facilities, also food and clothing. . . . Food and coal *can't be moved* without trucks and gasoline, and thousands of people are going to go through the winter anyway without heat in windowless houses.

As for the London Poles and the Polish political opposition that the Truman administration was trying to support, Brant reported that

> the government in exile [sic] has passed completely out of the thoughts of Poles in Poland. . . . I doubt if the masses of the people ever thought of it as a government.

Brant thought that it would be in American interests to extend immediate economic aid. With this aid, Brant argued that the Socialists (PPS) could emerge as the dominant force in Polish politics. Truman thanked Brant for his letter a few weeks later, commenting that "it was most informative and helpful."[15]

Brant's recommendation was seconded by PSL leader Stanisław Mikołajczyk when he came to Washington to see Truman in November. In a meeting with Durbrow on 8 November, Mikołajczyk proposed that the United States grant immediate loans of $150 million for basic goods to help Poland regain its independence from the Soviet Union. Mikołajczyk was referring in part to the economic independence of the coal mining industry in Silesia. Mikołajczyk argued that a loan for the coal mining industry would increase the amount of exportable coal so that Poland could offset the reparations shipments to the Soviets. Durbrow told Mikołajczyk about Lane's complaints about the exchange rate, Poland's barter trade agreements with the Soviet Union and other countries, and the ambassador's reservations about Poland's credit reliability. Durbrow also reminded Mikołajczyk of Congress's role in granting U.S. Export-Import loans, and added that Congress had recently been critical of the administration's compromising policy toward the communist governments in Eastern Europe.[16] A day later Mikołajczyk and the vice-chairman of the Polish Reconstruction and Supply Commission, Janusz Źóltowski, met with Truman and asked the president for credits to purchase industrial, agricultural and transport equipment, and loans to finance other reconstruction needs. Truman responded favorably to Mikołajczyk's requests and promised to tell Byrnes "to arrange for the extending of credits to Poland, so as to enable her to obtain supplies she urgently needs."[17]

Meanwhile, Lane was doing a little private diplomacy of his own that ran counter to the State Department's loan policy. In a meeting with Rajchman on 7 November, Lane outlined his own "personal" interest in an improved exchange rate, compensation for the nationalization of American property, freedom of the press, and an end to the secret police's harassment of the political opposition. Rajchman told Lane that the costs of running the U.S. embassy would be settled by a credit of zlotys from the Polish government, which could be refunded when Poland became a member of the International Stabilization Fund of the IMF. He also maintained that he had no information on arrests of the political opposition or on other political activities. Lane admitted to Rajchman that the press situation had improved and said that he had sent the State Department his approval of a three-year credit to Poland for the purchase of 1000 U.S. Army surplus trucks. Lane viewed it as an initial gesture of good will.[18]

The Polish leadership thought that Lane's statements represented the position of the U.S. government, but Byrnes did not authorize Lane to make a short-term Export-Import Bank loan contingent on political concessions. In a telegram to Lane on 9 November, Byrnes made it clear that for the time being the State Department preferred not to link political questions to loans from the Export-Import Bank. Byrnes wrote that "one of the primary purposes [for] advancing credits is to promote the economic foreign policy framed to further economic interests in this country."[19]

Byrnes thought that the United States could eventually bring economic pressure to bear on Polish politics,[20] but the political makeup of the Polish government and the structure of the economic system, except for its trade policies, were not primary but secondary interests of his economic diplomacy at this time; the economic recovery of Europe was more important. Therefore the State Department did not make a short-term loan contingent on the holding of free elections in Poland. Byrnes told Lane that the Polish government could be threatened with the denial of *further* loans if the Yalta and Potsdam agreements for free elections were not upheld.[21]

Lane was disappointed that Byrnes and the State Department would not take a tougher stand against any loans to the present Polish government.[22] In a dispatch to Washington on 13 November, Lane again argued that American loans would be used by the Polish government to strengthen its political standing, and that even a small loan now would show that the United States was largely unconcerned about the continuing terrorist activities of the secret police. Lane also argued that Poland's "Sovietized" economy made that country a bad credit risk. Finally, Lane pointed out that the Soviets were still stripping Poland of reparations from Silesia.[23]

In effect, Lane was championing the administration's secondary objective of fostering the development of a free and democratic Poland. Lane reminded Byrnes that loans would not help "in fulfilling our publicly expressed policy: the maintenance of a strong, free and independent Poland." Lane also interpreted any positive change in the Polish government's policies, such as a relaxation of censorship, as a direct result of American economic and diplomatic pressure. He counseled against any credits or loans (aside from the 1000 army surplus trucks) before the Polish communists relinquished their illegitimate hold on power.[24]

Byrnes informed Lane shortly thereafter that the United States was not in a position in 1945 to offer Poland any large, long-term loan anyway, except for a possible credit to buy American cotton. The secretary of state explained that short-term loans were a response to Mikołajczyk's appeals; the State Department hoped that the loans would benefit the Polish people, specifically the peasantry that supported the

PSL. Lane was satisfied with this exchange, and he agreed to a small loan to buy trucks, bulldozers, farm equipment and draft animals if measures were taken to ensure that the Polish people actually received the goods. He also suggested a loan to Poland to rebuild one port as a clear gesture of American good will. The ambassador continued to oppose any cotton or coal loan, however, maintaining that the Polish people would not benefit from it.[25]

Although Byrnes did not think that the United States was capable of granting Poland a long-term loan in 1945, he was still entertaining the idea of extensive aid for Poland in 1946. Durbrow, who as East European desk chief was in close contact with Lane and the embassy in Warsaw, supported Lane by arguing against any substantial loans for the present Polish government. Durbrow informed Lane in December that he had been trying to convince the rest of the State Department to take a stand against any immediate large-scale loans to Poland. Durbrow was worried that Rajchman had friends in the State Department who might be persuaded to grant these loans to Poland.[26]

Durbrow favored a short-term loan for the Polish coal industry, however. At the end of November, Durbrow told Stefan Litauer, the economic counselor in the Polish embassy in Washington, that the United States would probably grant loans to Poland. Durbrow did not mention any political contingencies but emphasized rather that the United States opposed the economic monopolies that the Soviets seemed to be creating in the Eastern European countries. Litauer assured Durbrow that this would not happen in Poland.[27]

III

During the course of the loan talks that began in the fall of 1945, the Polish negotiators flatly told U.S. officials that the Polish government would not make any political concessions for economic assistance. Bierut set the tone of the talks by heatedly telling Lane "that if Poland must accept an Allied Power's activity in the internal affairs of Poland as a price for economic assistance, then Poland would prefer not to have such assistance."[28] Polish officials thought they could be frank about rejecting American political demands because they fully expected the United States to follow a policy of punishing the Germans and aiding the victims of German aggression. Shortly before the

Potsdam Conference, Minc declared that "especially Poland has a right to aid in the form of goods to be purchased on credit."[29] The Polish press and other government officials often repeated this conviction that Poland had earned economic assistance from the United States.

The Polish government was also well aware of the importance of American aid for the development of the Polish economy and for the survival of the communist regime. At the end of 1945, economic officials in the Ministry of Industry and Trade noted that the

> duration of the transition period [of the Polish provisional government] depended on the speed of the restoration and the reconstruction of the Polish economy, and this process in turn depends on the scope, conditions and speed of imparting loans to Poland by the United States.

The ministry also said that it was "honored" that the American delegation at Potsdam had invited the Polish representatives to discuss loan and investment needs.[30] Nonetheless, the Polish communists never compromised their complete hold on political power.

Polish communist ideologues contributed to a false impression that American loan policy would be dictated primarily by economic necessity. They frequently predicted that the United States would be forced to grant loans to Poland to help stimulate European recovery, ultimately for the benefit of the American economy. In October, Lane observed that *Głos Ludu*, the Polish Workers' Party organ, was reporting about widespread unemployment in the United States and alleging that American workers were "destitute."[31] *Życie Gospodarcze* also maintained that the American economy was in crisis because of the conversion from a war-time to a peace-time economy. The journal reported that production in the United States had fallen 20 percent in August and that Polish economic recovery, as an integral part of European recovery, dictated that the U.S. government would grant Poland various forms of economic assistance. The Polish government also hoped to receive credits to purchase U.S. war surplus that had been produced in 1945 for the invasion of Japan.[32]

U.S. economic officials gave the Polish communist government indications that Poland was likely to receive some kind of assistance from the United States. Rajchman told Minc that at the Ottawa economic conference in November he had received assurances that Poland would "undoubtedly" receive an initial Export-Import Bank loan of $25 million and a credit of $40 million to buy U.S. Army surplus in Europe. Rajchman reported that the "administration, and above all Clayton, feels morally obligated." He warned, however, that the loan negotiations could depend on the state of Soviet-American relations after the upcoming Council of Foreign Ministers meeting in Moscow.[33] The ongoing debate within the U.S. government over loan policy toward Poland, however, caused considerable confusion among Polish officials about what Poland had to do to qualify for loans. Rajchman wrote Minc at the end of December that he had been conducting talks with the State Department for a month to obtain from them "in black and white" what it was that the Americans wanted.[34]

Although the Truman administration publicly championed the cause of Polish democracy, economic considerations dominated the loan negotiations themselves. American officials pressed the Poles to adhere to article seven of the Mutual Aid (or Lend-Lease) Agreement of 1 July 1942, which prohibited any trade agreements that gave one country a monopoly on trade with Poland.[35] When Rajchman asked the State Department about the loans in January 1946, the department repeated this demand. Rajchman explained that he could not guarantee that his government would accept the American proposals, but now he was at least satisfied that he understood the U.S. position. Rajchman assured the Americans that Poland would give the United States copies of all of Poland's commercial agreements, although he was probably not authorized to do so. Plainly the State Department was most interested in the Polish-Soviet trade agreements. The State Department did mention political demands at these meetings, which gave Rajchman the false impression that the State Department would completely disregard them.[36]

The Truman administration viewed a U.S. Army war surplus credit and a small Export-Import Bank loan for the coal industry as initial steps in economic cooperation between the two countries. At first the State Department made these six specific demands on Poland: 1) elimination of all forms of barriers to international commerce (article seven of the Lend-Lease Agreement), 2) participation in a general conference on trade and employment, and adherence to the protocols of that conference, 3) adherence to the Polish-American Trade Treaty of 1931, which "continues to accord to nationals and corporations of the United States, with regard to all forms of commercial activity, treatment no less favorable than that accorded to nationals and corporations of any other country," 4) the holding of general elections in accordance with the Potsdam agreements, and freedom of the press to report on the election, 5) the payment of adequate compensation to American owners of nationalized property, and 6) providing the United States with full information on Poland's international economic relations. On 12 January C. Burke Elbrick from the East European Division told Źółtowski that Export-Import Bank loans would not be available until the Polish government conformed with "announced policies" of the United States, which included the fourth provision of the proposed loan agreement, namely the holding of free elections.[37]

In reality, when Acheson relayed this proposal to Byrnes on 22 January, Acheson recognized that the State Department had not yet made a final decision on these conditions for a small Export-Import Bank loan.[38] Acheson thought that because the Soviet Union dominated barter trade with Poland in 1945, the Polish government would have difficulties adhering to the second condition on the principles of free trade. Acheson also thought that the Polish leadership would not promise to hold free elections. He was right about the Polish government's reluctance to commit to free elections, but the sixth condition (submission to the United States of Poland's trade agreements) proved to be a bigger problem for the Polish government than its general acceptance of the principles of the Open Door. Berman told Lane that there could be difficulties in relaying the provisions of the Polish-Soviet trade agreements to the United States, because the agreements stipulated that their contents could not be revealed to third parties.[39] In January 1946, Minc promised to give Lane information on Poland's trade treaties in order to meet the stipulations for the Export-Import Bank loan. The United States had to wait until that summer to receive copies of these treaties, however, and even then the Poles did not reveal all of the information in the Soviet trade agreements.[40]

In the course of the negotiations, the administration gave Polish officials more conflicting messages about the conditions that Poland had to meet for the loans. Lane insisted that his government would not grant any loans without Polish political concessions or satisfaction on the compensation issue.[41] Józef Olszewski, director of the Political Department in the Foreign Ministry, told the American chargé d'affaires in Warsaw, Gerald Keith, that Polish officials were in "a somewhat difficult situation when they did not know whether the

Ambassador [Lane] was expressing his own or the government's views."[42] On 26 January Byrnes instructed the U.S. embassy in Warsaw to "reiterate this Government's recognition of the right of the Polish Government to nationalize property and point out that Ambassador Lane's protest dealt only with the failure of the Polish Government to fulfill its obligations under the [Trade] Treaty of 1931." Byrnes added that he had told Polish Foreign Minister Rzymowski that the United States would not interfere in Polish internal affairs, but that he expected the Polish government to hold free and unfettered elections in accordance with the Potsdam agreement.[43]

It was clear to the Americans that the Polish leadership was confused and frustrated by the conflicting statements of Export-Import Bank officials and Byrnes on the one hand, and Lane and the East European desk on the other. At the end of January, Olszewski asked to confide in Keith privately about his concern that the embassy was going beyond Washington's orders in placing barriers in the way of loans. Olszewski said that American diplomats were constantly maintaining "that if this or that were not done the Poles would not be able to obtain loans." He said that he wanted to maintain a cordial relationship with the embassy and hoped that the embassy would better inform itself of Washington's policies in order to avoid such misunderstandings.[44] On 28 January Durbrow admitted to H. Freeman Matthews, head of the European Affairs Division, that the State Department needed to tell the Poles exactly what the United States wanted in return for the loans. He thought that this should be done through a policy letter to the Export-Import Bank. Durbrow recommended reducing the loan amount from $50 million to $25 million until the Polish government had signed an aviation agreement. He made no mention of Polish elections in this conversation.[45]

Poland's chances for the loans did not improve in 1946 when some American officials became increasingly convinced of Soviet interference in Polish economic affairs. Polish officials expressed amazement that the State Department still thought that loans to Poland might end up in the hands of the Soviets. One Polish diplomat lamented that "there still exists a fantastic picture [of Poland]: that we are occupied by the USSR, that all profits flow to them, and that credits for us are concealed aid for the USSR." Polish diplomats were aware, however, that the State Department, and especially the political divisions, did not believe that the Polish government was truly independent and negotiating in good faith. But some Polish officials thought that the administration's reservations about granting the loans were mainly economic, not political. They even thought that the final decisions for foreign loans were made in the Treasury Department rather than in the State Department.[46]

Much to Lane's satisfaction, Byrnes became concerned enough about the repression of the Polish political opposition in early 1946 that he began to rethink his loan policy. On 2 February Byrnes sent word to the U.S. embassy in Warsaw that guarantees of a free Polish press, cessation of political arrests, and the liberation of American citizens "must be met before American public funds can be put at the disposal of the Polish Provisional Government." Lane agreed that the United States should follow a "strong policy with respect to all of the Soviet dominated governments."[47] But two months later when the loan agreements were signed, these stipulations had not been met and were not in the text of the loan contracts. Indeed, on 22 February Clayton wrote the chairman of the board of the Export-Import Bank, William Martin, that if Poland adhered to most of the six conditions outlined in the State Department's proposal, the department would accept a loan of $50 million from the bank. Even if these conditions were not met, Clayton said that the State Department favored a loan of not more than $25 million in order to show the friendship of the U.S. government for the people of Poland.[48]

Export-Import Bank officials were generally favorable to a small loan for the Polish coal industry. The bank recognized that Western Europe desperately needed coal, and that a shipping shortage prevented the United States from delivering more of its own coal. The loan was intended to help Poland increase coal production and exports to Western Europe. In addition, bank officials were confident that the hard currency profits from the sale of coal to Western Europe would ensure Poland's capacity to repay the loan.[49]

In March, the Truman administration tentatively decided to grant Poland a $50 million dollar credit to buy U.S. Army war surplus equipment. Although Lane understood that the United States stood to take a total loss on this depreciating equipment sitting in Europe, he was vehemently opposed to this credit as well, calling it a "grave error."[50] On 14 March he cabled Byrnes to call for a halt to the surplus credit, citing the Polish government's arrests of PSL and former Home Army members, illegal searches of PSL headquarters, and attempts to stop the circulation of the PSL newspaper *Gazeta*

Ludowa. He warned that the credit would bolster the political standing of the present government and expressed reservations about continuing the Export-Import Bank loan negotiations. Lane recalled later that "I felt great concern over the Department's apparent intention to grant credits in spite of the bad faith so clearly shown on so many occasions by the Polish ruling clique."[51]

The urgent need for Polish coal in Western Europe finally convinced Byrnes to support the Export-Import Bank loan as well as the army surplus credit. The last roadblock to a loan agreement was removed on 29 March when a general accord was signed to settle the nationalization compensation issue through a bilateral commission. Byrnes then gave orders to sign the loan agreement in spite of his doubts that the Polish government would adhere to the agreement's provisions.[52] The Polish government indicated a willingness to compromise on several sensitive economic issues, however. On 8 April the Poles offered to show Lane in confidence the trade treaties with the Soviet Union, but also insisted that they could not be made public. They promised that all subsequent trade agreements would be open, even those with the Soviets.

The Polish negotiators would not budge on their refusal to include the clause on free elections in the loan agreement. Finally, the State Department offered to exclude this clause if the Poles promised to reaffirm the Potsdam election promises in a separate, simultaneously published document. Źółtowski thought that this was acceptable.[53] Byrnes agreed with this compromise and sent word of it to Lane on 15 April. Byrnes argued that the surplus credit and Export-Import Bank loan would show American support for the reconstruction of Poland. In addition, Byrnes thought that the Polish government's new election pledge would encourage Mikołajczyk and the PSL that the United States was standing firm in its support of a truly democratic Poland. Byrnes added that by insisting on this separate declaration on free elections, the United States was sending the Polish government a strong signal that further loans would be linked to the conduct of those elections.[54]

On 21 April Lane made one last attempt to persuade Byrnes to veto the proposed loan. Lane still thought that the Polish government should be asked to make political concessions:

> With the greatest earnestness of which I am capable I beg the Department not to approve the extension of any credit facilities at this time. When the terroristic [sic] activities of the security police come to an end, when freedom of the press is restored and when American citizens are released from Polish prisons then, and not until then, should US public funds be used to assist the Polish Provisional Government of national unity.[55]

Byrnes answered that the Polish government had agreed to the economic provisions of the loan agreement and had promised to make a separate statement promising to hold free elections. Byrnes reasoned that because the Poles had pledged to publish the text of the loan agreement, the Polish people would know that the United States had not forgotten them, and that the Polish government had made commitments to give them a free vote. He pointed out that the loan was intended solely for the Polish coal industry in order to increase exports to Western Europe. Byrnes promised that no further loans would be made until the political and economic situation had improved. Here Byrnes mistakenly thought that the United States had considerable leverage:

> The Poles have indicated they will endeavor to obtain additional substantial credits as soon as we will make them available. This gives us further means of pressure.[56]

Źółtowski, Rajchman, Durbrow and Emilio Collado, director of the Office of Financial and Development Policy in the State Department, met several times in April to negotiate the final loan agreement. On 24 April Clayton authorized Martin to vote in favor of the $40 million Export-Import Bank loan. Clayton told the bank's Board of Directors that "the agreements which have been reached with the Poles during the last week constitute a strong political commitment and an even stronger basic economic commitment." Clayton also told bank officials that

> State considers it desirable to go forward quickly on the loan before the Poles retract in any way the commitments they have made. . . . The Secretary and the Acting Secretary of State consider the political and economic commitments made by the Poles in the agreements just arrived to be very excellent and satisfactory.[57]

On 24 April Polish and American representatives signed the $90 million loan and credit agreement.[58] Significantly, the election clause was missing from the final draft of the loan agreement. The headline of a front page article in the *New York Times* read "U.S. Grants Credits to Poland on Promise of Free Election," but the newspaper also reported that "there was no mention of free elections in the text of the agreement itself."[59] Of course, the Polish government had no intention of holding "free and unfettered elections," but now the U.S. government could not legally withhold the loan if the Polish government did not keep this promise. Furthermore, because the election pledge was not in the final draft of the accord, the Polish press could publish the loan agreement without mentioning elections.[60]

In effect, the administration had decided not to link political concessions to the loan and credit package directly. In the spring of 1946, it was more important to the Truman administration to revive the Polish coal industry and the Polish economy than to withhold loans for political reasons. For the most part, the economic provisions of the treaty were acceptable to the Polish leadership.[61] The Polish government also agreed that it would use the Export-Import loan to buy coal cars, locomotives, and mining equipment, items that were in critical shortage in Poland.[62] Despite the Polish communists' propaganda about the threats to Poland's economic sovereignty, the Polish government allowed the United States, at least in this limited sense, to stipulate how Poland was to use the loans.

IV

Lane took the loan as a personal affront. He wrote Byrnes that either the State Department had no confidence in his evaluation of the situation in Poland, or "for reasons of which I am unaware it does not wish to accede to my recommendations."[63] Acheson tried to allay Lane's disappointment by relaying a statement from Polish Ambassador Oskar Lange promising that Polish elections would take place according to the Potsdam agreements.[64] Several days later Acheson sent Lane another cable in which he cited a "favorable" editorial on the loan in the *New York Times*.[65] Lane could not accept the State Department's position to grant the loans to achieve short-term economic goals, and he soon resigned his post.[66]

Two priorities that some historians cite for American economic policy in postwar Eastern Europe were actually secondary considerations in the case of this coal loan to Poland. First, no political concessions were directly tied to the loan agreement. Second, the importance of the Open Door for direct Polish-American trade was minimal; the Truman administration never considered Poland to be an important direct trading partner anyway. The Polish government could sidestep the vague Open Door principles in the agreement, and the State Department knew this. On the other hand, the administration was surprised when the Polish government adhered to the concrete financial provisions of its trade agreements.

There is also little evidence that Byrnes or other State Department officials really thought that the loan package would enable the Polish communists to become more politically independent from Moscow. In a note to Lane in May, Keith expressed a view of the Polish government that was rapidly gaining adherents in Washington: "We [the embassy staff] are unanimously in accord with your often expressed conviction that the Polish Government officials who make any of the vital decisions which have an effect upon our basic relations with Poland are Soviet tools."[67] The administration's frustration with Soviet meddling in Polish affairs and with the undemocratic actions of the Polish provisional government became immediately evident when the State Department suspended the loan agreement in May.

NOTES

1. Department of State *Bulletin*, 3 February 1946, 139.

2. Charles L. Mee, *The Marshall Plan: The Launching of Pax Americana* (New York: Simon and Schuster, 1984), 77.

3. United States Government, *Minutes of the Export-Import Bank*, 13 February 1946, Records Group 275, 6:110, National Archives, Washington D.C. (hereafter RG 275 with date, volume, and page number).

4. Acheson to Lane, 21 September 1945, RG 59, 860c.50, box 6381.

5. Lane to Byrnes, 25 September 1945, *FRUS, 1945* 5:377.

6. Lane to Byrnes, 4 October 1945, *FRUS, 1945* 5:383-386; Lane to Byrnes, 13 October 1945, ibid., 388-390; and Lane to Byrnes, 7 December 1945, RG 59, 860c.51, box 6385.

7. Memorandum of conversation, Rajchman, Emilio Collado, etal., 7 September 1945, RG 59, 860c.51, box 6385.

8. Memorandum of conversation, Rajchman and Gilpatric, 1 October 1945, RG 59, 860c.50, box 6381.

9. Memorandum by Young (associate chief of the OED) to Acheson, 25 October 1945, *FRUS, 1945* 5:392.

10. Lane to Byrnes, 27 December 1945, RG 59, 611.60c31, box 2847.

11. Lane, *I Saw Poland Betrayed*, 228; and Lane to Byrnes, 13 October 1945, *FRUS, 1945* 5:388-390.

12. Lane to Byrnes, 22 October 1945, RG 59, 860c.51, box 6385.

13. *New York Times*, 5 November 1945, 5.

14. Graebner, *America as a World Power*, 131-132. The head of the Polish American Congress, Charles Rozmarek, opposed loans without political concessions, but it does not appear that the lobbying pressure of the Polish-American community had much impact on the economic policy of the United States toward Poland at this time; See also Davis, *The Cold War Begins: Soviet-American Conflict over Eastern Europe*, 382, who argues that "the Polish-American vote was clearly a very important factor in the determination of United States Eastern European policy [in 1945]." There is no evidence in the State Department documents or in the Truman papers that the Polish-American lobby directly influenced this economic policy, however.

15. Irving Brant to Truman, 15 October 1945, Truman Papers, PSF, Subject File, box 186; Truman to Brant, 6 November 1945, ibid.

16. Memorandum of conversation, Durbrow and Mikołajczyk, 8 November 1945, *FRUS, 1945* 5:400-404; see also Hugh DeSantis, *The Diplomacy of Silence: The American Foreign Service, the Soviet Union, and the Cold War, 1933-1947* (Chicago: The University of Chicago

Press, 1980), 161, who claims that Durbrow, along with Bohlen and Matthews, refused to tie political strings to American financial aid. Here Durbrow mentions only economic considerations, but later he includes political concessions as well.

17. Polish embassy in Washington to the Department of State, 5 December 1945, *FRUS, 1945* 5:428-430.

18. Lane to Byrnes, 9 November 1945, *FRUS, 1945* 5:409-411; see Davis, *The Cold War Begins: Soviet-American Conflict over Eastern Europe*, 249, who states that "the only positive U.S. effort at all in the fall of 1945 to promote the holding of free elections was through the denial of American economic credits." This was true of Lane, but Byrnes differentiated between the objectives of a small, short-term loan and a larger loan. Eventually no political concessions would be tied to a $40 million Export-Import Bank loan for the coal industry.

19. Byrnes to Lane, 9 November 1945, *FRUS, 1945* 5:411.

20. See Lundestad, *The American Non-Policy Towards Eastern Europe 1943-1947*, 209, who contends that by November 1945 "there was also considerable doubt about the pressure which the United States could bring to bear in political as opposed to economic matters."

21. Byrnes to Lane, 9 November 1945, *FRUS, 1945* 5:411-412.

22. Lane, *I Saw Poland Betrayed*, 228.

23. Lane to Byrnes, 13 November 1945, *FRUS, 1945* 5:412-414.

24. Lane to Byrnes, 13 November 1945, *FRUS, 1945* 5:412-414; and Lane, *I Saw Poland Betrayed*, 229.

25. Byrnes to Lane, 24 November 1945, *FRUS, 1945* 5:419-420; Lane to Byrnes, 29 November 1945, ibid., 422-423; see also Paterson, *Soviet-American Confrontation: Postwar Reconstruction and the Origins of the Cold War*, 132, who contends that Byrnes and Lane were in agreement on this cotton credit.

26. Cable, "The United States and the Polish Question, 1939-1948," 311.

27. Cable, "The United States and the Polish Question, 1939-1948," 310.

28. Lane to Byrnes, 14 November 1945, *FRUS, 1945* 5:414-417; and Lane, *I Saw Poland Betrayed*, 229.

29. *Rzeczpospolita*, 25 July 1945, 3.

30. Undated memorandum (ca. December 1945), Ministry of Industry and Trade Records, File 51.

31. Lane to Byrnes, 20 October 1945, RG 59, 860c.50, box 6381.

32. *Życie Gospodarcze* 1 (5 December 1945): 5-8.

33. Rajchman to Minc and Jędrychowski, 30 December 1945, Ministry of Industry and Trade Records, File 51.

34. Memorandum of Rajchman to Minc and Jędrychowski, 30 December 1945, Ministry of Industry and Trade Records, File 51.

35. Memorandum of conversation, Durbrow, Clayton and J. Źółtowski, L. Rajchman, 5 December 1945, *FRUS, 1945* 5:427-428.

36. Memorandum of conversation, Rajchman, Litynski and Brown, Hooker, etal., 4 January 1946, RG 59, 611.60c.31, box 2847.

37. Proposed note to Poland, 8 January 1946, RG 59, 611.60c.31, box 2847; and memorandum of conversation, Elbrick and Źółtowski, 12 January 1946, *FRUS, 1946* 6:376-379.

38. Acheson to Byrnes in London, 22 January 1946, *FRUS, 1946* 6:383.

39. Lane to Byrnes, 7 March 1946, RG 59, 860c.51, box 6385.

40. Lane to Byrnes, 23 January 1946, RG 59, 711.60c, box 3426.

41. See Lundestad, *The American Non-Policy Towards Eastern Europe 1943-1947*, 212, who argues that the East European Division was in favor of the loan on economic grounds. Durbrow, like Lane, was opposed to a loan at this time. He later agreed to a small $25 million loan.

42. Keith to Byrnes, 24 January 1946, RG 59, 860c.51, box 6385.

43. Byrnes to Keith, 26 January 1946, *FRUS, 1946* 6:384-385.

44. Byrnes to Keith, 26 January 1946, *FRUS, 1946* 6:384-385; and Keith to Byrnes, 29 January 1946, ibid., 385-387.

45. Memorandum from Durbrow to Matthews, 28 January 1946, RG 59, 860c.51, box 6385.

46. Undated memorandum from the Polish embassy in Washington to Warsaw (ca. March 1946), Ministry of Industry and Trade Records, File 51. There is no evidence in the U.S. government documents that the Treasury Department was deeply involved in these loan decisions.

47. Byrnes in Paris to the U.S. embassy in Warsaw, 2 February 1946, RG 59, 860c.51, box 6385; Lane to Byrnes, 4 February 1946, *FRUS, 1946* 6:387; and Caffery to Byrnes, Clayton, etal., 4 February 1946, RG 59, 860c.51, box 6385.

48. Clayton to Martin, 13 February 1946, *FRUS, 1946* 6:393-395.

49. *Minutes of the Export-Import Bank*, 13 February 1946, RG 275, 6:109.

50. Lane, *I Saw Poland Betrayed*, 234.

51. Lane to Byrnes, 14 March 1946, *FRUS, 1946* 6:412-414; and Lane, *I Saw Poland Betrayed*, 234-236.

52. Paterson, *Soviet-American Confrontation: Postwar Reconstruction and the Origins of the Cold War*, 134.

53. Memorandum of conversation, Źółtowski, Collado, Durbrow, etal., 8 April 1946, RG 59, 860c.51, box 6385.

54. Byrnes to Lane, 15 April 1946, RG 59, 860c.51, box C-636.

55. Lane to Byrnes, 21 April 1946, *FRUS, 1946* 6:432.

56. Byrnes to Lane, 22 April 1946, *FRUS, 1946* 6:432-433.

57. *Minutes of the Export-Import Bank*, 24 April 1946, RG 275, 6:212-221.

58. Thomas McCabe (foreign liquidation commissioner) to Lange, 22 April 1946, *FRUS, 1946* 6:433-435; and Sekular, "Stosunki gospodarcze między Polska i Stanami Zjednoczonymy Ameryki po II wojnie światowej," 19. The terms of the surplus credit were twenty-five equal annual installment payments beginning on 1 July 1952 at 2 3/8 percent interest. Poland used only $37,670,000 of the $50 million army surplus credit, but used the $40 million Export-Import Bank loan in full by 1949, and repaid the loan by the late 1960s.

59. *New York Times*, 25 April 1946, 1, 4; see Cable, "The United States and the Polish Question, 1939-1948," 315-316, 322, who lists the six points of the original proposal but overlooks the fact that the election provision was not in the loan contract itself; see also Lukas, *Bitter Legacy: Polish-American Relations in the Wake of World War II*, 50, and Lundestad, *The American Non-Policy Towards Eastern Europe 1943-1947*, 211-212. They also make no mention that the promise to hold free elections was not in the final draft.

60. *Życie Gospodarcze* 1 (9 May 1946): 295-297; see Paterson, *Soviet-American Confrontation: Postwar Reconstruction and the Origins of the Cold War*, 133. Paterson also overlooks the separation of the election pledge from the draft of the loan agreement; see also Glinka-Janczewski, "American Policy Toward Poland Under the Truman Administration, 1945-1952," 237, who incorrectly writes that "the agreement had attached no conditions whatsoever to the financial assistance in question but had merely linked the economic assistance to the political freedoms."

61. Zyblikiewicz, *Polityka Stanów Zjednoczonych i Wielkiej Brytanii wobec Polski, 1944-1949*, 247; see also Davis, *The Cold War Begins: Soviet-American Conflict over Eastern Europe*, 374-375, who criticizes the inactivity of the United States in trying to facilitate the Open Door in Poland. Although the State Department was not confident that the Poles would adhere to the loan agreement, the provisions of the loan agreement tried to secure equal opportunity for the West to trade with Poland. Furthermore, there were some in the State Department who understood that it made economic sense for Poland to conduct barter trade with the Soviets in 1945. On the other hand, the stipulations for the loan show that (as Davis claims) "[the United States did not] initiate any action to block the conclusion of trade agreements between the Soviet Union and Eastern European countries." But according to Davis, the "economic and financial assistance to the Polish and Yugoslav governments was deferred pending the holding of such free elections." In Poland's case, this was simply not true.

62. United Nations Reconstruction and Relief Administration (UNRRA), Operational Analysis Papers, No. 1: *Transport Rehabilitation in Poland* (London: 1946), 6. The UNRRA estimated in December 1946 that Poland had a deficit of 1,086 locomotives and 83,000 wagons.

63. Lane to Byrnes, 25 April 1946, *FRUS, 1946* 6:436-437.

64. Acheson to the U.S. embassy in Warsaw, 25 April 1946, RG 59, 860c.00, box 6367.

65. Acheson to the U.S. embassy in Warsaw, 27 April 1946, RG 59, 860c.51, box 6385.

66. See Lundestad, *The American Non-Policy Towards Eastern Europe 1943-1947*, 212.

67. Keith to Lane, 15 May 1946, RG 59, 860c.51, box 6385.

Chapter Three

The Suspension of the Loan Agreement, 1946

I

Soon after the United States had signed the $90 million loan package in April 1946, the State Department had second thoughts. Some State Department officials, including Lane and Durbrow, were dissatisfied with the accord because it did not carry with it any specific political conditions. The Polish communists were not easing their repression of the political opposition in any way. Having bargained the election pledge out of the final loan agreement itself, the Polish government was not legally obligated to hold free elections. Instead, the communists used the loan agreement to their own political advantage.

On the other hand, the Polish government tried to adhere to the provisions of the loan accord, but Polish officials had some trouble giving the United States copies of trade agreements made with the Soviet Union. Moscow demanded that these agreements remain confidential. These developments prompted the Truman administration to suspend the loan agreement in May. This action angered and frustrated the Polish government and compromised any good will that might have resulted from the loan agreement.

II

As Lane and Durbrow had predicted, the Polish government used the $90 million loan agreement to legitimize the regime and to silence the political opposition. The East European Division complained that Polish press announcements and a speech on the loan by Premier Edward Osóbka-Morawski

> were both slanted to give the impression that the United States Government, by authorizing the credit, was supporting the policies and the continuation of the Polish Provisional Government and gave no indication that this Government is, in fact, pressing for the election of a truly representative government in Poland.[1]

The Polish press announced the signing of the loan on 28 April without publishing the actual text of the loan agreement. In a front page article *Rzeczpospolita* wrote that

> the most monstrous nonsense about us has been circulated and is being circulated by our own reactionary emigration and by international reaction. The loans granted to us by the United States are proof that . . . these attacks are slanderous and untruthful. The United States sees that we are working and therefore lent us [money].[2]

In addition to using the loan agreement to show that the United States supported the present Polish government, the Polish press used the loan accord to justify Poland's legal claim to Silesia. *Rzeczpospolita* argued that

> the loans were not granted to an indefinite Poland, but to a Poland whose boundaries rest on the Oder and Luscatian Neisse [Rivers]. Indirectly it is also an answer to Churchill and to all those politicians who are trying to question our western border.[3]

The newspaper also maintained that the loan was an American sanction for Polish participation in the reconstruction of Europe.[4]

In the Polish National Council, Osóbka-Morawski repeated that the loan agreement was a confirmation of Poland's desire for economic cooperation with all countries.[5] Democratic Party Deputy Adam Krzyżanowski applauded the government for acquiring the loan and predicted that the loans would have "great economic and financial importance, and above all, great significance in the foreign policy sphere." He urged the government to invite American economic experts to Poland in order to improve Polish chances for further loans.[6] New Polish Foreign Minister Zygmunt Modzelewski also expressed optimism about the loan's favorable impact on the Polish economy and viewed the loan as an indication that the United States was basing its relationship with Poland on mutual trust.[7]

Angered over this propaganda, Lane wrote Byrnes in Paris that Modzelewski was using the loan to claim that "the United States base their relations with us on ever growing confidence."[8] Lane then flew to Paris to tell Byrnes face to face that the Polish government was not adhering to the provisions of the loan agreement. The Polish press had not published a draft of the loan agreement, and the U.S. embassy in Warsaw had not yet received Poland's trade treaties. Much to the frustration of the Polish authorities, Lane also raised the issue of press freedom as another reason to suspend the loan package, although there was no mention of it in the agreement itself.[9] This time Lane succeeded in changing Byrnes's mind, and on 6 May Byrnes ordered a halt in the shipments of war surplus equipment to Poland and delayed the final signing of the $40 million Export-Import Bank loan contract.[10]

Lane was especially gratified that his advice was followed to suspend the loan package. Now he hoped that his superiors would withhold any aid until the Polish government made political concessions. The ambassador wrote Byrnes that

> the continued suspension . . . will in my opinion be the best step we can take in the protection of our interests. This credit should remain frozen until the Polish Government honors all its obligations to the United States.[11]

Lane and Keith also argued that Mikołajczyk's PSL was in favor of this action, on the grounds that the Polish government was using the loan as propaganda to claim that the United States supported the present regime. Furthermore, Mikołajczyk thought that the loan had given the PPR and the PPS confidence to continue and even escalate their repression of his PSL. Mikołajczyk now opposed the loan because he thought that it would enhance the communists' chances in the June referendum on the new structure of the Polish government.[12]

Acting Secretary of State Dean Acheson told the American press that the election issue and the censorship of the press in Poland were the grounds for the loan suspension, despite the fact that the Polish government was only legally bound to publish the loan agreement and a separate pledge to hold free elections.[13] On 17 May Byrnes instructed Lane to tell Bierut that the U.S. government was very concerned about the Polish government's press censorship and repression of the political opposition. Byrnes was especially disturbed about the censorship of a story sent to New York by *New York Times* correspondent Larry Allen. Allen's cable contained a speech by PSL leader Stanisław Bańczyk, in which Bańczyk criticized the undemocratic actions of the PPR and the PPS.[14] By this time some officials in the East European Division thought that even if the Polish government released the Bańczyk speech and supplied the trade treaties, the loans should remain frozen in light of the "disturbing political situation in Poland."[15]

It is unclear exactly why the text of the loan agreement was not published immediately in the Polish press, but Ambassador Lange understood that there would be debate in Warsaw over whether to publish the agreement and the election pledge at the same time. In a meeting with Acheson on 24 April, Lange expressed concern over the timing of the American press release of the loan agreement, for it was his understanding that the agreement was to be announced simultaneously in both countries.[16] Lange may have misinterpreted an agreement between the State Department and the Export-Import Bank that "the public relations officers of State and the Bank would collaborate and arrange for a simultaneous [press] release on April 25."[17] There was no clear agreement on the timing of the Polish and American press releases.

As for the censorship issue, at first the Polish authorities feigned ignorance of the blocked transmission of Bańczyk's speech, but later Modzelewski blamed an employee in the telegraph office.[18] The State Department continued to press the issue even though it was not sure of the reason for the delay.[19] The Associated Press finally received the story on 13 May.

The Polish government undoubtedly delayed the transmission of the speech, but Polish officials probably had little choice but to resist divulging the provisions of Soviet-Polish trade agreements.[20] The Polish government was legally bound to keep them secret. After weeks of stalling, Modzelewski promised to deliver the trade treaties by the second week of May, but by that time the suspension was already in effect. As for publishing the exact draft of the April loan agreement and the accompanying pledge to hold free elections, he claimed that Lange had not yet sent them to Warsaw.[21] During a meeting with Keith in Warsaw on 13 May, Modzelewski contended that the United States had not given his government "reasonable time" to publish the loan agreement. Keith thought that the Polish foreign minister was bluffing and that Modzelewski had "a deep down unfriendliness to the United States."[22]

Polish officials were completely surprised by the loan suspension, and it exacerbated an already testy relationship between the U.S. embassy and the Polish government. Lane tried to see Bierut several times to explain the action, but the Polish leader refused to receive him.[23] Modzelewski complained to Lane that the United States was treating Poland unlike any other country, and Modzelewski concluded that the suspension was another attempt to exert political pressure on Poland.[24] He was certainly correct.

The Polish press blasted the loan suspension. *Rzeczpospolita* wrote that "automobiles are rusting in American warehouses, and the United States has a considerable supply of locomotives which we so badly need." The newspaper claimed that this "pressure [is] intended to make us renounce our sovereignty at a price that threatens our interests and jeopardizes the friendship which the United States had, at every turn, shown our country."[25] *Życie Warszawy* accused the United States of "methods unprecedented in the history of diplomacy."[26]

Ambassador Lange warned that now his government had cause to wonder if it could count on the United States to aid Poland's reconstruction. He thought that Poland's economy should have more links to Western Europe, because the Soviets had little to offer in exchange for Polish coal. American economic assistance, he argued, would enable Poland to maintain an "independent position." If no American help was forthcoming, Lange said that "it would probably be necessary for Poland to seek Russia's economic aid."[27] When Poland and the Soviet Union conducted trade talks in Moscow in May, Lange told the State Department that there was an even greater chance that Poland would become economically dependent on the Soviet Union.[28] Although Lange was obviously trying to play on the Truman administration's fears that without American loans the Soviets would completely dominate the Polish economy, his analysis proved to be correct. Unfortunately for the Polish government, this reasoning no longer had much impact on American economic policy toward Poland.

In June, the *New York Times* and the *Washington Evening Star* reported that Lange had claimed that "Poland was no longer interested in the proposed $90,000,000 American credit to her because financial assistance had been obtained by Poland on generous terms from Russia."[29] Byrnes wrote Lane that "if this report is correct presumably no further action [on the loan] on our part is necessary."[30]

The Polish leadership did not miss a chance to compare the supposedly fruitful trade talks in Moscow with the American loan suspension. Minc claimed that Soviet help "has been furnished without impairment of Poland's economic and political freedom, and that no demands have been made on Poland for special concessions or insight into her trade treaties with other countries."[31] This indirect criticism of the United States undermined the efforts of some Polish officials who wanted to maintain close ties with the West. Obviously this propaganda did not put the Poland in a good position to lobby Washington for more economic assistance when the State Department finally lifted the loan suspension in late June.

There is little evidence that the Soviet-Polish trade talks influenced the Truman administration to reinstate the war surplus deliveries under the $50 million credit.[32] Soviet economic assistance to Poland was relatively small and the State Department knew it. The Soviet press reported on 27 May that Poland was forced to seek economic assistance from the Soviet Union as the result of the frozen American loans. The Soviets provided Poland with a much-needed 200,000 tons of grain in 1946, but this was a short-term credit purchase.[33] A Polish official told Lane in confidence that the Soviets had offered very little at the talks and that the Soviets had encouraged the Poles to seek all the assistance they could get from the West.[34]

The State Department lifted the loan suspension because of Polish compliance with some of the provisions of the loan agreement. In the second week of May, the Polish press published the five provisions of the loan agreement as well as Lange's note containing the government's pledge to hold free elections.[35] Acheson told the American press that the State Department was satisfied with these developments, but not with the continued press censorship and the missing trade treaties.[36] Nonetheless, on 23 May Acheson told Litauer and Źółtowski that only the problem of the trade treaties remained. The Poles promised to submit all of the details of the treaties, but by the end of May they had still not released this information.[37] The Polish leadership hoped that the loan would be reinstated before the referendum at the end of June in order to use that action as a sign of American support for the present regime.

Finally, on 14 June Osóbka-Morawski and Modzelewski told Lane that they would give the United States copies of the trade treaties within eight days, and that they would show the Americans in confidence the prices and quantities of the goods traded. Reluctantly, Lane recommended lifting the suspension of the army surplus credit before the referendum of 30 June so that the Polish government could not interpret the action as an American approval of the referendum results, which Lane feared would be fraudulent.[38]

On 26 June the $50 million army surplus credit was restored on the basis of the Polish promises of 14 June. The United States delayed the final signing of the $40 million Export-Import loan until the trade treaties were in hand, but again the Polish government stalled. Litauer informed the State Department that certain treaty information could be supplied immediately, but that the Poles might not be able to show everything to the Americans. The State Department told him that it expected to receive all the provisions of the treaties.[39]

After the United States had released the army surplus credit, Rzymowski promised to issue a statement to the press that the suspension had been a simple "misunderstanding." In the press release Rzymowski did not mention any of the political or economic issues that had been the actual grounds for the suspension. The *New York Times* reported the loan's release a day later, but did not mention any political reasons for the suspension other than the censorship issue.[40]

The Polish communist leadership had once again succeeded in divorcing political issues from the loan agreement. The Polish journal *Robotnik* claimed that the loan agreement (and a trade agreement with Great Britain) was

> a great victory for the foreign policy of our government. The fears of all those who stated, completely without basis, that our friendly relations with the Soviet Union do not make it possible for us

> to have favorable relations with powers of the West have been proven wrong.[41]

On 2 July the Polish government gave the trade treaties to Lane, but some parts of the Soviet agreements were still missing. A week later Osóbka-Morawski promised Lane that these were forthcoming, although he added that Poland was not obligated to provide the United States with this information. Lane wrote Byrnes that Osóbka-Morawski was very eager to have the army surplus credit reinstated and to finalize the Export-Import loan as soon as possible. Once again the ambassador thought it might be better to delay approval of the Export-Import loan until more time had passed after the referendum, because he knew that the communists had fixed the results to produce a convincing government victory. The State Department heeded Lane's recommendation and waited for the price information. When this information arrived at the U.S. embassy at the end of July, Lane said that some of the prices were still missing, including the price of the reparations coal.[42]

Lane made one final argument against the Export-Import Bank loan. Once again he complained that the exchange rate of 100 zlotys to one dollar was making life miserable for the embassy in Warsaw. Byrnes replied that the

> Department recognizes the seriousness of the exchange rate problem, but does not believe that new concessions can be requested at this stage of the Eximbank loan matter. Furthermore, as you know, the major purpose of the loan has been our interest in maximizing Polish coal deliveries to Europe.

On 1 August Lane reluctantly gave his approval to go ahead with the loan.[43]

Nonetheless, the trade treaty issue dragged on throughout the rest of the summer, and the State Department prevented the Export-Import Bank from signing the loan. The British government also lobbied the United States to deny Poland any assistance until the Polish government kept its promise to conduct free elections. When the $90 million loan package had been announced on 24 April, Foreign Minister Ernest Bevin had expressed "dismay" that the United States was granting loans for what he considered to be "paper commitments." Bevin argued that loans would only support the communists and not the democratic opposition.[44] When the loans were suspended in May, British diplomats encouraged the United States to demand free elections. When the Polish government met most of the economic criteria in the loan agreement, the State Department told the British government that the United States could not impose any new political demands on Poland.[45]

When the State Department's delaying tactics continued into the fall of 1946, the Export-Import Bank leadership demanded action because it had a tentative agreement with Poland and wanted to keep it. Bank Chairman William Martin told the State Department that the bank was in "a bad position because having once approved a commitment and being later over-ruled by the State Department there was nothing official in the record to show this action [suspending the loan]." In July, bank officials expressed their confusion over the reasons for the delay and hoped that Acheson and Clayton would explain the action at a bank board meeting. Bank officials were also upset about a report from the State Department that the loan was being held up because the department questioned Poland's ability to repay it. The bank had confidence that the Polish government could and would honor its debt.[46]

Finally, on 2 October Polish and American representatives signed the Export-Import Bank loan agreement. Over a year had passed since the Poles first asked for a loan at Potsdam. By this time the production of railroad cars in Poland had increased to nearly 500 a month,[47] prompting Polish officials to ask to shift $5 million of the loan from rolling stock to mining equipment. The State Department agreed because this would facilitate an increase in coal shipments to Western Europe.[48] The Export-Import Bank later revised the loan so that part of the $40 million was used for railway repair shop and signal equipment as well as for coal mining machinery.[49]

III

The loans received from the United States in the first year after the war fell far short of the Polish government's plans for foreign investment. At the end of 1945 the Polish government sent a note to the United States outlining investment needs of over $235 million for 1946-

1947, but Poland got only $90 million from the United States. As a result of this shortfall, the Polish government did not achieve its plan for coal and coke exports in 1946. The plan called for coal exports of 21,500,000 tons, but Poland exported 18,000,000 tons.[50] This was still an encouraging figure, because exports in 1945 had amounted to only 7,000,000 tons.[51] Other industries such as agriculture and textiles suffered more from the shortage in foreign loans, in part because Minc concentrated domestic investment in heavy industries.[52]

Although the $90 million loan package eventually contributed to Polish economic recovery, the prolonged loan negotiations and the loan suspension strained relations between the two countries and undermined the position of officials in the Polish government who favored closer ties to the West. Premier Osóbka-Morawski expressed dismay that purely economic criteria were not the basis of Polish-American economic relations, especially because the loan agreement contained only economic provisions. He warned that "your action in suspending the credit was a great blow to Polish pride especially when such matters as non-transmission of Allen's despatch on Bańczyk's speech were brought into the matter." Osóbka-Morawski also hoped that "in the future financial matters would be treated independently of other issues."[53]

The $90 million loan package and the prospect of additional loans did little to change the political behavior of the Polish government. The PPR and the PPS repeatedly warned that no political concessions would be made for economic assistance, and they were true to their word. The June referendum was fraudulent, and the persecution of the PSL and the remnants of the Home Army in the underground continued unabated in 1946. The result was a gradual severing of any significant economic exchanges between the two countries. The $90 million loan package proved to be the last American economic assistance to Poland during the Truman administration. The Truman administration's denial of any more relief for Poland after the end of UNRRA activities in 1947 (see Chapter 5) was one of the first manifestations of the administration's new hard line foreign economic policy.

NOTES

1. Memorandum from C. Burke Elbrick to Acheson, 2 May 1946, RG 59, 860c.51, box 6385.

2. *Rzeczpospolita*, 28 April 1946, 1.

3. *Rzeczpospolita*, 4 May 1946, 1.

4. Lane to Byrnes, 27 April 1946, RG 59, 860c.51, box 6385.

5. Polish National Council Records, 26 April 1946, 15.

6. Polish National Council Records, 27 April 1946, 259-260.

7. Polish National Council Records, 28 April 1946, 368.

8. Lane to Byrnes, 1 May 1946, RG 59, 760c.00, box 3990.

9. Acheson to the U.S. embassy in Warsaw, 6 May 1946, RG 59, 860c.51, box 6385. Acheson stated here that "the question of censorship is also a commitment taken by the Polish Government in connection with the credit." The promise to allow Allied press to cover the elections was part of the Potsdam agreement, and this pledge was part of Lange's separate statement on elections. This statement was not directly connected to the loan agreement itself.

10. Byrnes to Acheson, 6 May 1946, *FRUS, 1946* 6:448-449; and memorandum from Acheson to Elbrick, 8 May 1946, RG 59, 860c.51, box 6385. The Poles had already used $3.7 million of the surplus credit and over $10 million had been authorized for delivery. The final agreement for the Export-Import loan was not signed until 2 October.

11. Lane to Byrnes, 14 May 1946, RG 59, 860c.00, box 628.

12. Keith to Byrnes, 16 May 1946, RG 59, 860c.00, box 628; and Lane to Byrnes, 14 June 1946, RG 59, 711.60c, box 3426.

13. *New York Times*, 11 May 1946, 8.

14. Byrnes to Acheson, 17 May 1946, RG 59, 860c.51, box 6385.

15. Elbrick to Matthews (director of the European Affairs Division), 21 May 1946, *FRUS, 1946* 6:455-456.

16. Memorandum of conversation, Acheson and Lange, etal., 24 April 1946, *FRUS, 1946* 6:435-436.

17. *Export-Import Bank Minutes*, 24 April 1946, RG 275, 6:220-221.

18. Murphy (U.S. political advisor for Germany) to Byrnes, 4 May 1946, *FRUS, 1946* 6:445-448.

19. Memorandum of conversation, Acheson and John Balfour (minister counsel of the British embassy in Washington), etal., 29 May 1946, *FRUS, 1946* 6:452-453.

20. See Lukas, *Bitter Legacy: Polish-American Relations in the Wake of World War II*, 52. Lukas has no documentation to show that the Polish government's failure to publish the provisions of the loan agreement or to provide the United States with the texts of the its trade treaties was "more the result of bureaucratic bungling than a studied attempt to avoid commitments to the United States."

21. Murphy to Byrnes, 4 May 1946, *FRUS, 1946* 6:445-448.

22. Keith to Byrnes, 14 May 1946, RG 59, 860c.51, box 6385.

23. Lane, *I Saw Poland Betrayed*, 239.

24. Lane to Byrnes, 18 May 1946, RG 59, 860c.51, box 6385.

25. Quoted from *Rzeczpospolita*, 19 May 1946, in Keith to Byrnes, 19 May 1946, RG 59, 860c.51, box 6385.

19. Quoted from *Życie Warszawy* in Keith to Byrnes, 19 May 1946, RG 59, 860c.51, box 6385.

27. Memorandum of conversation, Benjamin V. Cohen and Oskar Lange, 25 May 1946, RG 59, 860c.50, box 6381.

28. Memorandum of conversation, Lange, Acheson and Thompson, 21 June 1946, *FRUS, 1946* 6:462-466.

29. *New York Times*, 23 June 1946, 1; and *The Congressional Record*, 79th Cong., 2nd sess., 92:A3706.

30. Byrnes (in Paris) to the State Department, 22 June 1946, RG 59, 860c.51, box 6385.

31. Quoted from *Kurjer Codzienny*, 12 June 1946, in Lane to Byrnes, 24 June 1946, RG 59, 860c.50, box 6381.

32. See Zyblikiewicz, *Polityka Stanów Zjednoczonych i Wielkiej Brytanii wobec Polski, 1944-1949*, 253.

33. *New York Times*, 28 May 1946, 10.

34. Lane to Byrnes, 15 July 1946, RG 59, 860c.51, box 6385.

35. Keith to Byrnes, 12 May 1946, RG 59, 860c.51, box 6385; and *Rzeczpospolita*, 13 May 1946, 4.

36. *New York Times*, 15 May 1946, 3.

37. Memorandum of conversation, Acheson, Elbrick, Litauer, and Źółtowski, 23 May 1946, *FRUS, 1946* 6:456-457.

38. Lane to Byrnes, 14 June 1946, RG 59, 860c.51, box 6385; and Lane to Byrnes, June 21, 1946, ibid.

39. Memorandum of conversation, Thompson, Elbrick, Litauer and Źółtowski, 25 June 1946, RG 59, 860c.51, box 6385.

40. Lane to Byrnes, 25 June 1946, RG 59, 860c.51, box 6385; Lane to Byrnes, 28 June 1946, ibid.; and *New York Times*, 27 June 1946, 5.

41. Quoted from *Robotnik*, 27 June 1946, in Lane to Byrnes, 28 June 1946, RG 59, 860c.51, box 6385.

42. Lane to Byrnes, 2 July 1946, RG 59, 860c.51, box 6385; Lane to Byrnes, 11 July 1946, ibid.; Lane to Byrnes, 23 July 1946, ibid.; and Lane to Byrnes, 1 August 1946, ibid.

43. Lane to Byrnes, 15 July 1946, RG 59, 860c.51, box 6385; and Byrnes to Lane, 17 July 1946, ibid.

44. Memorandum of conversation, Durbrow and G. Middleton (first secretary of the British embassy in Washington), 24 April 1946, RG 59, 860c.51, box 6385.

45. The Department of State to the British embassy in Washington, 12 July 1946, *FRUS, 1946* 6:474-475.

46. *Minutes of the Export-Import Bank*, 3 July 1946, RG 275, 6:323.

47. Memorandum of conversation, Lange, Litauer and Acheson, 22 August 1946, RG 59, 860c.00, box 6368.

48. Clayton to U.S. embassy in Warsaw, 24 September 1946, RG 59, 860c.51, box 6385.

49. Komitet Ekonomiczny Rady Ministrów, Protokoły Posiedzenia Prezydium i Plenum Komitetu Ekonomicznego [Economic committee of the council of ministers, protocols of the meetings of the presidium and plenary session of the economic committee], 6 September 1946, Archivum Akt Nowych, Warsaw (hereafter Economic Committee of the Council of Ministers, Protocols of Meetings, and date); and Clayton to the U.S. embassy in Warsaw, 27 September 1946, RG 59, 860c.51, box 6385.

50. Summary of needed investment, November 1945, Ministry of Industry and Trade Records, File 51; and Economic Committee of the Council of Ministers, Protocols of Meetings, 1 January 1946.

51. *Compendium Statystyczne Polskiego Handlu Zagranicznego w latach 1929-1938, 1945-1960*, 128.

52. Lane to Byrnes, 22 December 1945, RG 59, 860c.50, box 6381. Lane was concerned about the lack of investment in agriculture. In December, he wrote Byrnes that Minc had denied that the "peasant is being exploited to benefit the city workers."

53. Lane to Byrnes, 14 June 1946, RG 59, 860c.51, box 6385.

Chapter Four

The Change in U.S. Aid Policy, 1946-1947

I

By the summer of 1946, the Truman administration's immediate fears of a postwar depression in the United States had been allayed.[1] Although the administration had still not formulated a definite economic policy toward Poland, the hasty suspension of the $90 million loan in May, as well as the negligible political gain that the United States received from its substantial contributions to the U.N. relief effort in Poland bode ill for Poland's chances for more aid. The State Department rallied around George Kennan's "long telegram" in February, which advocated a firm containment policy toward the Soviet Union and its satellites. When the Truman Doctrine and Kennan's containment policy became the foundations of American foreign policy in Europe in 1947, the administration gradually shifted its main concern from the growth of European markets for American exports to a revival of the Western European economy to reduce the threat of communism.[2] American economic policy toward Poland did not change because the Open Door in that country closed; Polish trade with the West increased dramatically in 1946.[3] The Truman administration now viewed U.S. national security in terms of creating a strong non-communist Europe that was politically and economically tied to the United States.[4] The administration demanded that the Polish government conduct free elections in order to qualify for any more economic aid.

The $90 loan package to Poland failed to bring about a liberalization of communist rule in Poland, and the denial of further loans and relief also fell short of this goal. The political actions of the Polish communist government were unaffected American loans, or by the threat that further aid would be withheld. The political situation for the Polish opposition actually worsened in 1946. There were irregularities in the conduct of the referendum in June, and it was unlikely that the general elections, originally scheduled for the end of 1946, would be free and open. The result was the denial of any further loans or relief from the United States, so that by the time the Marshall Plan was announced in the summer of 1947, direct Polish-American economic relations were at an impasse.

Polish coal was so vital to the economic recovery of Western Europe, however, that the United States could not ignore Polish economic development.[5] Poland was the only Soviet bloc country that the Truman administration considered for more loans and relief aid. Even when no aid was forthcoming, the Polish government continued to export coal to Western Europe. Polish officials also persisted in their efforts to gain loans and favorable trade transactions with the West.

II

In spite of the outstanding political issues that prevented better relations between the United States and Poland in 1946 and 1947, the Polish government still sought to improve its trade relations with the United States and Western Europe. Although the Soviets viewed international economic cooperation with suspicion, the Poles made positive contributions to U.N. economic organizations such as the ECE Coal Commission for Europe and the ECE Subcommittee on Devastated Areas. Commerce Department official Thomas C. Blaisdell, Jr. commented in the fall of 1946 that the Subcommittee on Devastated Areas included two Polish officials who

> became our most useful allies. . . . In general, the people dealing with economic matters in the Polish Government are, with the exception of Minc, non-communists. They favor a policy of neutral economic orientation and as rapid as possible a revival of multilateral trade both with Eastern Europe and the West.

Blaisdell claimed that the Poles were doing everything possible to enhance their chances for economic assistance and increased trade; they had even proposed a European economic committee to further these goals. Blaisdell added that the Polish leadership was "interested in economic cooperation with the West for political reasons, in order to establish their independence.[6] Based on talks with Źółtowski and other Polish diplomats in Washington, Blaisdell recognized that the Commerce Department's Office of International Trade (OIT) took a more optimistic view of the prospects for commercial relations between the two countries than the State Department.[7]

The Polish government continued to ask for relief, loans and credits from the United States in late 1946. The U.S. embassy in Warsaw received numerous inquiries from Polish representatives about commercial exchanges. For example, in September 1946, the embassy responded favorably to a request from a Polish state trading company to buy chemicals in the United States and in the American occupation zone in Germany.[8] According to an American diplomat in Warsaw, the head of one of the Polish trading companies, Stanisław Szyszllo, had "recently been given the green light by the [Polish] Ministry of Commerce and Navigation to engage in foreign trade on a private basis." Szyszllo hoped for small credits to help develop various Polish export industries.[9] Ham was one of the major Polish exports to the United States before the war and the Polish government was interested in reviving this trade.[10] On the other hand, the embassy warned American businesses that the unfavorable exchange rate and the lack of clear commercial guidelines in Poland made it difficult to conduct trade with that country.[11]

Although some Polish officials worked hard to increase trade with the United States and Western Europe, their efforts were undermined by others in the Polish government who opposed a closer economic relationship with the West. A Polish economic representative in the United Nations, Jan Stańczyk, wrote Minc that American businessmen had complained to him about the uncooperative attitude of the Polish commercial mission in New York and the Polish embassy in Washington. Stańczyk reported that

> unfortunately the Commercial Mission not only does not attempt to engage in any close contact with interested parties, but even avoids discussions of commercial exchanges. . . . Interested parties especially complain about [economic] counselor [Zygmunt] Litynski, who behaves similarly to important [American] representatives of industry and finance.

Stańczyk also relayed a letter to Minc from Michael Mora, the director of World Trade Development in New Orleans, in which Mora wrote that Litynski had expressed no interest in the possibility of exporting Polish peat moss in exchange for cotton and cash. At that same time Minc was lobbying the State Department for a loan to buy cotton in the United States.[12]

The Polish government was aware that a few officials in the Truman administration were still concerned that a restrictive U.S. trade and aid policy would force Poland into the Soviet economic sphere, and the Poles played on this fear in their efforts to gain economic aid. In August, Lange emphasized that Poland desired and needed "a balanced economy, not tied up exclusively with either the Soviet Union or the West." Lange said that Poland could use up to one half billion dollars in loans, and warned that if Poland could not get help from the West it would have to look to the Soviets.[13] The State Department's Economic Affairs Division was one of the few agencies of the U.S. government that still argued in 1946 that the preponderance of Soviet trade with Poland was not necessarily discriminatory nor detrimental to Poland. The division's analysis of the Polish trade relationship with the Soviet Union concluded that

> respecting the question whether Poland has been forced into a trading structure which is at variance with her best interests from a strictly commercial standpoint, it is by no means clear that Poland is, in the over-all picture, placed at a disadvantage.

Economic affairs officials also did not think that Poland's trade with the Soviet Union automatically made Poland a bad credit risk, arguing that the coal industry gave Poland "substantial commercial and financial advantages, and gives her an essential raw material for the development of her own industries."[14]

The Polish leadership became very annoyed with the idea that the Soviets dominated the Polish economy. For example, when the Polish government was having difficulty buying U.S. Army surplus equipment in Western Europe with the $50 million credit, Modzelewski complained that the American authorities thought that half of Poland's purchases went to the Soviet Union, that the reconstruction of the Polish economy strengthened the economic potential of the Soviet Union, and that railroad cars went to the Soviet Union and never returned.[15]

In fact, the Polish government tried to keep trade with the Soviet Union below one third of Poland's total foreign trade. Berman claimed later that he had warned his government that if trade with the Soviets amounted to over 40 percent of Poland's trade, this would lead to Poland's complete economic dependence on the Soviet Union.[16] The proportion of Polish trade with the Soviet Union did in fact decrease significantly in 1946 and 1947. The Soviet share of Poland's imports dropped from a high of 90.6 percent in 1945 to 69.3 percent in 1946, and only 25.1 percent in 1947. The Soviet share of Poland's exports also decreased significantly from 92.8 percent in 1945 to 46.3 percent in 1946, and 28.4 percent in 1947.[17]

It is clear the Soviet Union did not force Poland to orient its trade eastward.[18] In fact, Poland conducted well over half of its trade in 1947 with developed capitalist countries.[19] The United States remained an insignificant trading partner, accounting for only 0.3 percent of Poland's exports in 1946, and slightly more in 1947. The $90 million loan package from the United States resulted in an increase in American imports from 1.1 percent of Poland's imports in 1946 to 15.9 percent in 1947.[20]

Some administration officials argued that the Polish government would use American economic aid to build the Polish army. The Polish government planned to use only an insignificant portion of its imports in 1947 for military purposes, however. According to Central Planning Office records, the estimated value of imports for the Polish Defense Ministry in 1947 was $1,749,832.[21] On the other hand, the Central Planning Office estimated that the cost of all imported capital goods in 1947 was $307,481,000. Of that latter figure over $59 million was earmarked for the coal industry, approximately $22 million for the textile industry, and nearly $62 million for agricultural equipment.[22]

III

The turning point in the State Department's economic policy toward Poland came in September 1946 when Secretary of State James Byrnes decided that the United States would reserve its limited aid funds for friendly countries only, specifically those outside of the Soviet sphere of influence. Byrnes thought that the administration needed to coordinate its economic policy in order to further the broader objectives of American foreign policy in Europe: "In a word we must help our friends in every way and refrain from assisting those who either through helplessness or for other reasons are opposing the principles for which we stand." Byrnes made it clear that these principles were not only economic but political.[23]

Truman was closely involved in the revision and coordination of economic policy toward the Soviet Union and Eastern Europe. After reading Kennan's "long telegram," Truman asked presidential advisor Clark Clifford to compile a summary report on Soviet-American relations. Clifford spoke with Acheson, General George C. Marshall, Secretary of Defense William Forrestal, Undersecretary of State Robert Lovett, and others close to the foreign policy-making process, and submitted a report to Truman at the end of September. Clifford supported Byrnes's new policy, recommending that in light of Soviet unwillingness to cooperate with U.S. economic and political proposals for Eastern Europe, American foreign economic policy should be integrated into the administration's political and strategic foreign policy objectives. Clifford said that if the Truman administration publicly denounced Soviet tactics in restricting democracy in Eastern Europe, then the United States should deny this area any economic assistance. Clifford emphasized the aggressive nature of Soviet communism and suggested that "economic aid granted to the Soviet Government or other governments within its sphere, and the fruits of private trade with persons inside these countries, will go to strengthen the entire world program of the Kremlin."[24] This new aid policy was intended to pressure the communist parties in Eastern Europe to hold free elections and to foster their independence from the Soviet Union. The United States followed this policy throughout the rest of Truman's presidency, even after the policy was obvious failing to achieve these objectives.

A major setback in Polish-American relations was Byrnes's speech in Stuttgart in September, in which he questioned the permanence of the Polish-German border. The speech dealt a severe blow to the political future of the Mikołajczyk's PSL and was condemned by all of Poland's political parties. A PSL deputy in the Polish National Council called for strong connections to the West but expressed his party's steadfast support for the present western border, and said that "whoever is with the Germans is against us, be it Byrnes, Churchill, or anyone else."[25]

Byrnes declared at Stuttgart that without a peace treaty with Germany, the United States did not recognize the permanence of the

Polish-German border. If Poland lost Silesia, its richest mineral and industrial region, the country would be left without any major exportable commodity. *Życie Gospodarcze* reported that coal comprised 90 percent of all Polish exports to the West and was therefore the "foundation of Polish trade policy and all Polish economic diplomacy."[26] Minc argued that

> without the western territory there is no reconstruction of the Polish economy. Without the western territory there is no Poland as a sovereign state.[27]

Byrnes's speech also had other important economic implications for Poland, because Byrnes said that German reconstruction would take precedence over rebuilding the Polish economy. The government-bloc Peasant Party (SL) criticized the PSL by claiming that Byrnes "would gladly approve if you [the PSL] would be willing to assist him in the reconstruction of Germany by impeding and delaying Polish reconstruction."[28] A PPR representative stated emphatically that Poland desired the "closest" and "friendliest" relations with the West, but that "our friends will be judged on their relations to Germany."[29]

The new American foreign economic policy manifested itself in September when the Truman administration suspended the unused portion of a $50 million Export-Import Bank loan to Czechoslovakia, which still had a democratically-elected government (the communists held key cabinet posts). Lane was pleased that Byrnes and the State Department had now come around to his tough position on economic assistance for Eastern Europe. He told embassy Chargé d'affaires Gerald Keith that the State Department's action on the Czechoslovak loan would set a precedent for similar economic policy toward Poland.[30] Polish officials feared this eventuality. Litynski wrote Finance Minister Jędrychowski that this action was part of an attempted economic blockade of the Slavic countries.[31]

Lane wrote Byrnes in early October recommending that the State Department send a note to the Polish government warning that if free and unfettered elections were not held soon, the United States would have to review its policy of economic assistance to Poland.[32] Great Britain, which had long favored Lane's tough approach, also urged Byrnes not to consider any additional aid until the Polish government had implemented the Yalta and Potsdam agreements on free elections. The only exception London was willing to consider was a loan tied to the export of Polish coal to Western Europe.[33]

Loan negotiations between Poland and the United States continued in the fall of 1946 because of Western Europe's desperate need for Polish coal.[34] The State Department was very concerned that there would be a coal shortage in Western Europe in the winter of 1946-1947, and Byrnes decided that any loan agreement would have to stipulate the amount of coal to be exported to Western Europe.[35] Lane reported to Washington that Minc was likely to ask the United States for another loan of $90 million ($20 million for electrical equipment and $70 for the coal mining industry) in return for Polish promises to export coal to Western Europe.[36] The Polish government indicated that this these stipulations were acceptable.[37]

Keith wrote Byrnes in November that he did not think that the Polish leadership actually expected to receive any more loans from the United States. On the other hand, Keith predicted that the Poles would continue to ask for them. Keith said that the recently announced Polish Three-Year Plan counted heavily on foreign investment from the United States and the IBRD.[38] In reality, the Polish government was quite optimistic about receiving another Export-Import Bank loan for the coal industry. Polish economic officials predicted in the fall of 1946 that the United States would grant additional coal industry loans of at least $20 million in 1947, and more loans in 1948. In order to speed up the loans, they recommended inviting an American coal industry expert to Poland.[39] The Polish representative to UNRRA, Feliks Bochenski, predicted that unless Poland received loans from the United States or Great Britain, his country would face a serious balance of payments problem after UNRRA relief shipments ended in 1947. Unlike his counterparts in the other economic agencies, however, Bochenski thought that the United States would only grant loans for the coal industry, but not for purchases of machinery, food, or raw materials.[40]

Bochenski was right. The State Department did not enter into serious loan negotiations for industries other than coal mining. The Poles still asked about a cotton loan for Poland's textile industry, but on 15 November the State Department informed the Polish embassy that there was "little possibility" for approval of a cotton loan from the Export-Import Bank. The department also said that the $27.5 million in Polish gold held in American banks would not be released until an agreement was signed to compensate American property losses in Poland.[41] The Polish embassy was still optimistic about eventually acquiring the cotton loan, but did not expect it at the present time.[42]

Minc went to Washington in December 1946 to finalize a nationalization compensation agreement and to hold general talks on trade and loans.[43] In the course of these discussions with State Department officials, Minc pointed out that compensation for nationalized American property depended solely on Polish balance of payments,[44] which in turn depended upon the Poland's ability to export coal.[45] Minc raised the possibility of another coal loan, but to his disappointment, Clayton told him that the IBRD would handle this loan request because the Export-Import Bank could not grant long-term loans. Clayton added that the Export-Import Bank had already committed its resources anyway. Minc feared that the IBRD would take too long to grant a loan,[46] and several days later he repeated his request for an Export-Import Bank loan of $60 million for mining equipment, port improvements, and railroad cars. He warned that if no loan were forthcoming, Polish coal exports to Western Europe would decline.[47]

On 18 December Minc met with Acheson to discuss loans and nationalization compensation. Encouraged by European Affairs Division Chief H. Freeman Matthews and Llewellyn Thompson, the new head of the East European Division, Acheson finally made it clear to Minc that political questions had to be resolved before the State Department would consider any more direct assistance for Poland. Minc feigned ignorance of Polish political matters, but assured Acheson that "the Polish Government had no intention of interfering with any opposition which restricted its activities to peaceful measures." This obviously excluded the PSL, which the Polish government claimed had close ties to the underground remnants of the Home Army. Minc contended that it would be to Poland's advantage to buy cotton from the West and to export coal westward, but he added that the restrictive American loan policy was blocking these commercial relationships. As a result, Minc said that Poland had to import cotton from the Soviet Union and was being drawn into the Soviet economic sphere.[48] Acheson countered that the State Department could not make decisions that were contrary to the wishes of the American people and grant loans to "countries which appeared to be accepting this help merely for the purpose of building up a domestic economy which would be joined to the closed economic system of the Soviet Union."[49] The dilemma for U.S. policy at this time was that without American loans Poland had little option but to turn to its eastern neighbor for trade and aid.

Minc was unsuccessful in acquiring either a cotton or a coal industry loan,[50] but an outline of a compensation settlement was initialed on 27 December. The two sides established a claims commission consisting of Polish and American representatives who would judge each petition for compensation. In return for this tentative agreement, the Truman administration authorized the release of the $27.5 million in gold held in U.S. banks.[51] On 12 March 1947 the Polish embassy in Washington informed the U.S. government of its willingness to sign a final compensation accord, but the State Department again hesitated, claiming that there were still legal problems to be settled. Józef Winiewicz, the new Polish ambassador in Washington, thought that the real reason for the delay was that if the United States signed the agreement (which compensated American property in all of the territory presently under Polish jurisdiction), the United States would be officially recognizing Poland's new border with Germany.[52]

Ironically, the Polish government realized that their acquisition of the gold that had been frozen in American banks could undermine their requests for additional U.S. economic assistance. The Polish embassy in Washington reported that unfriendly elements in the U.S. government now had a strong argument against further relief for Poland on the grounds that Poland had assets to buy grain from the United States. The embassy also warned that this gold could have a negative effect on the terms of payment and the amount of an IBRD loan or an Export-Import cotton loan.[53] On the other hand, the Poles could use the gold as collateral for loans from U.S. banks. While Minc was in Washington he was able to secure a $20 million loan at one percent interest from the Federal Reserve Bank, and a $31 million loan at 1.5 percent interest from Bankers Trust Company.[54]

By the end of 1946, the outlook for Polish-American economic cooperation was not very promising, and the Polish government's sharp criticism of U.S. economic policy became more frequent. In the Polish National Council, PPR representatives focussed their attacks on the inequities of the American economic system and alleged that it was undergoing constant crises.[55] In September, *Życie Gospodarcze* criticized American foreign economic policy for threatening the economic sovereignty of less wealthy countries, an argument that the

Polish government used over and over again after it was forced to reject the Marshall Plan in 1947.[56]

Obviously this propaganda jeopardized the ongoing loan negotiations. On 13 February Stanley Gruson of the *New York Times* reported that "Bierut did not agree . . . with the views expressed in the general Parliamentary debate last week that Poland's friendship with the West would be conditional on the West's aiding of this country economically." Gruson quoted Bierut as saying that "the present Government will do anything in its power to improve relations with the West, regardless of whether they extend us material aid."[57] In addition, Ambassador Winiewicz complained that "[Polish editors] are of inferior mentality and experience, are anxious to curry favor with the Gov [sic] and oftentimes, assume a policy that is more anti-American than even the gov't [sic] itself desires."[58]

Furthermore, the Polish government's own lack of policy coordination undermined practical economic relations with the United States. Modzelewski expressed dissatisfaction over his government's slow authorization to buy U.S. Army surplus with the $50 million credit. Modzelewski complained that his purchases were sometimes "paralyzed" because other countries were also competing for this equipment.[59]

Polish-American economic relations were dealt another blow at the beginning of 1947 when Congress questioned Clayton and Acheson about a possible conflict of interest in relation to the $90 million loan to Poland in 1946. Acheson had been a member of the law firm that was representing Poland in the loan negotiations. Acheson denied that he had a conflict of interest because he had resigned from the firm in 1941. The investigation ended there, but Polish Ambassador Winiewicz observed that as a result of this inquiry Acheson tried to avoid any more direct contact with Polish officials.[60]

Clayton's problems stemmed from the $100 million that the Export-Import Bank had set aside for cotton loans. Clayton was a major stockholder in the cotton firm of Anderson, Clayton and Company, which in 1940 had controlled about 15 percent of the world's cotton crop. In January 1947, Representative Paul Schaffer of Michigan accused Clayton of using his position in the government for personal profit. Clayton denied these accusations, arguing that he was only a stockholder and that the loans did not facilitate significant purchases of cotton. Little resulted from this investigation either, although the Polish government eventually blamed Clayton for denying Poland a cotton loan. Clayton opposed it on economic and political grounds, however, rather than on personal financial grounds.[61]

Despite the growing anti-communist attitude in Washington in 1947, the Polish government persisted in its efforts to develop a closer relationship with the Western economies. In May 1947, the government asked a Washington D.C. firm to do a large program of research and planning for industry in Silesia in order to integrate the area into the European economic community. Because of the deterioration in relations following the Polish rejection of the Marshall Plan, the job was never done.[62] Furthermore, Polish economic officials were still optimistic about receiving loans from the United States and the IBRD. In the revised Three-Year Plan for 1947-1949 they estimated that 20 percent ($800 million) of all investment funds would come from foreign sources.[63] Minc did not think this was an unreasonable estimate, and told Polish lawmakers that this forecast for foreign loans was not the result of his desire to isolate the Polish economy or to make it autarkic, but reflected rather a realistic assessment of the present economic and political situation in Europe. He also argued that the planned economy was in no way a barrier to trade with Poland. On the contrary, he maintained that the permanent and stable nature of the socialist economy made Poland a very reliable trading partner.[64]

Minc gave investment priority to heavy industry.[65] He wanted foreign loans for investment imports such as energy and electrical installations, machine tools, communications and port installations, and construction machines, but he also asked for loans to buy agricultural equipment.[66] The lack of any more U.S. loans put the PSL in an awkward position, because its peasant supporters were indirectly affected. The PSL hoped that if Poland received foreign loans for the industrial sector, more domestic investment funds would be freed for the agricultural and manufacturing sectors.[67] And when the Polish government did not receive any loans for the agriculture industry in 1947, it was forced to import grain.

At the end of 1946, Ambassador Lane indicated a little more flexibility in his position on economic assistance for Poland. Lane knew that it was probably futile to make free and fair elections a criterion for granting assistance, because the Polish government would not allow a PSL victory under any circumstances. Lane now argued that the United States should try to cultivate relations with the socialists in the PPS. Lane rested his hopes on party leader Józef Cyrankiewicz, who told

Lane that he wanted to maintain his party's independence from the PPR: "If I am compelled to capitulate to the Communists, it is because of 'realpolitik' and not because I want it."[68]

On 22 December Lane wrote Byrnes that he agreed that no aid should be offered to governments with an unfriendly attitude toward the United States, but also pointed out that

> there is a possibility that the Polish Government may at long last have realized the shortsightedness of its anti-American policy in light of its need for our financial and economic assistance, and may be willing to agree to conditions which should be essential prerequisites to our making any commitments to Minc.

Lane interpreted the recent conciliatory attitude of Modzelewski, Osóbka-Morawski, Rzymowski, and Lange as indications of Poland's desperate need for American loans. Lane still exaggerated American bargaining power, however, reasoning that the loans could be linked to less controversial issues such as the freeing of prisoners who claimed to have American citizenship, a nationalization compensation agreement, and an aviation accord.[69] But one week later Lane made it clear in a cable to Byrnes that he had not really changed his position on American loan policy: "We, however, should make it plain that the flouting of Polish Government obligations [i.e. free elections] must inevitably lead to our withholding financial and economic assistance."[70] In another cable to Byrnes in early January, Lane said an IBRD loan for Poland should include guarantees of Polish coal exports to Western Europe. Lane added that the administration should force Poland to reduce its deliveries of reparations coal to the Soviet Union and to refrain from trade policies (such as barter agreements) that reduced Poland's capacity to repay loans. Lane did not mention Polish political concessions in this cable.[71]

The Polish communists understood that economic concessions had to be made for loans, but they stood fast on their promise not to make any political compromises. A source in the Polish government told Lane that Minc was very satisfied with the results of the talks in Washington in December,[72] but others in the Polish leadership were unconvinced that the United States would waive its political demands.

New York Times Warsaw correspondent Stanley Gruson wrote that "the Government here expects the United States to exert economic pressure on it, no matter what else Washington decides to do." Gruson accurately predicted that "the Government is prepared to ask the people to suffer a little harder and a little longer and do without foreign investments." The reporter added that

> if the United States decides that economic pressure is sufficient to show its displeasure about the election campaign, then the Communist dominated Administration that will be returned to power next Sunday [the elections of 19 January] will be pleased.[73]

Gruson understood better than many American officials that the Polish government was stable enough to survive the lack of economic assistance from the United States.

On 6 January Byrnes wrote the U.S. embassy in Warsaw that Minc still wanted commitments for an Export-Import Bank loan to buy cotton and tobacco,[74] but that the State Department would not consider any more loans until there was a "lapse of sufficient time following elections to give assurances of internal stability essential for credit worthiness." Byrnes mentioned 1 February as the earliest possible date for a resumption of loan talks, but he did not indicate what impact of unfair election would have on American economic policy toward Poland.[75]

The results of the January election were a foregone conclusion. The government-bloc parties claimed over 80 percent of the vote, and the official tallies gave the PSL less than 11 percent. Lane thought that the defeat of the PSL was due in part to the State Department's disregard of his advice to follow a tougher economic policy, and he submitted his resignation shortly thereafter. Lane recommended against breaking diplomatic relations, however, contending that Poland was still desperate for American economic assistance. Lane thought that because of the harsh British criticism of the Polish elections there was a distinct possibility that the British ambassador would be declared persona non grata, but he wrote Secretary of State George C. Marshall, that "I do not believe that the Polish Government will take similar action towards me, or against any U.S. Ambassador succeeding me, because of its having to depend on the U.S. for financial and economic assistance."[76] During his final visit to the Polish Foreign Ministry Lane told Modzelewski that he "doubted whether Poland could thrive without the support of the United States."[77]

President Truman was extremely upset that the Polish elections had been so blatantly unfair. When Polish Ambassador Józef Winiewicz presented his credentials to Truman at the beginning of February, Truman curtly upbraided Winiewicz and his government for not keeping its promises to conduct free and fair elections.[78]

In order to control the damage that the elections might have on its foreign economic relations, the Polish government quickly moved to finalize another loan agreement. On 11 February Ludwig Grosfeld, the acting minister of shipping and foreign trade, told the U.S. embassy that his government was "most eager" to finalize a loan to purchase American cotton. Grosfeld warned that if the United States would provide the loan, Poland would have to buy Russian cotton. Fearing that his advice would again go unheeded, Lane advised against the cotton loan or U.S. approval of an IBRD loan until he could personally speak with his superiors in the State Department in Washington.[79]

Lane thought that the Polish leadership was bluffing about the possibilities of receiving aid from the Soviet Union. On 14 February he received information from the Polish Cardinal Hlond that the Soviet Union was "facing a serious economic and agricultural situation and that the Soviet Government will be unable to furnish any assistance to Poland." Hlond thought that this was the reason why the Polish government was trying to maintain economic connections to the United States.[80] Cyrankiewicz told Lane a few days later that the Soviet Union had turned down a Polish request for 500,000 tons in grain and that the Soviets could not furnish any financial assistance. Nonetheless, Cyrankiewicz repeated the argument that if the United States cut off economic aid, Poland would have to become even more economically and politically dependent on the Soviet Union. Cyrankiewicz also cultivated the idea that his party was trying to maintain its independence from the PPR. This argument worked on Lane again, who later that spring again argued that American loans to Poland might bolster the political position of the PPS.[81]

The Polish government followed a conscious strategy to portray itself as a coalition, however, in order to foster the idea that PPR did not have a monopoly on political power in Poland. In discussions with the State Department's East European Division, Ambassador Winiewicz lobbied for economic assistance by claiming that the Polish government had two competing groups, one "pro-West" and one "pro-East." He contended that the Soviet faction was gaining ground because of the American refusal of a cotton loan, the stillborn compensation agreement, Lane's attacks on the Polish government, and indications from Congress that Poland would not receive any more relief after the end of UNRRA relief operations in mid-year. Thompson told Winiewicz that he "did not think that this country would be willing to try to 'buy' Polish orientation to the West but rather that it was up to Poland, by its actions, to merit assistance from this country."[82]

The Polish government's warnings that without American loans Poland would have to become economically dependent on the Soviet Union were not all bluff. Lane and the State Department, as well as most Polish officials, did not think that the Soviet Union could provide Poland with any significant economic assistance in 1947. During trade talks with the Soviets in Moscow in March, however, Minc was able to convince Stalin that the market price of reparations coal shipments to the Soviets was greater than the reparations that Poland was receiving from the Soviet occupation zone in Germany. Stalin agreed to halve these coal shipments. The Soviets also granted Poland a $28.9 million gold loan, returned the Polish railroad cars that they had held since the end of the war, and gave Poland part of the German merchant fleet as reparations.[83] One Polish economic expert at the talks later commented that the gold loan was a "great help in facilitating the acquisition of many immediate needs."[84] Ironically, the Poles planned to use the gold as collateral for loans to purchase food and investment goods in the United States.[85]

IV

After the elections in January, the State Department ended any more consideration of a cotton loan, although Polish inquiries about it continued throughout the spring and summer.[86] Winiewicz told Marshall in August that Poland had been forced to ask the Soviet Union for cotton, and that the refusal of a American cotton loan had caused "embitterment and further turning to the East."[87] By refusing to negotiate any more loans for Poland, the United States lost what little influence it had over Polish economic developments.[88] For example, with a cotton loan the United States had the opportunity to link the Polish textile industry to the West. The entire prewar Polish textile industry had been technically adapted to American cotton and the United States had been Poland's traditional supplier.[89] The Polish government wanted to reestablish this relationship, but eventually it had to turn to the Soviet Union for cotton. The Poles received 26,710 tons from the Soviet Union in 1946 and only 2,225 tons from the United States. Soviet cotton exports to Poland increased significantly in 1948 to 61,500 tons.[90] In addition, Polish cotton textile exports to the Soviets increased by over 90 percent from 1946 to 1948.[91]

Furthermore, some of Poland's industries proved to be less dependent on American loans than Truman administration officials thought. For example, in 1947 Poland's textile industries produced 97 percent of the 1938 production levels, and in 1948 this figure increased to 130 percent. In comparison, Great Britain realized only 80 percent of its 1938 production in 1947, and approximately 118 percent in 1948.[92] Textile exports became an important sector of Poland's external trade.[93] Textile exports to developed capitalist countries more than doubled from 1946 to 1947.[94]

Certainly additional loans beyond the $40 million U.S. Export-Import loan would have helped Poland hit its targets for coal production, but Poland achieved 99.8 percent of the plan for coal production in the first quarter of 1947, 100 percent in the second, 102.5 percent in the third, and 107.7 percent in the fourth.[95] The Polish government intended to export about one third of the coal produced in 1947, and this figure was nearly reached.[96] The Polish government also kept its promises to increase coal exports to Western Europe. The coal exported to developed capitalist countries increased dramatically from 3.7 percent of all exported coal in 1945 to 30.3 percent in 1946, and then to 44.1 percent in 1947.[97] As a result of the Export-Import Bank loan and heavy Polish investment in this industry, coal production increased from 12,881,000 tons in 1946 to 17,566,000 tons in 1947.[98]

Although the textile and coal industries did quite well, without a doubt the Polish economy as a whole suffered from the lack of American loans. Investment that was channeled into these two export industries left deficits in other sectors of the economy, most notably in agriculture. From 1945 to 1949, only 22 percent of Poland's foreign obligations were covered by foreign credits. The highest figure was 39.6 percent in 1947 when the Polish government benefitted from the

$90 million loan package from the United States. Only 10.3 percent of Poland's foreign obligations were covered by foreign credits in 1948.[99] Changes in Minc's investment plans for 1947 also reflect the lack of loans and credits from the United States and Western Europe. Poland received loans and credits of $153 million in 1946,[100] but in 1947 Poland got only half of the foreign loans that had been planned in the 1946 draft of the Three-Year Plan. The final draft that was completed in July 1947 lowered the plan for foreign loans approximately 32 percent (from 2.8 billion zlotys to 1.9 billion zlotys), but Poland received only about three fourths of these loans (1.4 billion zlotys).[101] Certainly this lack of economic assistance hurt Polish economic recovery by significantly reducing the government's ability to purchase much-needed capital goods. In April 1947, the Central Planning Office had to establish a hierarchy of the most essential imports to be purchased on the open market.[102]

V

After returning to Washington, Lane sent a letter to Marshall expressing his disappointment over the lack of policy coordination within the State Department. He noted that "the Soviet and Polish government authorities are, of course, aware that the department has not stood as an integrated whole with respect to Polish matters, especially those of an economic nature."[103] Unfortunately, Lane had made a significant contribution to the State Department's inconsistent economic policy toward Poland. Frequently he had gone beyond orders to conduct his own personal diplomacy, and his stubborn attitude had only fueled the growing conflict between the Polish government and the Truman administration. Ironically, Lane's input into final decision-making on economic policy toward Poland was not decisive. An indication of the relative disregard that the State Department in Washington had for the opinion of its ambassador in Warsaw is this recollection of the new ambassador, Stanton Griffis: "[I was never] given a clear, concise statement of what the policy of the Department was toward any of the countries to which I was appointed." Before going to Poland, Thompson told Griffis (perhaps in a reference to Lane), "above all, young man, not too much zeal."[104]

NOTES

1. Georg Vancura, "Die Entwicklung nach dem Ende des Weltkrieges" [The development after the end of the world war], *Schweizerische Zeitschrift für Geschichte* 29 (1979): 447; Pollard, *Economic Security and the Origins of the Cold War, 1945-1950*, 31-57; and Witold Jurasz, *Wpływ zagranicznej polityki ekonomicznej USA na rozwój polskiego eksportu do Stanow Zjednoczonych w latach 1946-1947* [The effect of U.S. foreign economic policy on the development of Polish export to the United States in the years 1946-1947] (Warsaw: Polish Institute of Foreign Affairs, 1971), 5.

2. Gaddis, *Strategies of Containment*, 23, 57. As Gaddis points out, the Truman administration realized that there were limits to Congress's generosity. On the other hand, administration officials had not yet given up on the idea that the dollar could be used to influence political events in Eastern Europe.

3. Paterson, *Soviet-American Confrontation*, 117; and see Kolkos, *The Limits of Power*, 199. The Kolkos also argue that the United States began to emphasize political developments in 1946, but mainly because the United States was shut off from the "economic penetration" of Eastern Europe.

4. Pollard, *Economic Security and the Origins of the Cold War, 1945-1950*, 5.

5. Lukas, *Bitter Legacy: Polish-American Relations in the Wake of World War II*, 89. Lukas argues that between the fall of 1946 and the spring of 1947 the United States decided to rebuild Germany rather than Poland. But Polish coal was still essential to Western European recovery, and despite the political developments in Poland, this was the only Eastern European country that the United States still considered for more loans.

6. "Report on Session of U.N. Devastated Areas Subcommittee in London, 31 July-14 September 1946," Papers of Thomas C. Blaisdell, Jr., box 7, Folder 2, Truman Library, Independence, Missouri (hereafter Blaisdell Papers with filing information).

7. Blaisdell letter, 3 December 1946, Blaisdell Papers, box 7, Folder 2.

8. Report by Clifford C. Taylor (counselor for economic affairs) in *World Trade Directory Report*, 16 September 1946, RG 84, box 18.

9. Memorandum of conversation, F.J. Dubas and Stanisław Szyszllo, 14 January 1947, RG 84, box 37. The Ministry of Navigation and Commerce (Ministerstwo Zeglugi i Handlu) is often translated as the Ministry of Shipping and Foreign Trade, which will be used here. In March 1947, this ministry was dissolved and its work was taken over by the Ministry of Industry and Trade.

10. Lane to Byrnes, 4 September 1946, RG 84, box 18.

11. Taylor to the Smith-William Corporation, N.Y., 17 July 1946, RG 84, box 18.

12. Stańczyk to Minc, 24 July 1946, Ministry of Industry and Trade Records, File 51; Michael Mora to Stańczyk, 18 July 1946, ibid.; and Józef Winiewicz, *Co pamiętam z długiej drogi życia* [What I remember from the long trail of life] (Poznan: Wydawnictwo Poznańskie, 1985), 465.

13. *New York Times*, 18 August 1946, 24.

14. Memorandum by Brown and Moore, 20 November 1946, RG 84, box 18.

15. Modzelewski to Jędrychowski, 19 November 1946, Ministry of Industry and Trade Records, File 51.

16. Berman interview in Torańska, *Oni*, 353.

17. *Compendium Statystyczne Polskiego Handlu Zagranicznego w latach 1929-1938, 1945-1960*, 207; and Alton, *Polish Postwar Economy*, 280.

18. See Pollard, *Economic Security and the Origins of the Cold War*, 36, who writes that Soviet trade with Eastern Europe "soared" after the war. Although this trade had been insignificant before the war, postwar Soviet-Polish trade was geographically determined and was for the most part mutually beneficial.

19. *Compendium Statystyczne Polskiego Handlu Zagranicznego w latach 1929-1938, 1945-1960*, 57. After the Cold War started, this figure dropped to a low of 31 percent by 1954; and Długosz and Szczepaniec, *Stosunki handlowe Polski z rozwiniętymi krajami kapitalistycznymi*, 109. Długosz reports that this figure was 23.5 percent in 1954.

20. *Compendium Statystyczne Polskiego Handlu Zagranicznego w latach 1929-1938, 1945-1960*, 295; and Sekular, "Stosunki gospodarcze między Polska i Stanami Zjednoczonymy Ameryki po II wojnie światowej," 36.

21. Ministry of National Defense plan of imports for 1947, Centralny Urząd Planowania, Akty [Central planning office, records], File 2393, Archiwum Akt Nowych, Warsaw (hereafter Central Planning Office Records with filing information).

22. Memorandum on capital goods to be ordered abroad in 1947, December 1946, Central Planning Office Records, File 610.

23. Byrnes to Acheson, 24 September 1946, *FRUS, 1946: The Near East and Africa* (Washington: U.S. Government Printing Office, 1969), 7:223-224.

24. "American Relations with the Soviet Union: A Report to the President by the Special Counsel to the President," 24 September 1946, in Thomas H. Etzold and John L. Gaddis, eds. *Containment: Documents on American Policy and Strategy, 1945-1950* (New York: Columbia University Press, 1978), 64.

25. Polish National Council Records, 22 September 1946, 302.

26. *Życie Gospodarcze* 1 (15 November 1946): 869-870.

27. Polish National Council Records, 21 September 1946, 126; Zygmunt Modzelewski, *Polityka Zagraniczna Polski: Artykuły i Przemówienia* [Polish foreign policy: articles and speeches] (Warsaw: Państwowe Wydawnictwo Naukowe, 1960), 42-43. According to Modzelewski, investment in this area was heavy, amounting to almost $600 million by the middle of 1947, much of it from UNRRA relief and the U.S. Army surplus credit.

28. Polish National Council Records, 20 September 1946, 59.

29. Polish National Council Records, 22 September 1946, 349.

30. Cable, "The United States and the Polish Question, 1939-1948, 356.

31. Litynski to Jędrychowski, 18 November 1946, Ministry of Industry and Trade Records, File 51.

32. Lane to Byrnes, 2 October 1946, *FRUS, 1946* 6:497-498.

33. Gallman to Byrnes, 3 October 1946, RG 59, 860c.51, box 6385; British embassy to the Department of State, 17 October 1946, *FRUS, 1946*, 6:510-511; Gallman to Byrnes, 31 October 1946, RG 59, 860c.51, box 6385; and Zyblikiewicz, *Polityka Stanów Zjednoczonych i Wielkiej Brytanii wobec Polski, 1944-1949*, 279.

34. Zyblikiewicz, *Polityka Stanów Zjednoczonych i Wielkiej Brytanii wobec Polski, 1944-1949*, 292. There is no evidence that the "promising Polish market" had anything to do with further loan considerations for Poland, as Zyblikiewicz argues.

35. Paterson, *Soviet-American Confrontation: Postwar Reconstruction and the Origins of the Cold War*, 157.

36. Lane to Byrnes, 28 September 1946, RG 59, 860c.51, box 6385; Lane to Byrnes, 1 October 1946, ibid.; see also Lundestad, "The American Policy Towards Poland 1943-1946," 26. There is no evidence to support Lundestad's contention that "the difficulty in having such a [coal export to Western Europe] guarantee written into any aid agreement was probably one reason for the [$40 million Export-Import Bank] credit in the end being tied to the holding of the elections." The election pledge was not a part of the actual loan agreement, and the Poles, needing to gain hard currency through its coal exports to Western Europe, were more than willing to guarantee these shipments.

37. Gallman (in London) to Byrnes, 1 October 1946, RG 59, 860c.51, box 6385.

38. Keith to Byrnes, 25 November 1946, *FRUS, 1946* 6:521-523.

39. Economic Committee of the Council of Ministers Records, Subcommittee of International Economic Affairs, 1 October 1946, File 136.

40. Memorandum from St. Dobrowski, (director of the Foreign Division in the Central Planning Office) to Bobrowski, 21 October 1946, Central Planning Office Records, File 1930.

41. Acheson to Keith, 22 November 1946, *FRUS, 1946* 6:519-520.

42. Memorandum of meeting, Źółtowski, Hickerson and Thompson, 15 November 1946, Ministry of Industry and Trade Records, File 51.

43. Minc to the Polish embassy in Washington, 28 November 1946, Ministry of Industry and Trade Records, File 51.

44. See Lange to Acheson, 2 May 1946, *FRUS, 1946* 6:439. Lange repeatedly made this distinction, arguing that a more rapid recovery of the Polish economy with American aid would enable the Polish government to pay equitable compensation.

45. Memorandum of conversation, Acheson, Thompson, Minc, Źółtowski, etal., 11 December 1946, RG 59, 860c.5034, box 6383.

46. Memorandum of conversation, Clayton and Minc, etal., 13 December 1946, RG 59, 611.60c31, box 2847.

47. Memorandum of conversation, Minc, Źółtowski, Thorp and Thompson, etal., 12 December 1946, RG 59, 860c.50, box 6381.

48. Undated memorandum, Truman Papers, PSF, Subject File, box 186. For more than a century before the Second World War Poland received more than half of its cotton imports from the United States.

49. Memorandum of conversation, Acheson and Minc, etal., 18 December 1946, *FRUS, 1946* 6:541-542.

50. Department of State *Bulletin*, 5 January 1947, 28.

51. The gold was turned over to the Poles in January 1947. Almost $2 million more had already been used in August 1946 as the Polish contribution to the IBRD.

52. Winiewicz, *Co pamiętam z długiej drogi życia*, 448.

53. Note from Źóltowski, Litynski, etal. to Modzelewski, Minc, etal., 1 January 1947, Ministry of Industry and Trade Records, File 51.

54. Marshall to the U.S. embassy in Warsaw, 4 February 1947, RG 59, 860c.51, box 6385; and Sekular, "Stosunki gospodarcze między Polska i Stanami Zjednoczonymy Ameryki po II wojnie światowej," 19. The interest rate on the Federal Reserve Bank loan was later raised to 1.6 percent.

55. Polish National Council Records, 21 September 1946, 181; and ibid., 22 September 1946, 332.

56. *Życie Gospodarcze* 1 (August 1946): 570-574.

57. *New York Times*, 13 February 1947, 16.

58. Lukas, *Bitter Legacy: Polish-American Relations in the Wake of World War II*, 82.

59. Modzelewski to Jędrychowski, 19 November 1946, Ministry of Industry and Trade Records, File 51.

60. *New York Times*, 17 January 1947, 10; ibid., 18 January 1947, 7; and Winiewicz, *Co pamiętam z długiej drogi życia*, 393.

61. Mee, *The Marshall Plan: The Launching of Pax Americana*, 79.

62. Robert Nathan (president of Nathan and Associates) to Marshall, 20 May 1947, RG 59, 860c.50, box 6382.

63. Foreign credits in the Three-Year Plan, 29 October 1946, Central Planning Office Records, File 1930.

64. Polish National Council Records, 21 September 1946, 130. After the elections in January, Minc complained that the private and cooperative trading enterprises were not operating in the interests of the economy as a whole, but were interested only in profits. He gradually eliminated them, increasing nationalized trade from 80 percent of all of

Poland's trade in 1946 to 90 percent in 1949. This development did not result in a drop in trade with the Western Europe, however.

65. See Alton, *Polish Postwar Economy*, 5.

66. Balance of payments and trade balance, August 1946, Central Planning Office Records, File 1930.

67. Polish National Council Records, 21 September 1946, 138-139.

68. Cable, "The United States and the Polish Question, 1939-1948," 374.

69. Lane to Byrnes, 22 December 1946, *FRUS, 1946* 6:546-548.

70. Lane to Byrnes, 31 December 1946, *FRUS, 1946* 6:554.

71. Lane to Byrnes, 9 January 1947, RG 59, 860c.51, box 6385.

72. Lane to Byrnes, 10 January 1947, RG 59, 860c.51, box 6385.

73. *New York Times*, 13 January 1947, 6-7.

74. See Ministry of Industry and Trade Records, File 51. As early as July 1946 the Polish Tobacco Monopoly expressed interest in buying tobacco in the United States. Several U.S. tobacco firms responded positively to the idea.

75. Byrnes to U.S. embassy in Warsaw, 6 January 1947, RG 59, 860c.51, box 6385.

76. Lane to Marshall, 23 January 1947, *FRUS, 1947: Eastern Europe and the Soviet Union* (Washington: U.S. Government Printing Office, 1972), 4:413.

77. Lane to Marshall, 24 February 1947, *FRUS, 1947* 4:421; see Cable, "The United States and the Polish Question, 1939-1948," 376, who assesses the Lane's tour in Warsaw this way: "The tragedy of the ambassadorship of Lane was that different options were not exercised by the State Department, flexibility was often lacking, economic policies were clumsily pursued, and ultimately the Socialists were driven by economic necessity in the arms of the anti-Western elements within the Polish Government." Cable agrees that the administration's economic policies were poorly constructed and poorly implemented. As for the Socialists, it is unlikely that any economic policy the United States might have followed would have seriously affected the internal political situation in Poland. As they often told the Americans, the communists in the PPR were not going to allow the United States to meddle in Poland's domestic politics for any price.

78. Truman meeting with Winiewicz, 4 February 1947, Truman Papers, PSF, Presidential Appointments File (Daily Sheets), 1947.

79. Lane to Marshall, 15 February 1947, RG 59, 860c.51, box 6385; and Lane to Marshall, 24 February 1947, *FRUS, 1947* 4:421.

80. Lane to Marshall, 15 February 1947, RG 59 860c.00, box 629.

81. Lane to Marshall, 17 February 1947, *FRUS, 1947* 4:418-419.

82. Memorandum of conversation, Thompson and Winiewicz, 3 April 1947, RG 59, 711.60c, box 3426.

83. Różański, *Śladem wspomnień i dokumentów, 1943-1948*, 463-467, 478; *New York Times*, 7 March 1947; Zyblikiewicz, *Polityka Stanów Zjednoczonych i Wielkiej Brytanii wobec Polski, 1944-1949*, 302; *Compendium Statystyczne Polskiego Handlu Zagranicznego w latach 1929-1938, 1945-1960*, 258; and Jerzy Ciepielewski, "Współpraca Gospodarcza Polski z Europejskim Krajami Socjalistycznymi," [Economic cooperation of Poland with the socialist countries of Europe], in *Gospodarka Polski Ludowej, 1944-1955* [The economy of Peoples' Poland], eds. Janusz Kalinski and Zbigniew Landau (Warsaw: Książka i Wiedza, 1986), 421. At the closing ceremonies of the trade talks in Moscow, Beria asked Różański how much coal Silesia would produce. The Pole answered 46 million tons for 1947, and 57.5 million for 1948. Beria said that the Germans had mined 93 million tons in 1943, and Różański replied that this had been done with slave labor. Beria retorted that the Poles had no lack of prisoners themselves. Although the reparations coal shipments were halved, through barter agreements with the Soviet Union coal exports to the Soviets remained stable from 1946 to 1947.

84. Różański, *Śladem wspomnień i dokumentów, 1943-1948*, 463.

85. Janusz Kalinski, *Plan Odbudowy Gospodarczej, 1947-1949* (Warsaw: Książka i Wiedza, 1975), 271.

86. Prezydium Rady Ministrów, Akty [Presidium of the council of ministers, records], March, 1947, File 290/1-/10, Archiwum Akt Nowych, Warsaw (hereafter Presidium of the Council of Ministers Records, with filing information); memorandum of conversation, Litynski, Elbrick, etal., 25 July 1947, RG 59, 860c.51, box 6385; Ute Daniel, *Dollardiplomatie in Europa: Marshallplan, Kalter Krieg und U.S. Aussenwirtschaftspolitik, 1945-1952* [Dollar diplomacy in Europe: the Marshall plan, the cold war and U.S. foreign economic policy] (Düsseldorf: Droste Verlag, 1982), 159; and Lundestad, *The American Non-Policy Towards Eastern Europe 1943-1947*, 220.

87. Memorandum of conversation, Marshall, Winiewicz, and Thompson, 6 August 1947, *FRUS, 1947* 4:440.

88. See Paterson, *Soviet-American Confrontation: Postwar Reconstruction and the Origins of the Cold War*, 49, who criticizes the administration's refusal to discuss a Russian loan. Paterson writes that the Truman administration "used loans as a diplomatic weapon before negotiations began rather than as a diplomatic tool at the conference table." This is not true in the case of Poland, as loan negotiations continued into 1948.

89. Paterson, *Soviet-American Confrontation: Postwar Reconstruction and the Origins of the Cold War*, 392.

90. Ciepielewski, "Współpraca Gospodarcza Polski z Europejskim Krajami Socjalistycznymi, 420. Cotton imports from the Soviet Union jumped from 17,400 tons in 1945 to 26,710 tons in 1946, and then to 28,300 tons in 1947; see also Nicolas Spulber, *The Economics of Communist Eastern Europe* (Boston: MIT Press, 1957), 416, who claims that Soviet cotton exports to Poland were 38,300,000 tons in 1947.

91. *Compendium Statystyczne Polskiego Handlu Zagranicznego w latach 1929-1938, 1945-1960*, 259.

92. United Nations Economic Community for Europe (ECE), *Economic Bulletin* 1:1 (1949): 29; *Compendium Statystyczne Polskiego Handlu Zagranicznego w latach 1929-1938, 1945-1960*, 138. Cotton textile production in general increased from 17,423,000 meters in 1945 to 43,201,000 meters in 1947, and increased to 76,485,000 meters in 1948; and Quarterly output of coal and cotton goods, 1947, Central Planning Office Records, File 386. Cotton fabric production ranged from 91 percent of the Polish plan in the first quarter of 1947 to 93.3 percent in the last quarter. These figures are probably reliable because they were not published in 1948 and were classified material.

93. Central Planning Office, *Sytuacja Gospodarcza Polski*, 125. Textile exports increased from 13.8 percent to 18.0 percent of Poland's total exports for 1946 and 1947.

94. *Compendium Statystyczne Polskiego Handlu Zagranicznego w latach 1929-1938, 1945-1960*, 163; and Długosz and Szczepaniec, *Stosunki handlowe Polski z rozwiniętymi krajami kapitalistycznymi*, 166.

95. Quarterly output of coal and cotton goods for 1947, Central Planning Office Records, File 386.

96. Memorandum on expected raw material exports in 1947, Three-Year Plan (1947-1949), Central Planning Office Records, File 610; Central Planning Office, *Sytuacja Gospodarcza Polski*, 25. Coal

and coke exports represented 62.7 percent of all Polish exports in 1946 and 45.9 percent in 1947; "Comparison of coal exports," Three-Year Plan (1947-1949), Central Planning Office Records, File 610. Poland exported 14,000,000 tons out of the 46,000,000 tons produced (30 percent) in 1946, and in 1947 20,000,000 tons out of 60,000,000 tons; *Compendium Statystyczne Polskiego Handlu Zagranicznego w latach 1929-1938, 1945-1960*, 128; and United Nations, ECE, Coal Division, "United Nations Monthly Bulletin of Coal Statistics," (December 1950): 5.

97. Długosz and Szczepaniec, *Stosunki handlowe Polski z rozwiniętymi krajami kapitalistycznymi*, 115.

98. *Compendium Statystyczne Polskiego Handlu Zagranicznego w latach 1929-1938, 1945-1960*, 128.

99. Wojciechowski, "Handel Zagraniczny Polski," 376.

100. Thompson, "The New Poland," *Foreign Policy Reports* 23:1 (December 1947): 233. Ninety million dollars came from the United States, $24 million from Great Britain, $38 million from Sweden, and $11 million from Switzerland; and undated report, Central Planning Office Records, File 788. This report shows the total credit figure to be even higher for 1946 ($179,424,000).

101. Central Planning Office, *Sytuacja Gospodarcza Polski*, 134; and Alton, *Polish Postwar Economy*, 273. Sweden granted another credit of 360 million krone ($100 million) in March 1947, and Great Britain lent $24 million more in June.

102. Memorandum on planning and balance of payments, 11 April 1947, Central Planning Office Records, File 610.

103. Lane to Marshall, 29 April 1947, *FRUS, 1947* 4:425-427.

104. Stanton Griffis, *Lying in State* (Garden City: Doubleday and Co., 1952), 151-152.

Chapter Five

The Denial of U.S. Relief Aid for Poland, 1947

I

By the spring of 1947 the Truman administration had decided on a foreign economic policy to aid Western Europe and to deny assistance to Eastern Europe and the Soviet Union. Some officials in the administration viewed Poland an exception in Eastern Europe, however, because of the importance of the Polish economy to the reconstruction of Western Europe. But if Polish coal exports continued to flow into Western Europe, the administration saw no reason to give Poland any more economic assistance until there was a true democratization of the Polish regime, or at least until there were tangible signs that Poland was not a Soviet satellite. When the Polish government virtually eliminated the political opposition after the fraudulent elections of January 1947, the chances for Poland to receive direct economic assistance from the United States were very slim.

One of the first manifestations of the Truman administration's new foreign economic policy was the omission of Poland from an American relief program that Congress passed in 1947. Long before the UNRRA ended its relief mission in Europe at the end of 1947, some officials in the State Department thought that this international relief effort was not serving American political objectives in Eastern Europe. By the end of 1946, most of the State Department agreed that the United States should administer further relief programs unilaterally. The Truman administration's decision to eliminate Poland from a $300 million relief package in 1947 was based on political considerations rather than on humanitarian grounds, and this decision showed that the chances were slim for further economic cooperation of any kind between the two countries.

II

Direct trade between Poland and the United States was negligible in the first year after the war, but UNRRA shipments to Poland from 1945 to 1947 (the United States contributed 72 percent of these goods) helped the Polish government to overcome a chaotic postwar economic situation.[1] The official Polish press regularly reported the UNRRA deliveries, and government officials often expressed their appreciation for these relief supplies. The fact that the United States was the largest contributor to the UNRRA was seldom mentioned, however. Occasionally the government-bloc parties in the Polish National Council acknowledged the American contribution to UNRRA, but generally their praise of the UNRRA was for the international economic cooperation that this relief effort exemplified.[2]

The United Nations hoped that its relief operations would have a humanitarian and non-political character, but soon after its creation the UNRRA was fraught with political problems. In May 1945, the State Department had to decide whether to invite the Polish government-in-exile in London or the Lublin Committee sponsored by Stalin to the first meetings of the UNRRA. In the interests of avoiding political debate within UNRRA, the State Department decided not to invite a Polish delegation to the meetings.[3]

When the war ended in May, the State Department wrote a position paper that called for U.S. administration of its own relief program.[4] Based on very sketchy evidence, administration officials became increasingly dissatisfied with the early U.N. relief efforts in Poland. They were troubled by reports that the Soviets were using the little aid that they could give to Poland for propaganda purposes, such as the opening of a fancy food store in Warsaw.[5] The administration also reacted negatively to the Polish government's demand to distribute UNRRA goods, and to the naming of a Soviet official to head the UNRRA mission in Poland.[6] In addition, the Americans had evidence that the Polish government might be distributing UNRRA aid on the basis of political utility, because there were complaints from the peasants that the goods were not reaching them. In July 1945, the PSL contended that although there was widespread destruction in five of the Kielce districts, the area had not received one UNRRA package.[7]

In early August 1945, Polish officials told Lane of their disappointment over the delays in UNRRA deliveries. Lane assured them that the United States was not preventing the relief from getting to Poland for political reasons, which was true.[8] Transportation problems and the destruction of the Polish ports of Gdańsk and Gdynia were responsible for the delays. In fact, the first relief shipment came by rail through Constanza, Rumania in April, and it was not until September that the first shipment arrived by sea at Gdynia. After the transportation situation had improved, Poland received 500,000 tons of UNRRA goods in the second half of 1945, as well as increased aid from the Red Cross. These goods enabled Poland to overcome the most difficult initial recovery period,[9] and the Polish communist government reaped the political benefits.

Nonetheless, friction developed between the Polish government and UNRRA officials over the amount of relief Poland was receiving. In early 1946, the UNRRA reduced grain deliveries to Poland to 350,000 tons, 150,000 tons less than the Polish government had requested. In February, Gomułka complained to Lane that UNRRA food supplies to Poland were being cut in an effort to extract political concessions from the Polish government. Despite this criticism and the dominant presence of Americans in the UNRRA, there is little evidence that the UNRRA made decisions to distribute relief on a political basis.[10]

The Polish government could not afford to jeopardize the American contribution to the UNRRA, however. The Polish communists were most concerned that their popular support would erode if they could not supply the populace with basic necessities. The government depended on UNRRA relief to quickly rebuild the economy. President Bierut took a more diplomatic approach in his plea to Truman for increased grain shipments to Poland through the UNRRA:

> Considering that Poland's quota of entire UNRRA [grain] supplies constitutes only a few percent, my government hopes that . . . the needs of Poland, which has suffered so painfully from the war and from the pillaging German occupation, will be taken into careful consideration.

Truman replied that the UNRRA was an international organization and that the United States was bound to its decisions.[11]

Truman commissioned former President Herbert Hoover in 1946 to study each European country's grain requirements. On 14 May Hoover reported to the director of UNRRA, Fiorello La Guardia, that after September Polish grain needs could be covered with the present levels of UNRRA supplies. Lane agreed with Hoover and thought that both La Guardia and the UNRRA were exaggerating Polish grain needs. Lane was especially concerned about the political gain that the Polish government was reaping from the aid. American economic analysts in Poland also agreed with Hoover and Lane, but their lobbying did not change La Guardia's mind. After meeting with Polish representatives in April, LaGuardia ordered three grain shipments bound for England and Norway to go to Poland.[12]

Polish economic officials were very pleased with this development and thought that La Guardia's assessment of the economic situation would put Poland in good stead for new forms of economic aid.[13] Their optimism was not very well founded, however, and the reduction in American grain shipments to Poland continued to strain Polish-American relations in 1946. On the other hand, attempts by the Polish embassy in Washington to increase relief shipments to Poland were undermined by attacks on UNRRA by Polish government officials. For example, in 1946 Władysław Gomułka accused the UNRRA of giving Germany and Italy better treatment than Poland.[14] In November, Rajchman urged Modzelewski to

> stop the attacks on UNRRA, which are useless in the matter of [attaining] grain and fats. . . . Loyal press campaigns do not result in quicker deliveries and will be understood as attacks on UNRRA, which (in our own interest) we must assist.[15]

As the UNRRA gradually decreased its relief activities in Europe in 1947, the Polish government had to use its precious hard currency reserves to purchase grain.

III

The Polish government hoped to receive a sizeable share of a new American relief fund that Congress proposed in 1947. The Polish leadership thought that regardless of the political situation in Poland or the state of Soviet-American relations, as a victim of German aggression Poland would certainly receive more humanitarian relief aid.

United Nations relief aid was instrumental in spurring Polish economic recovery, and the UNRRA estimated that Poland would need $134 million in additional relief immediately after the UNRRA ended its relief operation in 1947.[16] Furthermore, the UNRRA determined at the end of 1946 that Poland's barter trade agreements, American loans, and German reparations from the Soviet Union would not meet Poland's food requirements or fill more than half of its minimum needs for capital equipment. Because Poland could cover only 60 percent of its imports with export earnings, the UNRRA predicted that Poland would have a $221 million trade deficit in 1947.[17] At the beginning of 1947 the Polish government was spending a great deal more on food and textile raw materials than it had estimated in the Three-Year Plan,[18] and the dollar shortage was indeed becoming critical.

There was virtually no support left in the U.S. government for international relief efforts, however. In October 1946, Ambassador Lane recommended that the administration withdraw its support for UNRRA relief, because this aid had not resulted in improved relations between the two countries or in better prospects for free elections.[19] Not only the Truman administration was frustrated with the lack of political benefits that the United States was accruing from UNRRA relief, but Congress was also becoming more and more concerned over reports that the Polish government was distributing relief on political rather than on humanitarian grounds. For example, at the end of 1946 it came to the attention of Congress that UNRRA grapefruit juice was being used to make cocktails in exclusive Warsaw restaurants.[20] The State Department maintained its public support for international relief efforts, however. In reference to a possible American relief program after the end of UNRRA operations, the State Department told the Polish government that the United States "preferred to work out methods of assistance with the other major powers."[21] This was no longer the case.

When the United States announced its own relief program for Europe in January 1947, Poland was on the list of possible recipients. The State Department proposed a total relief fund of $350 million, which the administration would distribute to all needy countries.[22] Both Truman and Secretary of State Marshall wanted to include Poland on the list in part to deflect criticism that the aid package was an anti-communist measure.[23]

Ambassador Winiewicz thought that Poland's chances of receiving relief were enhanced by what he thought was his government's relatively fair treatment of the political opposition (especially the PSL) after the communist victory at the polls in January 1947. In addition, Winiewicz credited a recent visit to the West by Foreign Minister Modzelewski for silencing attacks on the Polish government. Winiewicz thought that it was likely that Poland would receive further relief aid even if the U.S. government viewed his government as a Soviet satellite, because the Americans wanted to show their support for the Polish people. Winiewicz took this view because the American press was characterizing the political situation in Poland as a struggle between the unrepresentative Polish government and the Polish people. Winiewicz wrote Minc that American newspapers generally argued that "we do not like the Government, but beyond the Government is a poor, terrorized society which needs our help."[24]

Polish officials thought that it was inconceivable that Poland would be left out of the American relief program, and they assumed that the government's political actions would have little bearing on this humanitarian aid. In the Polish Diet a PPS deputy declared that "economic assistance for Poland from the wealthy countries is our right which we have earned." Premier Cyrankiewicz was also very optimistic about post-UNRRA aid from the United States, but he recognized that beyond the end of UNRRA operations" other forms of assistance for Poland have not yet been clearly defined."[25]

The Polish government knew that without American aid Poland would experience a grain shortage in 1947. In 1946, the Central Planning Office estimated the cost of grain imports at $32.5 million in 1947, from a total cost of $132 million for all food imports.[26] The U.S. proposal for the UNRRA budget for the first quarter of 1947 allocated only $26 million in food supplies for Poland. Polish economic officials estimated that Poland would face a deficit of 105,000 tons of grain and 9,000 tons of meat in the first quarter of 1947. On this basis the Poles requested an extra $10-12 million from the UNRRA.[27]

At the end of 1946 Mikołajczyk told U.S. embassy Chargé d'affaires Gerald Keith that the Soviets were making matters worse by buying grain in southeast Poland. The PSL leader warned that famine conditions could develop there. Rather than influencing the State Department to grant Poland increased grain supplies, however, Mikołajczyk's report inadvertently strengthened American officials' belief that the Polish economy was being exploited by the Soviets, and that American aid would end up in their hands.[28]

Although the UNRRA mission in Warsaw agreed with the Polish government's assessment that there would be a severe grain shortage in Poland in 1947, Clifford C. Taylor and the other economic counselors in the U.S. embassy in Warsaw thought that Poland could supply its own needs.[29] The State Department was also of little help in facilitating grain sales to Poland. In October 1946, Rajchman asked Clayton if Poland could use $15 million of the $50 million U.S. Army surplus credit for food supplies, but Clayton told him that this was probably legally impossible.[30] When Clayton met with Winiewicz in February 1947 to discuss Poland's grain allocation for March, the Polish ambassador asked for 50,000 tons and promised that part of this grain would be paid for with the gold that had been frozen in American banks. Clayton replied that Poland would get what the United States could sell, but that the Unites States had a lack of transport and a shortage of exportable wheat. Nonetheless, Winiewicz evaluated the meeting optimistically. Indeed, later that day the Department of Agriculture informed Winiewicz that Poland would be sold 47,000 more tons for the month of April (for a total of 80,000 tons). Administration officials told Winiewicz that decisions on these shipments would be made within a week, but final approval was delayed for political reasons.[31]

The United States had other non-communist customers that were given first priority, and the Polish diplomats in Washington recognized that they were at a disadvantage when France and other Western European countries asked to purchase American grain. Hoover also lobbied the administration to ship grain to Germany and Austria in order to cover shortages there. Canada was another possible grain supplier for Poland, but Canada was selling most of its surplus to Great Britain. As a result, the Polish embassy in Washington recommended that its government turn to Argentina to buy wheat.[32]

American authorities again delayed grain sales to Poland in June, while they settled deliveries to Germany and France.[33] The Polish embassy reported to Warsaw that "despite announcements of an excellent harvest in the United States, the huge European grain deficit as well as the [American] tendency to make political allotments are causing great difficulties in acquiring grain."[34] Winiewicz claimed that American officials were even preventing Canada from selling grain to Poland by using their virtual veto power in the international system of licensing grain purchases. He informed Warsaw that "the Canadian

Ambassador Hume Wrong, despite the best will and proper understanding for our need, was also not in a position to help."[35]

Winiewicz was also concerned that conflicts between the PPS and the PPR over the agricultural situation in Poland would have a "fatal effect" on American grain sales to Poland. In order to gain the confidence of the Polish people, the PPR was trying to convince them that the food situation was under control, when in fact it was not. The American press asked Winiewicz about the truthfulness of official Polish government reports that the food supplies in Poland were adequate. The Polish ambassador replied that it was necessary for his government to behave calmly and to reassure the country that there would be no major food shortages.[36]

Polish diplomats worked hard to bring the State Department over to their side on the relief issue. Winiewicz wrote Warsaw that "we are preparing a campaign among the members of the [State] Department in order to counteract possible opposition to granting us aid."[37] Fortunately for the Poles, in early 1947 the State Department was still in favor of relief aid for Poland and lobbied Congress to include Poland in the $350 million relief program.[38] Acheson told the Senate Foreign Relations Committee on 15 April that the administration favored aid to all who needed it. Acheson assured the committee that the Polish government would have to agree to certain conditions in order to receive relief, conditions which "are calculated to provide adequate assurance that relief aid would reach the people needing it and would not be used to promote the political aims of the Government." Acheson also pledged that the United States would demand "full publicity in the country [which] would insure that the people would know the American source of help . . . and demonstrate to them that we have not forgotten them." Acheson told Congress that the United States would supervise distribution of the relief aid.[39]

The State Department was still concerned that the Soviets would benefit indirectly from American relief to Poland, however. Acheson cabled the U.S. embassy in Warsaw on 25 April for information regarding Soviet grain and munitions credits, grain shipments, and the terms of a Soviet gold loan to Poland.[40] Keith reported that although the Soviets had not advanced any gold or currency to Poland in 1946,[41] they had supplied some "normal" supplies for the Polish Army and had bartered grain for Polish coal, zinc, lead, and other raw materials.[42] Evidently the State Department was not very concerned about these transactions and continued to support for relief for Poland.

The State Department did not have many allies to keep Poland on the list of recipients, however. In April, the Joint Chiefs took a strong stand against any more assistance to countries under Soviet control. They listed Poland sixteenth on a list of countries in need of relief, but advocated "no aid of any sort to Hungary, or to Czechoslovakia and Poland."[43] The House of Representatives also tried to attach an amendment to the relief bill excluding Poland or any other governments "dominated" by the Soviet Union. The amendment had a surprising opponent in former Ambassador Lane, who spoke out sharply against the Polish government in the American press but advocated continued relief for the Polish people, as long as the Polish government met Acheson's stipulations. Lane argued that a distinction should be made between the Soviet-imposed regime and the Polish people. He said that American support for the people would bolster their friendship with the United States. When the bill passed on 31 May, Poland and Hungary were the only Soviet bloc countries listed for possible aid. The administration retained the power to decide whether they actually received assistance.[44]

Debate over relief for Poland continued in Washington throughout the summer. The Polish embassy in Washington was optimistic about Poland's chances for a sizable relief package until they received word in June that Poland would probably get no more than $10 million in relief in 1947.[45] But Poland's rejection of the Marshall Plan in July virtually ended the State Department's support for any more direct loans from the U.S. government, and it also hurt Poland's chances for a cut of the $350 million aid package.

The findings of an American fact-finding mission to Poland in July dashed Polish hopes for American relief. The mission was headed by Colonel R.L. Harrison of the Department of Agriculture, who spent four days touring Poland. Winiewicz was optimistic about the visit and the chances that Harrison would find Poland in need of more relief aid; he described the colonel as "a person with many independent ideas and [one who] is firm in carrying out that which he thinks is right." Winiewicz told his superiors that "it is worth trying to win him over."[46] But when Harrison reported to Washington that Poland could meet its own minimum food requirements for 1947, the administration decided against any relief aid for Poland.[47] The Harrison visit also jeopardized Poland's grain purchases from the United States.[48] Ambassador Winiewicz blamed Poland's grain shortages on the Harrison mission, which he said had gathered its information in only one weekend and had spent the rest of the time relaxing in a resort area.[49]

The manner in which the mission collected its evidence was hardly scientific. When U.S. Ambassador Stanton Griffis asked Harrison how he could arrive at such a conclusion about the Polish agricultural situation in only four days, Harrison replied that

> he simply went to four parts of Poland and looked at the 'behinds' of the citizenry, male and female. [He reported that] confidentially they are uniformly large.[50]

The head of the Central Planning Office, Czesław Bobrowski, recalled later that Harrison had employed some curious fact-finding methods in Poland. On a trip with Harrison from Warsaw to Lublin, Bobrowski tried to follow a route that would show Harrison the most devastated and barren communities in the area. He remembered that "the [purpose of the] trip was difficult from the standpoint of the high consumption of alcohol on the way. On the other hand, discussion was minimal, because our companion dozed most of the time." Bobrowski thought that Harrison probably caught glimpses of areas that had not been destroyed and had based his report on half-drunk recollections. Bobrowski asked sarcastically, "perhaps he woke up at the wrong moment?"[51]

The Truman administration had other information on Poland's food situation that contradicted the Harrison report, but after the Poles rejected the Marshall Plan in July this evidence had no impact on changing the administration's policy. On 25 July Representative George Sadowski of Michigan entered a statement in the *Congressional Record* from a former UNRRA official in Poland claiming that although the Polish people had benefitted greatly from UNRRA aid, the food situation was now "grave" as a result of the end of UNRRA operations in Poland.[52] In addition, a Central Intelligence Agency report in August found that the International Emergency Food Council had allotted Poland 382,000 metric tons of grain for 1947-1948 so that Poland could overcome food shortages.[53]

A UNRRA study conducted in the summer of 1947 also concluded that food consumption of the non-farm population in Poland in that year would be below the FAO's level of emergency subsistence. According to the FAO, this level could not "be long maintained without causing ill-health." Furthermore, the study estimated the cost Poland's grain needs for 1947 at $153.5 million, which was an increase of $21.5 million over UNRRA predictions.[54] A report by the director of CARE found that the average caloric intake in Poland was on the decline, and that there were approximately 3 million hungry children in Poland.[55] The Polish Catholic church also estimated that 90 percent of Poland's six million children were underweight and that 20 percent had active tuberculosis. The fact that Poland was trying to buy grain in the United States with its precious hard currency was further proof of Poland's urgent need for food relief.[56] The Polish grain shortage was so serious in the summer of 1947 that Poland made purchases of grain with the gold received from the Soviet Union earlier in the year.

The Polish government expressed sincere surprise over Washington's decision to exclude Poland from the aid package, and told the Polish people that the United States was unconcerned about their welfare. *Rzeczpospolita* reflected either the wishful thinking of the Polish leadership or the leadership's total misunderstanding of the anti-communist sentiment in the United States by asserting that "certainly the American public will not understand the motives for the denial [of aid]."[57] A Catholic priest wrote that it was difficult to understand how the Harrison report found no need for further relief: "We hope that the matter of assistance for Poland will be considered objectively and that prejudicial attitudes will be eliminated."[58] In order to deflect this criticism and to show that the United States was still interested in the Polish people and Poland's economic recovery, the State Department sent Christian Herter, the future secretary of state under Dwight D. Eisenhower, on a goodwill visit to Warsaw in September.[59] Herter's mission did not accomplish much in the way of improving Polish-American relations.

IV

The Truman administration's decision to exclude Poland from the relief program in 1947 was an unexpected blow to Poland's economic recovery plan. United Nations relief shipments dominated Poland's imports in 1945 and 1946, accounting for 73 percent and 69 percent of Poland's total imports.[60] That figure dropped to 15 percent in 1947, leaving a huge gap in much-needed agricultural supplies and industrial equipment.[61] Although food, clothing, and medical aid comprised the bulk of UNRRA relief aid, by 1947 over $95 million in aid had been committed to industrial rehabilitation, and nearly $76 million to agricultural recovery.[62] Furthermore, about 80 percent of the Polish government's fluid income in the first half of 1946 came from sales of UNRRA supplies to the Polish people.[63] The Polish government expected another $90 million in food assistance in 1947, but the actual amount fell far short of its requests.[64] As a result, the Polish government was forced to turn to the Soviet Union for help. The Soviets supplied Poland with 100,000,000 tons of grain in October 1946, and in February 1947 the Soviets agreed to send another 110,000,000 tons.[65] The Polish economy was becoming increasingly dependent on the Soviet economy for grain, cotton, and other goods that Poland could not get from the United States.

NOTES

1. Department of State *Bulletin*, 31 March 1946, 542. Trade with the United States represented only 0.7 percent of total Polish trade in 1946; *Compendium Statystyczne Polskiego Handlu Zagranicznego w latach 1929-1938, 1945-1960*, 294; and Thompson, "The New Poland," 232. UNRRA relief amounted to approximately 40 percent of all Polish imports from 1945 to 1947. The United States contributed almost $350 million of the $481 million UNRRA aid to Poland in those years.

2. Polish National Council Records, 21 July 1945, 59-60; and ibid., 29 December 1945, 23-24.

3. Memorandum from Grew to Truman, 16 May 1945, Truman Papers, PSF, Subject File, box 186; and memorandum from Truman to Stettinius, 19 May 1945, ibid.

4. State Department briefing book paper, "Suggested United States Policy Regarding Poland," 29 June 1945, *FRUS, 1945* 1:784-785.

5. William J. Donovan memorandum to Truman, 20 June 1945, Truman Papers, Rose Conway File, box 15.

6. Gardner, *Economic Aspects of New Deal Diplomacy*, 312. The Soviet was soon replaced.

7. Polish National Council Records, 23 July 1945, 144.

8. Lane to Byrnes, 6 August 1945, *FRUS, 1945* 5:361-363.

9. "UNRRA's Help to Poland," undated, Central Planning Office Records, File 3792; and Zyblikiewicz, *Polityka Stanów Zjednoczonych i Wielkiej Brytanii wobec Polski, 1944-1949*, 176, 336.

10. See Lane, *I Saw Poland Betrayed*, 220. The Soviets assumed that the United States would use relief for political purposes, but Lane claimed that "this showed a lack of [Soviet] comprehension of the United States' approach to humanitarian problems." There is no evidence that the United States had a policy to use UNRRA relief to extract political concessions, which is why the administration decided to conduct its own relief program so it could do just that.

11. Department of State *Bulletin*, 31 March 1946, 542.

12. Cable, "The United States and the Polish Question, 1939-1948," 250, 254.

13. *Przegląd Socjalistyczny* 2 (1 September 1946): 38. The Poles were probably referring here to loans from the IBRD.

14. Cable, "The United States and the Polish Question, 1939-1948, 248.

15. Rajchman to Modzelewski and Minc, 26 November 1946, Ministry of Industry and Trade Records, File 51.

16. Zyblikiewicz, *Polityka Stanów Zjednoczonych i Wielkiej Brytanii wobec Polski, 1944-1949*, 307.

17. UNRRA, *Foreign Trade in Poland*, 45.

18. Central Planning Office, *Sytuacja Gospodarcza Polski*, 135.

19. Lane to Byrnes, 8 October 1946, *FRUS, 1946* 6:506-508.

20. *Life*, 16 December 1946, in the *Congressional Record*, 80th Cong., 1st sess., 93: A-2534.

21. Memorandum of conversation, Rajchman and Cleveland and Posniak (European desk), 15 July 1946, RG 59, 860c.50, box 6381.

22. Winiewicz to Modzelewski, Minc, etal., 9 February 1947, Ministry of Industry and Trade Records, File 51.

23. Lundestad, "The American Policy Towards Poland 1943-1946," 27.

24. Winiewicz to Minc, Berman, etal., 25 February 1947, Ministry of Industry and Trade Records, File 51.

25. Polish Government, Sejm Ustawodawczy, *Sprawozdanie Stenograficzne*, Akty [Polish legislative diet, stenographic records], 8 February 1947, 23, 74 (hereafter Polish Diet Records with date and page number). The Polish Diet replaced the Polish National Council after the elections in January 1947.

26. Program of imports and exports for 1947, Central Planning Office Records, File 2398.

27. Economic Committee of the Council of Ministers, Subcommittee of Foreign Economic Affairs, 20 January 1947, File 137.

28. Keith to Byrnes, 17 November 1946, *FRUS, 1946* 6:514-516.

29. Lane, *I Saw Poland Betrayed*, 223.

30. Memorandum of conversation, Clayton and Rajchman, 11 October 1946, RG 59, 860c.51, box 6385.

31. Winiewicz to Modzelewski, Minc, etal., 25 February 1947, Ministry of Industry and Trade Records, File 51; and Edward Iwaszkiewicz and Rajchman to Minc, etal., 25 February 1947, ibid.

32. Iwaszkiewicz and Rajchman to Minc, etal., 25 February 1947, Ministry of Industry and Trade Records, File 51.

33. See Zyblikiewicz, *Polityka Stanów Zjednoczonych i Wielkiej Brytanii wobec Polski, 1944-1949*, 309, who writes that the Department of Agriculture announced in July that Poland would be allowed to buy 20.5 thousand tons of grain from a pool of 1,407 thousand tons. The Bizone, on the other hand, was allotted 466 thousand tons.

34. Iwaszkiewicz to Minc, etal., 21 May 1947, Ministry of Industry and Trade Records, File 51.

35. Winiewicz, *Co pamiętam z długiej drogi życia*, 395.

36. Winiewicz to Warsaw, 25 May 1947, Ministry of Industry and Trade Records, File 51.

37. Winiewicz to Modzelewski, Minc, etal., 25 Feb. 1947, Ministry of Industry and Trade Records, File 51.

38. Iwaszkiewicz and Rajchman to Minc, etal., 25 February 1947, Ministry of Industry and Trade Records, File 51; see also Zyblikiewicz, *Polityka Stanów Zjednoczonych i Wielkiej Brytanii wobec Polski, 1944-1949*, 291. Although there is no record of this exchange in the Truman Papers or in State Department documents, Zyblikiewicz claims that Truman assured Winiewicz in early February that Poland would receive further relief.

39. Department of State *Bulletin*, 20 April 1947, 757.

40. Acheson to the U.S. embassy in Warsaw, 25 April 1947, RG 59, 860c.51, box 6385.

41. Lane to Byrnes, 24 September 1946, RG 59, 860c.51, box 6385; Lane to Byrnes, 28 September 1946, ibid.; and Clayton to Bevin, undated, ibid. The Polish press announced in September 1946

that Poland would receive a Soviet loan of $25 million in gold, which could be used as collateral for a larger IBRD loan. Actually, Poland signed the loan agreement with the Soviet Union six months later.

42. Keith to Marshall, 28 April 1947, RG 59, 860c.51, box 6385.

43. "U.S. Assistance to Other Countries from the Standpoint of National Security (JCS 1769)," 29 April 1947, *FRUS, 1947: General; The United Nations* (Washington: U.S. Government Printing Office, 1973), 1:738-750. Hungary was listed eighth on this list, Czechoslovakia fifteenth.

44. House debate on the Colmer amendment, 28 April 1947, *Congressional Record*, 80th Cong., 1st sess., 93:4219, 4178.

45. Winiewicz to Warsaw, 18 June 1947, Ministry of Industry and Trade Records, File 51; and Zyblikiewicz, *Polityka Stanów Zjednoczonych i Wielkiej Brytanii wobec Polski, 1944-1949*, 308.

46. Winiewicz to Modzelewski and Minc, 3 July 1947, Ministry of Industry and Trade Records, File 51.

47. Report of Harrison to Marshall, 18 July 1947, Department of State *Bulletin*, 3 August 1947, 223.

48. Winiewicz to Warsaw, undated (ca. September 1947), Ministry of Industry and Trade Records, File 51.

49. Winiewicz, *Co pamiętam z długiej drogi życia*, 394-395.

50. Griffis, *Lying in State*, 202.

51. Bobrowski, *Wspomnienia ze stulecia*, 154.

52. Statement by Melvin P. McPherson (former chief of distribution for UNRRA in Poland), 25 July 1947 *Congressional Record*, 80th Cong., 1st sess., 93:A-3863.

53. "Soviet and Satellite Grain," 2 August 1948, Truman Papers, PSF, Intelligence File (CIA Reports, 1948), box 255.

54. UNRRA, *Foreign Trade in Poland*, 40-41.

55. *Głos Ludu*, 1 August 1947, in Central Planning Office Records, File 1194; *Rzeczpospolita*, 29 July 1947, in ibid. The United Nations estimated that 2,300 calories was the average daily requirement. Most Poles were getting between 1700-1900 calories daily.

56. Lukas, *Bitter Legacy: Polish-American Relations in the Wake of World War II*, 88.

57. *Rzeczpospolita*, 27 August 1947, in Central Planning Office Records, File 1194.

58. *Tygodnik Warszawski* 3 (17 August 1947): 1.

59. *New York Times*, 9 September 1947, 4.

60. Sekular, "Stosunki gospodarcze między Polska i Stanami Zjednoczonymy Ameryki po II wojnie światowej", 16; and Wojciechowski, "Handel Zagraniczny Polski", 374. Of the total $480 million in UNRRA goods that Poland received from 1945 to 1948, over 83 percent came in the critical first two years (21 percent in 1945, and 62 percent in 1946).

61. Sekular, "Stosunki gospodarcze między Polska i Stanami Zjednoczonymy Ameryki po II wojnie światowej", 16.

62. "UNRRA Program of Relief and Rehabilitation: Supplies Summary Report," June 1947, Ministry of Industry and Trade Records, File 3824a; and Alton, *Polish Postwar Economy*, 269.

63. Thompson, "The New Poland," 232.

64. Notes on the balance of payments, 11 April 1947, Central Planning Office Records, File 610.

65. Różański, *Śladem wspomnień i dokumentów, 1943-1948*, 461-462.

Chapter Six

Poland and the Marshall Plan, 1947-1948

I

In June 1947, Secretary of State Marshall announced his extensive American aid plan for the reconstruction of Europe. Although the offer was made to Eastern Europe and the Soviet Union, State Department officials did not really expect the Soviets to participate in the European Recovery Program (ERP). They were not at all surprised when Molotov walked out of the Paris conference of foreign ministers, where the essentials of the plan were to be hammered out. Nor were they surprised when Moscow ordered Poland and Czechoslovakia not to attend that conference.[1] Even before the communist coup in Czechoslovakia in February 1948, U.S. officials assumed that the governments of Eastern Europe had no choice but to fall into line with the Soviet Union on most political and economic issues. The State Department already referred to the Eastern European countries as Soviet satellites, and Poland's rejection of the Marshall Plan only confirmed the department's belief that the Soviet Union exercised complete control over that country.[2]

There is no question that Poland had to take its cue from Moscow before making major foreign policy decisions such as acceptance of the Marshall Plan. Poland's decision not to participate in the ERP was not a reflection of an overall Soviet plan to isolate the entire Soviet bloc economy from the West, however, or to sabotage the ERP, as some high level officials in the State Department thought. There was no significant change in Polish foreign economic policy after the Soviet bloc rejection of the Marshall Plan. The Polish government still exercised considerable freedom of movement in the economic sphere and continued its efforts to increase commercial relations with Western Europe and the United States.[3] Poland made an important contribution to the success of the ERP, especially through the export of coal to

Western Europe.[4] Unfortunately for the Polish communists this cooperation did little to change their image as Soviet puppets.

The Polish government had mixed feelings about Marshall's announcement of a comprehensive economic recovery plan for Europe. On the one hand the Polish leadership hoped to gain reconstruction funds from the ERP, but on the other they did not want this new initiative to jeopardize negotiations for loans from the IBRD or Poland's chances for American relief aid (see Chapter 5). Despite denials from Marshall and the State Department, the Polish rejection of the Marshall Plan had a major impact on the department's final decisions to leave Poland out of any other aid or loan packages. Only because of the need for Polish coal in Western Europe was Poland even considered for IBRD loans after 1947.[5]

II

It is well known that the Polish government hoped to participate in the Marshall Plan.[6] In early July, Premier Cyrankiewicz told the press that he was not familiar with the details of the Plan but that "Poland took a positive attitude toward it."[7] *Życie Gospodarcze* viewed the Marshall Plan in Marxist terms as an outlet for excess American capital but also wrote that

> the Plan is undoubtedly a bold concept, and could establish an epoch in world economic history. Europe needs today everything that the United States can deliver.

The journal also praised the Plan as a possible "harbinger of new international cooperation."[8]

Like many in the Polish government, Ambassador Winiewicz thought that Poland would play an important role in the Marshall Plan, because Silesian coal was indispensable to Western European recovery. In June, Winiewicz told State Department counselor Benjamin Cohen that a recently negotiated reduction of coal shipments to the Soviet Union was an indication that Poland desired to integrate its economy with Europe's by increasing coal exports to Western Europe. According to Winiewicz, Cohen replied that Poland should not count on Marshall aid, for the American public and Congress would never allow assistance to a communist country.[9] Winiewicz maintained his optimism, however, informing Warsaw on 21 June that "the Marshall Plan will be realized above all in light of coal, about which the United States is mainly concerned." Winiewicz understood that the Truman administration thought that German economic recovery was of paramount importance and was contemplating a full-scale reconstruction of the Bizone, so he warned his government that rejection of the Marshall Plan would result in the rapid reconstruction of the coal industry in the Ruhr. The ambassador recommended that Poland immediately declare its participation in the plan and that Warsaw ask Paris and London for their opinions of the recovery program.[10]

Of course, the Polish government realized that the Marshall Plan would put Poland in an uncomfortable position if the Soviet Union rejected it. When Molotov left the Paris conference in June, Minister of Industry Minc happened to be in Prague. The Czech minister of foreign trade, Hubert Ripka, remembered later that Minc told him that "the situation is becoming complicated for you and for us." Minc maintained his optimism, however, telling Ripka that surely the Soviet Union would take into consideration the economic problems of the two countries and understand that "we need American help."[11]

To their dismay, Winiewicz and his superiors in Warsaw soon realized that the Marshall Plan had political as well as economic objectives. In early July, shortly before Poland formally rejected further talks on the plan, Winiewicz wrote Foreign Minister Modzelewski and Minc that the dollar shortage in Europe was not the primary reason for the Marshall Plan; rather, the United States intended to use the plan to prevent economic chaos in Europe because it feared that the Soviets might benefit from an unstable economic situation there.[12]

On orders from Moscow, the Polish government announced on 9 July that Poland would not participate in the Marshall Plan discussions. In his memoirs, Winiewicz deemphasized Stalin's directive to reject the Marshall Plan, claiming that he himself played a more important role in Poland's decision. According to Winiewicz, his report to Warsaw indicating that Congress would not vote Marshall funds for any communist country persuaded the Polish government not to take part in any further discussions of the plan. Poland was not forced to reject the Marshall Plan, he said; it elected not to participate, knowing that Congress would not vote for aid to Eastern Europe anyway.[13]

If Winiewicz's version of the events is true, then the Soviets and the Poles made a serious diplomatic blunder, because their rejection of the Marshall Plan enabled the West to blame the uncooperative attitude of the communists for the economic and eventual political division of Europe. Their participation in the Paris conference would have put the onus on Congress to reject inclusion of the Soviet bloc in the Marshall Plan.

Berman and Bobrowski recalled later that the Soviet Union wavered on whether to participate in the Marshall Plan until Stalin decided to reject it.[14] Stalin did not want to risk having a wedge driven between the Soviet Union and Eastern Europe if Congress did the unexpected and voted funds for Poland or Czechoslovakia.[15]

After Stalin handed down his decision, the Polish government's expressions of opposition to the Marshall Plan more often reflected Moscow's line than real Polish reservations. Polish officials cited the possible loss of economic sovereignty as one reason Poland would not participate in the ERP. In applying for loans from the United States and the IBRD, however, the Polish government had already agreed repeatedly to stipulations that obligated Poland to develop certain sectors of its economy. For example, the $40 million Export-Import Bank loan was earmarked, with Warsaw's agreement, for the coal mining industry. Further loan negotiations with the Export-Import Bank, as well as with the IBRD, while unfruitful, did not fail because of any unwillingness on the part of the Poles to allow these agencies a say in where the money would be spent. Furthermore, Poland was still a cooperative member of other multilateral economic organizations, such as the ECE and the FAO, and the Polish government abided by decisions made in these bodies.[16]

On the other hand, the specter of a resurgent Germany taking part in the ERP was a very real threat to Poland, and the Poles, like the French and other ERP participants, offered compelling arguments against German reconstruction.[17] Before the announcement of the Marshall Plan, Polish officials told British and French diplomats in Warsaw that German reconstruction at the expense of the rest of Europe was unacceptable.[18] On 11 July Cyrankiewicz declared that Poland would not take part in a plan to reconstruct Germany, because a revived Germany could pose a new threat to the security of Europe.[19] On that day the front page headline of the PPR organ *Głos Ludu* was "We do not want German dominance in Europe."[20]

Both communist and non-communist Poles agreed that Poland was too dependent on the German economy in the interwar period, and they did not want their country to reprise its role as colonial provider of raw materials and food to Germany. *Rzeczpospolita* complained that "foreign capital proposes to concentrate the entire metallurgy industry in Germany, leaving to us the role of delivering coal and agricultural products."[21] In October, the vice director for economic organization in the Central Planning Office, Stanisław Rączkowski, was invited to participate in a discussion on the Marshall Plan hosted by Eleanor Roosevelt. Rączkowski explained that Poland was not participating in the Marshall Plan because his government could not accept German dominance of industrial production in Central and Eastern Europe again. He cited as evidence the fact that before the war the Germans had produced two thirds of the machine tools in Europe.[22]

The Polish leadership still hoped that Poland could participate indirectly in the ERP, but German reconstruction remained a stumbling block. On 12 July Minc told the IBRD that Poland might still participate in the Marshall Plan, but he reiterated that his country feared taking part in any organization that intended to reconstruct Germany faster than Poland. Minc also expressed reservations about the Marshall Plan organization proposed by the British and the French, which he said would be some kind of "confidential club" in which Poland would have no voice. Minc preferred to deal directly with the United States for aid.[23]

Although Polish officials did not mention it publicly, the economic competition that a reconstructed Germany would offer Poland was of equal concern to them. The Ruhr was second only to Silesia as a source of coal in Europe, and if German coal displaced Polish coal in European markets, Poland's economic recovery would be dealt a severe blow. In August, Great Britain and the United States decided to re-industrialize the Bizone. Winiewicz protested to the State Department. The reconstruction of Germany, he declared, was "contrary to the principle of priority for the reconstruction of countries devastated by German aggression, as well as to the principle not to exceed in Germany the average of the standard of living of [other] European countries."[24] He stressed that Poland still needed help and added that there should be no political strings attached to economic aid.[25]

The Poles had another legitimate reason for opposing the Marshall Plan. If it was enacted and they rejected it, they would probably lose reparations from Germany.[26] By mid-June 1947 Poland had received over $35 million in reparations from all of Germany, including the German areas occupied by Poland.[27] That was not all clear gain. Reparations received from the Soviet zone did not balance the forced shipment of coal to the Soviets at prices far below market levels. Reparation coal shipments to the Soviets totaled almost $11 million in 1947 and over $8 million in 1948.[28] After the Marshall Plan was announced, reparations received from the western zones of Germany slowed to a trickle.[29] But the Poles did not have many options. By far the most important reparation that Germany had made to Poland was Silesia, and as Berman later recalled, the Polish leadership feared that if they defied Moscow and joined the ERP, Poland would face the loss of Silesia to East Germany and the establishment of a new twentieth-century Duchy of Warsaw.[30] Poland's only choice was to seek aid from the West independent of the Marshall Plan. Moscow did not hinder that effort.

Most officials in the Truman administration did not expect any cooperation from the Soviet Union and Eastern Europe for the Marshall Plan, which Marshall had launched in part to prevent Stalin from capitalizing on a Western European economic collapse.[31] In his memoirs, President Truman accused the Soviet Union of wanting to sabotage the Marshall Plan even before Molotov walked out of the Paris conference in June.[32] One historian of the Marshall Plan contends that after Molotov left Paris, "policymakers on both sides of the Atlantic now expected the Soviet Union, together with its Communist supporters in the West, to do everything possible to retard recovery and sabotage the Marshall Plan."[33]

The propaganda that the Polish government leveled against the plan seemed to be designed to undermine it. Berman called the plan "anti-European, anti-British, anti-French and anti-Italian, only not anti-fascist."[34] Many delegates in the Polish Diet charged that the Western zones of Germany were being run by ex-Nazis. If the United States was determined to rebuild Germany rather than Poland, said one PPR representative in December, then Poland would have to rely on its own resources to reconstruct its economy.[35]

Poland's commercial policy belied this propaganda. Instead of turning inward economically, Poland continued its efforts to gain reconstruction assistance from the Export-Import Bank and the IBRD, and persisted in trying to negotiate favorable trade agreements with Western Europe. Records of the negotiations for an IBRD loan reveal that Poland was willing to play a positive role in Western European recovery.

III

The Polish government had good reason to be optimistic that Poland would be indirectly included in the ERP as a coal supplier to Western Europe through loans from the IBRD. Ambassador Winiewicz wrote Warsaw in September that the subject of the significance of Polish coal exports for European reconstruction was on the agenda in Paris.[36] Although Poland was not a participant in the Marshall Plan, the Committee for European Economic Cooperation (CEEC) expected Poland to play an important role in the ERP. In September, the CEEC estimated that the sixteen ERP countries would have to import forty-one million tons of coal from the United States in 1948, and seventeen million tons from Poland. For 1951 the estimate was six million tons for the United States and thirty-one million tons for Poland.[37] Dr. Tadeusz Lychowski, head of the Economics Division in the Polish Foreign Ministry, thought that neither Germany nor Great Britain would be capable of covering the increased demand in Western Europe, but that with loans Poland could export even more than thirty-one million tons in 1951.[38]

Ambassador Winiewicz lobbied hard for American aid outside of the parameters of the Marshall Plan, especially in the wake of the poor Polish harvest of 1947.[39] In a speech in Portland, Oregon, on 19 December, the Polish ambassador summarized Poland's cooperative efforts in the IBRD, the FAO, and other international economic organizations, and indicated that Poland wanted to continue cooperating with these agencies. He pointed out that Poland had normal diplomatic relations and trade agreements with fourteen of the sixteen participants in the ERP, and declared that the Polish government wanted to expand those economic contacts. Winiewicz again emphasized the immorality of rebuilding Germany first while Germany's victims lagged behind economically, but he also sounded a note of conciliation and compromise on German reconstruction: "I do not say that Germany must be ruined economically, but I stress that Germany should not be reconstructed sooner than other countries of Europe."[40]

Although the U.S. government had virtually rejected any more economic assistance for Poland by the fall of 1947, the demand for Polish coal in Western Europe was so great that Poland was the only country in Eastern Europe considered for more Export-Import Bank loans after the rejection of the Marshall Plan by the Soviet bloc. Anti-communist sentiment in the United States, however, which was reflected in both the Truman Doctrine and the Marshall Plan, made direct American aid to Poland politically impossible by the end of 1947, so Poland was forced to turn to the IBRD as its last hope for significant reconstruction assistance. The State Department still saw the IBRD as the source for long-term reconstruction loans to supplement Marshall Plan aid, and there was a good chance that Poland would receive a loan.[41] Poland had been a cooperative member of the IBRD since its inception in 1946 and had gold and hard currency on deposit at the bank.[42]

The Poles were very optimistic about their chances for a loan. They thought that the bank's charter, which prohibited political considerations from influencing lending, put them in a good position for loans.[43] The Polish Minister of Finance, Konstanty Dąbrowski (PPR), hoped that the IBRD would consider a loan to Poland solely on the basis of the government's ability to repay. Dąbrowski reflected his party's thinking that the IBRD was truly an international institution that was not completely controlled by Washington.[44] In April 1947, Dąbrowski promised the Polish Diet that the IBRD had "especially significant importance" for Poland.[45] It seemed only a question of how much money they would get. Minc set his sights high. In the summer of 1947, Poland requested loans of $600 million over a period of four years or more for reconstruction purposes.[46]

At first the State Department's Economic Affairs Division and the IBRD leadership favored granting loans to Poland. At a joint session of the IBRD and the IMF in Savannah, Georgia, in 1946, Edward Drozniak, President of the Polish National Bank, recalled that "everywhere we met with great interest in the matter pertaining to the reconstruction of economic life in our country, and with much understanding and favorable, positive opinion of our achievements to date."[47] But again the State Department gave the Polish government conflicting signals on the possibilities for an IBRD loan. In the fall of 1946, when the IBRD began consideration of a loan to Poland in return for promises to export coal to Western Europe, the administration counseled against it, reasoning that Polish coal exports were increasing anyway. Loan negotiations went ahead anyway when Acheson told the IBRD in November that "preliminary discussions" of a small Polish loan were acceptable to the State Department. Acheson reported to Byrnes that the IBRD's executive director had assured him that "the Bank would in no case wish to allot more than $75-$100 million to Eastern European countries this year, and possibly not more than $50 million to one." Among the countries of Eastern Europe, Poland was undoubtedly the best candidate for a loan, and the bank promised Acheson that top priority would be given to reconstruction projects with ties to "Western European economic needs which would help insure hard money proceeds for interest and amortization."[48]

Clayton, head of the Economic Affairs Division, favored an IBRD loan, especially after the harsh winter in Europe in 1946-1947. Poland had provided about 15 percent of Western European coal needs in 1946, and Clayton hoped that this percentage could be significantly increased through a loan for the Polish coal industry. He also thought a loan would make Poland less dependent on the Soviet Union. In the fall of 1947, when the CEEC decided to use Ruhr coal to supply Europe, Clayton opposed offering Marshall funds to Poland or any of the Soviet bloc countries, but he still supported an IBRD loan for the Polish coal industry. The European Affairs and East European Divisions in the State Department argued against the loan because of the political situation in Poland, and their pressure eventually convinced Emilio Collado, the U.S. executive director of the bank, to postpone a decision on the Polish coal loan.[49] These dilatory tactics continued for the next two years, much to the frustration of the Polish government.

Despite their propaganda about the Marshall Plan's threat to the economic sovereignty of Poland, Polish leaders recognized that they would have to make some compromises in order to receive IBRD loans, even if it meant accepting a degree of dependence on the West. One PPS delegate in the Polish National Council argued that in order to obtain loans, Poles would have to "speak the language of these [capitalist] countries and assure them minimum economic profits, which would justify the investment of their reserves in the reconstruction of Poland."[50] These concessions were necessary, because the loans were indispensable to complete Poland's reconstruction plans. The government's Three-Year Plan for the period 1947 to 1949 estimated that Poland would need $600 million in foreign loans, $375.5 million of which would come in the form of loans from the IBRD.[51]

In the summer of 1947, Polish negotiators in Washington asked for $130 million from the IBRD specifically for the coal industry and related industries, arguing that this credit was necessary to increase exports to Western Europe.[52] The Poles also expected additional IBRD loans for the agricultural industry, which Minc accorded second priority. The Polish negotiators argued that Polish agricultural exports would put an end to the shortage in Western Europe; therefore, loans to Poland were loans for the good of all Europe.[53]

The Polish government invited an IBRD fact-finding mission to Poland in June. The bank accepted, but let it be understood that in accepting the invitation the bank was not indicating what position it would take on the loan requests.[54] At the news conference announcing the visit, the IBRD made it clear that Western European reconstruction took priority over Polish reconstruction, but IBRD officials argued that the importance of Polish coal to Western Europe overrode ideological and political considerations.[55]

For one month the mission met with Polish economic officials and surveyed Poland's general economic situation, focussing particularly on the coal industry in Silesia. Minc told the mission that Poland was willing to give the bank a "certain voice" in deciding the quantity and destination of coal exports, and he offered a guarantee that part of the profits from coal exports would go to repay the loan. Although the Polish government had recently used the threat to economic sovereignty as an excuse for rejecting the Marshall Plan, Minc now said that provisions such as these were acceptable. He did stipulate, however, that the conditions of the loan must not be worse than those applied to other countries, such as France. Minc also told the mission that the Polish government would agree to insure the repayment of the loan but that the actual terms of repayment would have to await direct negotiations with the IBRD in Washington.[56]

Minc's assurances were sincere. Several months earlier the Poles themselves had proposed to bind an IBRD loan to coal exports to Western Europe. At that time the executive director of the IBRD, Eugene Black, delayed action on the loan saying that the bank was dependent on funds from American banks and that a loan to Poland would hurt confidence in the bank. "We do not want to commit suicide," he told Czesław Bobrowski.[57] Black was generally negative about any loan to Poland, and after one fruitless talk with him Ambassador Winiewicz recalled being overwhelmed by a sense of hopelessness:

> I was so upset that I dropped in for a drink at the bar in the Hotel Mayflower. I left equally angry . . . . All the tries and efforts [went] without result.[58]

By August, Warsaw was expressing impatience with the delay on its loan requests. Dąbrowski told a British correspondent that if Poland did not get a loan soon, it would withdraw from the IBRD.[59]

A loan to Poland made simple economic sense, and there were some in the IBRD who lobbied for it. William Welk, chief of the bank's East European Department of Loans, argued that the Polish government was in a difficult political situation and was forced to take its cue from Moscow on some foreign policy positions. After discussions with Polish representatives at the Marshall Plan conference in Paris, Welk reported that the Poles had a strong desire to participate in the conference but were forced to leave by the Soviets. Welk claimed that in daily economic affairs, however, the Poles had "independence to a great degree" and that Poland desired to increase its commercial exchanges with Western Europe. Welk also found that Poland had a great shortage in grain and machinery. Because the United States was the only country that could supply these commodities in any great quantity, Poland would have to depend on foreign loans if it was to buy such items at all.[60]

The Poles still had reason to expect a loan, because IBRD President John J. McCloy favored lending money to Poland throughout 1947 and 1948, although he too had political reservations. The Polish leaders were very concerned about what effect the Marshall Plan would have on the availability of IBRD loans, but McCloy assured them that a loan would be evaluated on its own merits. He told the Polish representative to the IBRD, Leon Barański, that the IBRD would only get involved in the Marshall Plan, or more specifically in the reconstruction of the Ruhr, if the Ruhr were administered by an international consortium. Barański relayed this information to Winiewicz and said that in his opinion, based on this meeting with McCloy, the chances for a Polish coal loan were still very good.[61]

On the other hand, Robert L. Garner, vice president of the IBRD, believed that because the Poles had refused to participate in the Paris economic conference, the Poles would have to reduce Minc's original request for a total of $600 million in loans, and that any loan they received would have to be targeted for the coal industry for increased exports to Western Europe. But even this loan was in trouble, according to Garner, who said that it was "not possible to disregard the question whether the [Polish] government is an independent organ, or a part of a foreign power."[62]

Throughout the fall of 1947 the IBRD continued to give the Polish embassy in Washington the impression that Poland's chances for a loan were very good. At the beginning of September the bank's press chief told a Polish embassy official that the Polish government would receive part of its loan requests, but that the precise amount depended on how much coal Poland would guarantee to supply Western Europe. Soon afterward the bank informed Winiewicz that Poland's chances for a loan had improved, because European recovery would stagnate without an increase in Polish coal exports. Winiewicz also expressed optimism about the IBRD loan because some Republicans had come out against a special session of Congress to discuss the Marshall Plan and because there was considerable opposition to the Plan in the United States. If the Marshall Plan hit a snag, Winiewicz thought Poland's immediate chances for a loan would improve. Therefore, he recommended that the government put firm pressure on the bank to make a quick decision on the coal loan.[63]

Foreign Minister Modzelewski made a personal plea for loans during a visit with Marshall in September. He stressed that Poland was counting on good relations with the West as well as with the East and asserted that Poland's friendship with the Soviet Union did not preclude a fruitful relationship with the United States.[64] Modzelewski also told Marshall that Poland expected to export thirty-five million tons of coal in 1949 but that present exports were only twenty million tons because of a lack of capital for new machinery. One third of this total was going to the Soviet Union, two thirds to the rest of Europe. In order to increase exports, Modzelewski said, Poland needed credits and loans from the United States and the IBRD. Marshall was generally in favor of a small coal loan and promised to speak to McCloy about it. Marshall knew, however, that giving a loan to Poland at this time would undermine the administration's lobbying strategy in Congress, making it difficult to portray the Marshall Plan as an anti-communist measure.[65]

Although the loan negotiations were moving slowly, the Polish government remained hopeful that the IBRD was not taking orders directly from the United States. At the Council of Governors meeting of the IBRD and the IMF in London at the beginning of October, the new Polish minister of finance, Karol Alexandrowicz, reported to Minc that while the U.S. delegation held the "dominant position" at the conference, it did not have the power to dictate to the other nations. He called Eugene Black's argument that the bank could not lend money to Poland because such a loan would be unacceptable to American financiers and to the American public one of the "pretexts" bank officials for refusing the loan. Alexandrowicz did not think that the United States would be able to deny a loan to Poland for political reasons. He declared that because Poland was a dues-paying member of the bank and had adhered to all of the bank's statutes, it was in a good position to receive a loan. He also said that because the Ruhr was to be reconstructed, Poland surely had a moral right to a loan.[66]

McCloy's visit to Silesia in early October gave the Polish government another opportunity to lobby for the loan. McCloy told the Poles that although their long-term prospects were good, there was little chance of their receiving a loan very soon. McCloy was probably stalling because of the uncertain fate of the Marshall Plan and because the State Department opposed the loan. Minc told McCloy that Marshall had indicated to Winiewicz in September that the State Department would raise no objection to the IBRD loan. In reality Marshall had said no such thing, although he had told Winiewicz that he had personally appealed to Congress for relief aid after the end of the U.N. relief effort in 1947. On 7 October Ambassador Griffis asked the State Department for clarification, and Undersecretary of State Robert Lovett replied that the department was still studying a proposal for a $47 million loan for the coal industry and had not reached a decision.[67]

After McCloy returned to Washington, he and Winiewicz met to discuss his findings. The IBRD president talked about his visit with "enthusiasm" and said that he and Minc had gotten along very well together. He told Winiewicz that he thought Poland was well administered and was making a rapid economic recovery. He also said that the Polish loan request was the "best substantiated and justified" among the many loan requests received by the bank. Winiewicz waited impatiently for the meeting to end so that he could send off a dispatch to Warsaw reporting the good news. Later he admitted that he had "colored the telegram too optimistically."[68]

On 15 October the State Department requested an opinion on loans for Poland from the ambassador in Warsaw. Griffis confirmed that McCloy's visit seemed to have convinced the Polish government that it would soon receive an IBRD loan. He himself thought that lending money to a Soviet-dominated country was inadvisable. He cited the possibility that the Soviets could force the Poles to break the conditions of the loan. His dispatches gave further credence to the idea that the Soviets were running and exploiting the Polish economy. "It is perfectly obvious that a dollar to Poland is a dollar to Russia," he told Marshall. He recommended approval of the coal industry loan, however, because of the need for Polish coal in Western Europe.[69]

Once again, Poland's chances for a loan were hurt by its own remarkable economic recovery. A Foreign Policy Association report in December found that the Polish economy was rebounding so quickly that it might be possible for Poland to fulfill most of its goals in the Three-Year Plan without the $600 million in loans it was requesting from the IBRD. The report predicted that if Poland needed any assistance, the Soviet Union would provide it.[70]

Ambassador Griffis agreed. He advised Marshall that the Polish government was "doing a really excellent job of economic control, development and organization throughout the nation."[71] In January 1948, he told the press that Poland's economic condition was excellent: "The people are well fed and countrywise [sic] the food situation stacks up well with the food available here in the States." In his opinion, Poland could recover without a loan, although perhaps not as quickly as it would otherwise. He thought (mistakenly as it turned out) that the Polish government had virtually given up on an IBRD loan anyway. Griffis reaffirmed his support for a loan for the coal industry, however. He predicted that Poland could increase the fifty million tons of coal it would produce in 1948 to sixty million tons in 1949.[72]

Because Polish coal exports to Western Europe were already on the rise, the State Department decided to delay the loan negotiations. In January, McCloy felt that he could not keep the Poles waiting any longer, and he told Lovett that a decision had to be made on their loan immediately. He said that a rejection of their loan request would be embarrassing to the bank, because the bank's charter expressly forbade making or refusing loans on a political basis. McCloy assured Lovett that every possible condition had been included in the loan contract to provide for coal shipments to Western Europe. He expected the Poles to accept the contract soon.[73]

McCloy was already aware that the secretary of commerce and one or two members of the National Advisory Council on International Monetary and Financial Problems (NAC) were against the loan. McCloy wanted the State Department's opinion, because Minc had claimed that Marshall had said that the State Department would not object to the loan. Lovett told McCloy that this was not the case, and suggested that there were indeed grounds for rejecting the loan. For one thing, the American public would not support loans to a communist country dominated by the Soviet Union, and a loss of support in the United States might affect the ability of the bank to raise funds in the future. McCloy countered that 60 percent of the bankers with whom he had spoken supported the loan. Lovett then offered another argument against the loan, which McCloy found more convincing. He claimed that because the normal flow of Polish coal was from east to west, both the loan and the stipulations contained in the loan contract were superfluous.

Lovett then proceeded to ask what McCloy's position would be if the State Department member on the NAC took a stand against the loan. McCloy replied that "this would clearly remove his problem with respect to declining the loan on political grounds, since it would not be the Bank that turned it down but the United States representative under instructions from the NAC."[74] McCloy, who was also concerned with Soviet actions in Eastern Europe, could in this way legally deny a loan to Poland and deflect criticism of loan making on a political basis. McCloy may have had some misgivings about this decision. According to Polish Central Planning Office official Stanisław Rączkowski, McCloy said later that the biggest mistake he made as president of the bank was not granting Poland the coal loan.[75] Undoubtedly it would have increased Polish coal shipments to Western Europe and would have speeded economic recovery.

At the end of February, Ambassador Griffis and the embassy in Warsaw reversed their position and appealed to Washington to reject the IBRD loan, arguing that Polish coal exports to Western Europe would continue to rise anyway. Griffis also warned Marshall that, judging by the virulence of the attacks on the United States in the Polish press, a loan would not bring about any profound change in Polish attitudes toward the West.

> We feel [that the] slanderous and outrageous attacks on the U.S. will continue with or without the loan. . . . If the loan is small (47 million) the U.S. will be attacked for niggardliness; if large, for attempting to purchase Poland's soul.

Griffis repeated his conviction that a "dollar to [a] satellite is a dollar to the U.S.S.R."[76]

IV

The communist coup in Czechoslovakia in February virtually ended any serious consideration of an IBRD loan for the Polish coal industry, but fears of a European coal shortage kept negotiations going throughout the first half of 1948. The United States would give no further help to Poland, although in 1948 it became obvious that neither Ruhr nor costly U.S. coal could fill Western Europe's needs. Nonetheless, Poland's failure to gain loans from the IBRD did not lead the Polish government to restrict coal exports to Western Europe or to end cooperative efforts to expand intra-European trade. In fact, through its coal exports Poland made an important contribution to the rapid pace of Western European economic recovery.

When Marshall proposed his plan for European recovery in 1947, officials in the Truman administration had no intention of restricting East-West trade. They merely wanted to develop the pattern of intra-European trade that existed before the war.[77] The embargo of exports to the Soviet bloc developed out of an idea associated with the Marshall Plan, that the United States should regulate its export of scarce items that Western Europe needed by means of a licensing program.[78] But as fears of a possible war with the Soviet Union increased in 1948, the licensing program became an export embargo involving virtually all industrial products. Although the Commerce Department and Joint Chiefs of Staff opposed making an exception for Poland, the State Department lobbied for a looser set of licensing controls for that country, because they feared that the Polish government might eliminate its coal exports to Western Europe or take other steps to sabotage the Marshall Plan.[79]

The Polish government did not respond in kind to the imposition of the licensing program, however. Rather, the Polish government persisted in its efforts to increase trade of all kinds with Western Europe. In 1946 Poland had provided about 15 percent of Western Europe's coal; by 1949 it was providing some 25 percent.[80] And although the Polish government's export plan for 1948 gave priority to the Soviet Union, Sweden came next, followed by Denmark, Czechoslovakia, Norway, Austria and France.[81]

The Coal Division of the ECE was fully aware of Western Europe's need for Polish coal. It predicted that the Marshall Plan countries would need an additional fifty-eight million tons in 1948, fifty million tons in 1949, forty-two million tons in 1950, and thirty-seven million tons in 1951. Great Britain and West Germany could not fill this need, so the CEEC factored Polish coal into the reconstruction plan.[82] The importance of this coal to the recovery program was underscored when the Economic Cooperation Administration (ECA) authorized $11.2 million in ERP funds in 1948 (and several million more dollars by mid-1949) to purchase Polish coal.[83]

The pace of Western European recovery was threatened by the ERP countries' purchases of large quantities of high-priced U.S. coal. At the end of 1948, the State Department sent a report to President Truman recommending that the United States offer to sell cotton to Poland in return for increased coal exports to Western Europe.[84] Some congressmen and hard-liners in the administration were concerned that Western Europe was trading strategic items for Polish coal, and Harriman, now heading the Economic Defense Staff (EDS) of the ECA, thought that his agency could better coordinate the gradually emerging embargo of strategic items to the Soviet bloc if U.S. cotton were provided to the ERP governments to trade for Polish coal. The State Department, the Department of Agriculture, and the Food and Agricultural Division of the ECA all supported Harriman's idea, because there was a cotton surplus in the United States in 1949. Opposition came from the Economic Affairs Division in the State Department, the Joint Chiefs, and the Coal Branch of the ECA, which sought to replace Polish coal with American coal exports.[85]

The assistant to the secretary of agriculture, Dr. E.D. White, visited Poland in May to discuss the possibility of the cotton-for-coal exchange. White discovered that the Polish authorities were eager to reestablish Poland as a market for American cotton, especially because Poland had been forced to use dollars to buy approximately 50,000 tons of it on the open market in 1948, and present stocks would be sufficient for only about six weeks. The Poles proposed to purchase approximately 25,000 tons of cotton in 1949 in return for shipments of one and one half to two million tons of coal to Western Europe. The EDS was inclined to favor this exchange in order to replace Austrian dollar payments for Polish coal and to halt shipment of strategic materials by Denmark to Poland. In addition to increasing coal exports to Western Europe, the Poles offered to export up to 30,000 tons of rye. White favored the exchanges and urged the State Department to take immediate action before the Poles looked elsewhere for cotton. The new U.S. ambassador to Poland, Waldemar Gallman,[86] agreed, reasoning that the cotton-for-coal exchange would reduce Poland's economic dependency on the Soviet Union, and would possibly result in a drop in the Polish price of coal, which at the time was set to match the high cost of American coal.[87]

The U.S. embassy in Warsaw told the Polish government that it should negotiate with the European countries with which they hoped to exchange cotton for coal, but the Poles still preferred to deal directly with the United States. Lychowski hoped for political reasons that Poland would not have to go through ECA channels to purchase cotton. Obviously the Soviet Union would have frowned on such direct cooperation with agencies of the ERP, but evidently there was no pressure from Moscow to halt trade with Western Europe or even with the United States. Lychowski also wanted to eliminate American coal from the European market as soon as possible, even though the price of Polish coal would then drop to a normal level.[88] Poland would still benefit from an increase in the demand for its coal. Given the high cost of shipping American coal to Western Europe, the State Department favored such an arrangement, as long as Western Europe did not exchange strategic commodities for coal.[89] When the cotton shortage eased by the end of the summer, the Poles agreed to deal directly with Western European governments for American cotton.[90]

There was a serious lack of coordination between the Truman administration, the Marshall Plan agencies, and U.N. economic organizations on the question of East-West trade. Both the Office of European Economic Cooperation (OEEC) and the ECA called for an increase in trade between Eastern and Western Europe during the four-year period of the ERP,[91] while the administration's emerging embargo policy was working against this development. The American delegation to the ECE also contradicted the hard line licensing policy of Commerce Secretary Charles Sawyer[92] and the Joint Chiefs by encouraging East-West commercial exchanges. According to Polish representatives there, the United States did not try to limit East-West trade in any way, and "wholly supported" a Polish proposal to replace American coal with European coal, which would give Poland a secure place in the market.[93] The Poles also introduced a resolution to the ECE on 29 July calling for increased intra-European trade.[94]

After the outbreak of the Korean War and the adoption of Secretary of State Dean Acheson's plan to militarize the containment strategy, the United States put an even stricter embargo into effect and formulated a new coal export policy to reduce Western Europe's dependence on Polish coal. Nonetheless, Polish export tendencies did not change. On the average, Poland exported over thirty million tons of coal each year from 1948 to 1952. The figure rose steadily through 1950 and then dipped slightly in 1951 and 1952. About one third of all Polish coal exports went to Western Europe in 1951; about one fourth went West in 1952, when the impact of U.S. exports created a glut in the coal market.[95] Without Polish coal European recovery would have been seriously retarded.[96]

Throughout 1948 and 1949, in the face of the U.S. embargo on trade and financial assistance to the Soviet bloc and American efforts to bring the ERP countries into line with the export licensing program, the Polish government continued to expand its commercial relations with Western Europe. The Poles thought that one of the main requirements for the development of East-West trade was the flow of Western investments into Eastern Europe, and they were optimistic about the opportunities for commercial exchanges.[97] According to American observers, the Polish delegation to the ECE was consistently cooperative, and was the only Soviet bloc country to propose an expansion of trade between Eastern and Western Europe.[98]

Because there was a dollar shortage in Europe, and because European countries were obliged to use Marshall funds to buy essential goods from the United States, it was natural that Western Europe should look to Eastern Europe to fill out its trade needs.[99] Western European trade with Poland rose steadily until the United States began to pressure the ERP countries to follow a stricter embargo policy after 1951. In 1948, Western European exports to Poland were valued at $161 million. That figure increased to $218 million in 1949. Exports dropped back down to $164 million in 1950, but rebounded to $195 million in 1951. Many of the imports from Western Europe were capital goods that were denied export licenses in the United States. Polish exports to Western Europe followed the same course as Polish imports, rising in value from $296 million in 1948 to $325 million in 1949, dropping to $239 million in 1950, and increasing again to $305 million in 1951, when Western European rearmament created a greater demand for Polish coal.[100]

Unable to obtain financial assistance from the United States or the IBRD, Poland turned to the Soviet Union and Western Europe. The Soviet Union's economic recovery allowed it to step in to fill some of Poland's trade needs. In May 1948, the Soviets agreed to deliver 200,000 tons of grain to Poland. The two countries signed another agreement in December that called for $500 million in trade for four years and an eight-year, $450 million credit for Poland to buy industrial equipment.[101] In 1950 the Soviets granted the Poles another eight-year credit of $100 million for investment goods.[102] Of course, this financial assistance was modest compared to Marshall Plan aid, but it furthered the integration of the Polish and Soviet economies.

Much to the dismay of the U.S. government, the ERP countries that were receiving Marshall funds were making credit agreements with Poland at the same time. For example, in the spring of 1948 Great Britain granted Poland a £6 million credit to purchase British capital goods and a £1.5 million credit to buy wool and other raw materials. Although private banks made the credit agreements, the British government guaranteed them.[103] Britain also looked to Poland for trade that did not have to be conducted in dollars. In early 1949, Poland and Great Britain agreed to exchange $600 million worth of goods over five years.[104] On March 19 Poland and France signed an agreement for a $60 million credit in return for compensation of nationalized French property in Poland. By May Poland had also received smaller credits from Sweden, Switzerland, Italy and Denmark.[105] Far from working to sabotage Western European recovery under the ERP, Poland established itself as one of the ERP countries' most important and reliable trading partners.

NOTES

1. See Michael Hogan, "The Search for a Creative Peace: The United States, European Unity, and the Origins of the Marshall Plan," *Diplomatic History* 6 (Summer 1982): 267-285; and Charles P.Kindleberger, "The Marshall Plan and the Cold War," *International Journal* 23 (Summer 1968): 369-382.

2. See Kovrig, *The Myth of Liberation: East-Central Europe in U.S. Diplomacy and Politics since 1941*, 86, who writes that "by the summer of 1948, with Czechoslovakia and Hungary firmly in Moscow's embrace, East-Central Europe (excluding Yugoslavia) had acquired a monolithic appearance that neither invited nor deserved a particularly differentiated involvement on the part of the West."

3. Contrast this view with J. R. Thackrah, "Poland: Internal Developments and Effects on Anglo-American Relations, 1945-1947," *East European Quarterly* 20 (September, 1986): 281, who claims that after the announcement of the Marshall Plan, "it was clear, however, that State [sic, Stalin] put considerable pressure on Poland to cut itself off from any negotiations with the West." Of course, Stalin pressured the Polish leadership to reject the Marshall Plan, but he allowed the Poles to continue other negotiations for economic aid.

4. Historians of the Marshall Plan have overlooked the important role that Polish coal played in Western European recovery. Michael Hogan's *The Marshall Plan: America, Britain, and the Reconstruction of Western Europe, 1947-1952* (Cambridge: Cambridge University Press, 1987) is the best of the Marshall Plan studies, but as the title implies, the indirect contribution of Poland to the ERP is beyond the scope of his work. Alan Milward, in *The Reconstruction of Western Europe, 1945-1951* (Berkeley: University of California Press, 1987), also concentrates on Western Europe and devotes little space to the role of East-West trade in the recovery program. The same is true of other monographs on the Marshall Plan, such as Hadley Arkes's *Bureaucracy, the Marshall Plan, and the National Interest* (Princeton: Princeton University Press, 1972), Imanuel Wexler's *The Marshall Plan Revisited: The European Recovery Program in Economic Perspective* (Westport, Conn.: Greenwood Press, 1983), Charles L. Mee's *The Marshall Plan: The Launching of Pax Americana* (New York: Simon and Schuster, 1984), or Joseph M. Jones' *The Fifteen Weeks* (New York: The Viking Press, 1955).

5. Lundestad, "The American Policy Towards Poland 1943-1946," 26.

6. See Ripka, *Czechoslovakia Enslaved: The Story of the Communist Coup d'Etat*, 52. The Czechoslovak communists also decided to accept an invitation to participate in the ERP until Stalin told them not to go to Paris.

7. *Głos Ludu*, 6 July 1947, 1.

8. *Życie Gospodarcze* 2 (July 1947): 518-519.

9. Zyblikiewicz, *Polityka Stanów Zjednoczonych i Wielkiej Brytanii wobec Polski, 1944-1949*, 318-319; Winiewicz, *Co pamiętam z długiej drogi życia*, p. 396; and Margaret Dewar, *Soviet Trade with Eastern Europe, 1945-1949* (London: Royal Institute of International Affairs, 1951), 43. In early 1948, the Soviets agreed to limit their claims on reparations coal to 6.5 million tons annually.

10. Winiewicz to Warsaw, 21 June 1947, Ministry of Industry and Trade Records, File 51.

11. Ripka, *Czechoslovakia Enslaved: The Story of the Communist Coup d'Etat*, 53.

12. Winiewicz to Modzelewski and Minc, 3 July 1947, Ministry of Industry and Trade Records, File 51.

13. Winiewicz, *Co pamiętam z długiej drogi życia*, 396; see also Milward, *The Reconstruction of Western Europe, 1945-1951*, 69, who writes that after Molotov's departure from the Paris conference in June, the Czechs and the Hungarians were told not to participate in the CEEC, "and Poland's interest in the proceedings died an understandable death."

14. *Trybuna Ludu* [Tribune of the people], 26 November 1987, 1; Torańska, *Oni*, 309.

15. See Charles Kindleberger, "The Marshall Plan and the Cold War," 378, who underestimates Stalin's fear that the Marshall Plan would have undercut his political control of Eastern Europe: "what the Machiavellis among us never understood was why the Soviet Union did not join the Marshall Plan and disrupt it, as they have done with many organizations. . . . It would have been simple to agree in principle and object in practice."; see also Hogan, "The Search for a 'Creative Peace': The United States, European Unity, and the Origins of the Marshall Plan," 282-284; for an account of Stalin's directive to Czechoslovakia to reject the Marshall Plan, see Ripka, *Czechoslovakia Enslaved: The Story of the Communist Coup d'Etat*, 56-62.

16. Editorial note on the telegram from the U.S. embassy in Warsaw to Acheson, 14 July 1949, *FRUS, 1949* 5:135-136; the U.S. Resident Delegation to the ECE to Acheson, 16 June 1950, *FRUS, 1950: Central and Eastern Europe and the Soviet Union* (Washington: U.S. Government Printing Office, 1980), 4:1049; and Department of State Policy Statement, 27 November 1950, ibid.

17. See Hogan, *The Marshall Plan: America, Britain, and the Reconstruction of Western Europe, 1947-1952*, 33, 50, for a discussion of the reservations raised by the British and especially the French against a high level of German production without international control; see also Robert A. Pollard and Samuel F. Wells, Jr., "1945-1960: The Era of American Economic Hegemony," in eds. William H. Becker and Samuel F. Wells, *Economic and World Power: An Assessment of American Diplomacy Since 1789* (New York: Columbia University Press, 1984), 141-143, for a discussion of French opposition to German reconstruction.

18. Andrzej Skowronski, "Security and Cooperative Policy: The Origins," *Polish Perspectives* 21 (December 1978): 19.

19. Gajda, *Polska Polityka Zagraniczna, 1944-1971*, 62.

20. *Głos Ludu*, 11 July 1947, 1.

21. *Rzeczpospolita*, 26 July 1947, quoted in Central Planning Office Records, File 1194.

22. Interview by author with Stanisław Rączkowski, 10 March 1988, Warsaw.

23. Notes of conference, Minc and E.G. Burland, 9 July 1947, Ministry of Industry and Trade Records, File 51; and Zyblikiewicz, *Polityka Stanów Zjednoczonych i Wielkiej Brytanii wobec Polski, 1944-1949*, 322.

24. Winiewicz to Marshall, 29 August 1947, Department of State *Bulletin*, 5 October 1947, 741.

25. *New York Times*, 7 December 1947, 21.

26. Bobrowski in *Trybuna Ludu*, 26 November 1987, 1; see also Hogan, *The Marshall Plan: America, Britain, and the Reconstruction of Western Europe*, 61-62, 175-176, for a discussion of France's opposition to halting reparation shipments from Germany.

27. Reparations from Germany, undated document, Central Planning Office Records, File 1930; and Różański, *Śladem wspomnień i dokumentów, 1943-1948*, 441.

28. Polish coal exports for 1947, Central Planning Office Records, File 787; and plan for imports and exports for 1948, 15 October 1947, ibid., File 2400.

29. Zyblikiewicz, *Polityka Stanów Zjednoczonych i Wielkiej Brytanii wobec Polski, 1944-1949*, 366. The total value of reparations that Poland received from the Bizone in the first eleven months of 1948 was nearly $1.2 million.

30. Torańska, *Oni*, 309.

31. Ambrose, *Rise to Globalism: American Foreign Policy 1938-1976*, 154.

32. Adam Ulam, *The Rivals: America and Russia Since World War II* (New York, 1971), 128.

33. Hogan, *The Marshall Plan: America, Britain, and the Reconstruction of Western Europe, 1947-1952*, 55.

34. Jakub Berman, "In the Struggle for the Peaceful Development of Postwar Europe," *Nowe Drogi* 2 (March, 1948): 7-16.

35. Polish Diet Records, 29 December 1947, 67.

36. Winiewicz to Warsaw, 11 September 1947, Ministry of Industry and Trade Records, File 51.

37. Report by Lychowski on the "Report of the Paris Conference on the Marshall Plan," 14 October 1947, Ministry of Industry and Trade Records, File 51; and "Economic Cooperation General Report," Truman Papers, PSF, Subject File, box 163.

38. "Report of the Paris Conference on the Marshall Plan," 14 October 1947, Ministry of Industry and Trade Records, File 51.

39. *New York Times*, 13 August 1947, 20.

40. Winiewicz speech to City Club of Portland, Oregon, 19 December 1947, *Congressional Record*, 80th Cong., 1st sess., 93: A-4918-4919.

41. Lundestad, *The American Non-Policy Towards Eastern Europe 1943-1947*, 399.

42. Memorandum on planning and the balance of payments, 11 April 1947, Central Planning Office Records, File 610. The Polish government honored the Bretton Woods agreements by depositing $4.9 million in the IMF and $2.5 million in the IBRD.

43. See translation of articles from *Les Nouvelles Economiques*, 14 November 1947, and *The Economist*, 14 February 1948, in Central Planning Office Records, File 1930. The Polish leadership underestimated the role that politics would play in the IBRD and the extent to which the United States controlled the organization. The United States had 34 percent of the votes in the IBRD, Great Britain 27.8 percent. Furthermore, most of the countries of Central and South America supported the United States in the bank, and thus the Americans had virtual veto power over loan requests. The loans granted in 1947 indicate the extent to which the bank was channeling money where the United States wanted it to go. Although Poland did

not get a loan, Great Britain received a $240 million loan, France $125 million, and Holland $46 million. Mexico, Belgium, Chile, Turkey and Denmark also received smaller loans. The total loaned to January 1948 was $472.7 million.

44. Polish National Council Records, 21 September 1946, 151.

45. Polish National Council Records, 15 April 1947, 40.

46. Winiewicz, *Co pamiętam z długiej drogi życia*, 397; and Kwiatkowski to the Polish embassy in Washington, 10 June 1947, Central Planning Office Records, File 1930.

47. *Rzeczpospolita*, 30 April 1946, 6.

48. Acheson to Byrnes, 5 October 1946, *FRUS, 1946* 6:504-506.

49. Lundestad, *The American Non-Policy Toward Eastern Europe*, 216-217; Lukas, *Bitter Legacy: Polish-American Relations in the Wake of World War II*, 84; and Pollard, *Economic Security and the Origins of the Cold War*, 45.

50. "Ninth Session of the National Council on New Economic Problems," *Przegląd Socjalistyczny* [Socialist review] 2 (March 1946): 7-12.

51. Balance of payments, Three-Year Plan, undated document, Central Planning Office Records, File 610. Poland expected $10 million from the IBRD in 1947, $140.5 million in 1948, and $225 million in 1949.

52. H. Szyr in Warsaw to Topolski in Katowice, 12 June 1947, Ministry of Industry and Trade Records, File 51; and communiqué on the IBRD visit to Poland (20 June-20 July 1947), 23 June 1947, Central Planning Office Records, File 1930.

53. Communiqué on the visit of the IBRD delegation in Poland (20 June-20 July 1947), 23 June 1947, Central Planning Office Records, File 1930; see also Karpinski, *Twenty Years of Poland's Economic Development*, 110. Given the record of Polish coal exports to Western Europe, and Poland's desperate need to acquire hard currency to buy machinery in the West, the IBRD had little reason to doubt the Poles' sincerity. Of course, it was in Poland's interest to export as much coal as possible; in 1949 coal exports represented 60 percent of the foreign currency earned from all Polish exports.

54. Note from the IBRD to the Polish embassy in Washington, 10 June 1947, Central Planning Office Records, File 1930.

55. *New York Times*, 11 June 1947, 1.

56. Notes of conversation, E.G. Burland (head of the IBRD mission to Poland) and Minc, 10 July 1947, Ministry of Industry and Trade Records, File 51.

57. Bobrowski, *Wspomnienia ze stulecia*, 154.

58. Winiewicz, *Co pamiętam z długiej drogi życia*, 399.

59. Griffis to Marshall, 5 August 1947, RG 59, 860c.51, box 6385.

60. "Current Polish Economy," report by William Welk (director of the East European Department of Loans, IBRD), August 1947, Central Planning Office Records, File 1930.

61. Winiewicz to Modzelewski and Minc, 3 July 1947, Ministry of Industry and Trade Records, File 51.

62. *Bulletin of America*, 9 September 1947, in Ministry of Industry and Trade Records, File 51.

63. Winiewicz to Warsaw, 9 September 1947, Ministry of Industry and Trade Records, File 51; and Winiewicz to Warsaw, 11 September 1947, ibid.

64. Winiewicz, *Co pamiętam z długiej drogi życia*, 436-437.

65. Memorandum of conversation, Modzelewski and Marshall, etal., 26 September 1947, *FRUS, 1947* 4:446-452; see also Pollard, *Economic Security and the Origins of the Cold War*, 147-153; Paterson, *On Every Front: The Making of the Cold War*, 64; and Ambrose, *Rise to Globalism: American Foreign Policy 1938-1976*, 143. Truman went before Congress in March to plead for ERP funds to stop the threat of communist takeovers in Europe.

66. Report on the Council of Governors meeting of the IBRD and the IMF, 2 October 1947, Central Planning Office Records, File 1930.

67. Griffis to Marshall, 7 October 1947, RG 59, 860c.51, box 6385; and Lovett to the U.S. embassy in Warsaw, 14 October 1947, ibid.

68. Winiewicz, *Co pamiętam z długiej drogi życia*, 397.

69. Griffis to Marshall, 15 October 1947, RG 59, 860c.51, box 6385.

70. *New York Times*, 10 December 1947, 22.

71. Griffis to Marshall, 15 November 1947, *FRUS, 1947* 4:549.

72. Griffis memorandum, January 1948, The Papers of Stanton Griffis, General File, box 8, Truman Library, Independence, Missouri (hereafter Griffis Papers with filing information).

73. Memorandum of conversation, McCloy and Lovett, 19 January 1948, RG 59, 860c.51, box 6385.

74. Memorandum of conversation, McCloy and Lovett, 19 January 1948, RG 59, 860c.51, box 6385. The NAC transmitted instructions to the U.S. executive director of the IBRD.

75. Interview by author with Rączkowski, 10 March 1988.

76. Griffis to Marshall, 25 February 1948, *FRUS, 1948: Eastern Europe and the Soviet Union* (Washington: U.S. Government Printing Office), 4:520-521.

77. See Kindleberger, "The Marshall Plan and the Cold War," 378.

78. See Arkes, *Bureaucracy, the Marshall Plan, and the National Interest*, 108. The ECA had the power to restrict shipments to certain ERP countries if the goods were then shipped to non-participating countries.

79. Some historians have claimed that the Soviet Union and the Eastern European governments actively tried to sabotage the ERP, but there is no evidence that Poland used discriminatory trade policy or any other economic policy to prevent Western European reconstruction. See David Horowitz, *The Free World Colossus: A Critique of American Foreign Policy in the Cold War* (New York: MacGibbon and Kee, 1965), 80-81, who writes that "the Communist parties of Europe began a campaign to oppose the Marshall Plan be all means available to them. The effect was to lend substance to fears of sabotage and subversion."; see also Louis Halle, *The Cold War as History* (New York: Harper and Row, 1967), 123ff.

80. Lundestad, *The American Non-Policy Towards Eastern Europe 1943-1947*, 216; ECE, *Economic Bulletin* 4:3 (1952): 43; and ECE, Coal Division, "United Nations Monthly Bulletin of Coal Statistics" (December 1952): 74-75. It is important to note the relatively high exports of Polish coal to West Germany and West Austria, areas that were still occupied by the United States. The free inter-zonal trade within these countries undermined the American embargo, and there was significant trade with Poland in machinery embargoed by the United States. Austria imported 1.48 million tons of coal from Poland in 1949 and slightly less in 1950. When the United States increased its coal exports to Western Europe after the Korean War, this amount dropped to 1.1 million tons in 1951, and 979,000 tons in 1952. West Germany also imported 106,000 tons of hard coal from Poland in 1949,

and 211,000 tons in 1950. That figure dropped to 115,000 tons in 1951 when the Ruhr supplied West Germany's needs. As a result of American coal imports and increased German production, the Polish share of Western European coal use was back down to 15 percent in 1951.

81. Wexler, *The Marshall Plan Revisited: The European Recovery Program in Economic Perspective*, 273; William Diebold, "East-West Trade and the Marshall Plan," *Foreign Affairs* 26 (July 1948): 715. The CEEC estimated that Poland would export sixteen million tons of coal to the West in 1948, twenty-four million tons in 1949, seventy-seven million tons in 1950, and thirty million tons in 1951; plan for coal exports, 1948, Central Planning Office Records, File 2392; and "Poland: Economic Power," *Szabad NEP* (12 May 1948) in Ministry of Industry and Trade Records, File 3004. The plan called for a total of 24.8 million tons in exports in 1948, and thirty-five million tons in 1949. About 55 percent of these exports were targeted for Western Europe. Actual exports to Western Europe amounted to 11.9 million tons in 1948, and 12.6 million tons in 1949.

82. ECE, *Quarterly Bulletin of Coal Statistics for Europe* 1:4 (1952): 8; and Janusz Litwin, "Rola polskiego węgla w gospodarcze europejskiej," [The role of Polish coal in the European economy] *Świat i Polski* [The world and Poland] 3 (31 October 1948): 7. The ECE estimated that Poland would mine seventy million tons of coal that 1948, and eighty million tons in 1949 and 1950.

83. Wexler, *The Marshall Plan Revisited: The European Recovery Program in Economic Perspective*, 79.

84. "Poland," undated document, Truman Papers, PSF, Subject File, box 186.

85. Memorandum from the Polish government to the U.S. embassy in Warsaw, 19 May 1949, Records of the Agency for International Development (AID), Records Group 286, Economic Cooperation Administration, Economic Defense Staff, Country Subject Files, box 3 (Poland), National Archives, Washington (hereafter RG 286 with filing information); Acheson to the U.S. embassy in Warsaw, 15 February 1949, RG 59, 611.60c31, box 2847; and Acheson to Geneva, 21 April 1949, RG 84, General Records, box 98.

86. Letter of Stanton Griffis, 11 March 1948, Griffis Papers, box 8, Scrapbook File. Gallman succeeded Griffis on 8 July 1948. Griffis, like Lane before him, had been unsuccessful in developing any rapport

with the Polish government. But then not much could have been expected from a man who allegedly said in 1939 that Hitler was a wise man, or toward the end of his tour in Warsaw thought that the United States and the Soviet bloc could not get along "because here in the East of Europe, there is so little human happiness or sense of humor. . . . I earnestly believe that if the Russians and the Slavs could learn to laugh they could more nearly understand us and we might live together in peace and understanding."

87. Memorandum from Polish government to U.S. embassy in Warsaw, 19 May 1949, RG 286, Country Subject Files, box 3; and Gallman to Acheson, 20 May 1949, RG 59, 611.60c31, box 2847.

88. Memorandum to the Polish government from the U.S. embassy in Warsaw, 19 May 1949, RG 84, General Records, box 99; and memorandum of conversation, James F. Hodgson, Thomas D. Bowie (economic counselors, U.S. embassy in Warsaw) and Tadeusz Lychowski (director of the Economic Section, Ministry of Foreign Affairs), 24 June 1949, ibid.

89. Acheson to Paris (OEEC), 14 July 1949, RG 84, General Records, box 99.

90. Lyon (embassy counselor) to Acheson, 1 August 1949, RG 84, General Records, box 99.

91. Wexler, *The Marshall Plan Revisited: The European Recovery Program in Economic Perspective*, 78.

92. Sawyer replaced Harriman on 6 May 1948.

93. Notes on the present matter of the ECE, 4 September 1948, Ministry of Industry and Trade Records, File 3004; see also Hogan, *The Marshall Plan: America, Britain, and the Reconstruction of Western Europe, 1947-1952*, 236ff. Hogan gives evidence that the serious dollar shortage threatened to undermine European reconstruction efforts. It made simple economic sense for Western Europe to trade for Polish coal rather than to buy American coal with scarce dollars.

94. United Nations ECE, Economic and Social Council, 7th sess., "Annual Report of the ECE. Poland: Draft Resolution," 29 July 1948.

95. *Compendium Statystyczne Polskiego Handlu Zagranicznego w latach 1929-1938, 1945-1960*, 128; see also ECE, *Economic Bulletin* 4:3 (1952): 43. United States coal exports to Western Europe increased dramatically in 1951. Exports amounted to 30.4 million tons in 1949, and dropped to 27.1 million tons in 1950. But in 1951 this figure

jumped to almost fifty-eight million tons. The United States share of Western European coal imports was 15 percent in 1949, one percent in 1950, 31 percent in 1951, and 33 percent in 1952.

96. See Hogan, *The Marshall Plan: America, Britain, and the Reconstruction of Western Europe, 1947-1952*, 393, and Milward, *The Reconstruction of Western Europe*, 388, for a discussion of the coal shortages in Europe from 1947 to 1952.

97. Notes on the present matter of the ECE, 4 September 1948, Ministry of Industry and Trade Records, File 3004.

98. Porter to the State Department, 27 May 1949, RG 84, General Records, box 98; Porter to Acheson, 31 May 1949, *FRUS, 1949* 5:120-122.

99. See Hogan, *The Marshall Plan: America, Britain, and the Reconstruction of Western Europe, 1947-1952*, 236ff.

100. ECE, *Economic Bulletin* 3:2 (1951): 58. The latter figure can be explained in part by the sharp decline in U.S. exports to Poland, which were valued at $55.5 million in 1948, $8.9 million in 1950, and only $800,000 in 1953.

101. Janusz Kalinski, "Zmiana Dekoracji" [Decorative changes], *Przegląd Tygodniowy* [Weekly review] 7 (1988): 1; and Kalinski, *Plan Odbudowy Gospodarczej, 1947-1949*, 271-272. This included equipment for steel, cement, chemical and automobile factories, as well as machinery for the energy, coal, petroleum, textile, and paper industries.

102. Różański, *Śladem wspomnień i dokumentów, 1943-1948*, 515; Spulber, *The Economics of Communist Eastern Europe*, 434-435; and Paterson, *Soviet-American Confrontation: Postwar Reconstruction and the Origins of the Cold War*, 135-136. Although it can be argued that the Polish Six-Year Plan was an inappropriate blueprint for the most efficient reconstruction of the economy, or that the increased commercial relations between Poland and the Soviet Union hastened the integration of the two economies, there is no evidence to show that trade with the Soviet Union in this period was, as Paterson writes, "more beneficial to itself [the Soviet Union] than to the Poles." Of course, this trade and Soviet aid was balanced by the continued reparations shipments of Silesian coal at about one tenth of the market price.

103. Douglas (counselor at U.S. embassy in London) to Marshall, 23 April 1948, RG 59, 860c.51, box 6385.

104. Zyblikiewicz, *Polityka Stanów Zjednoczonych i Wielkiej Brytanii wobec Polski, 1944-1949*, 363. Poland was to receive wool, sisal, tin, raw materials and investment goods. Poland's exports included agricultural products, timber, minerals, industrial metal products, textiles, and chemicals.

105. Article by William L. Shirer, *New York Herald Tribune*, 2 May 1948, cited in *Congressional Record*, 80th Cong., 2nd sess., 94: A3173-A3174.

Chapter Seven

The Strategic Embargo of Poland, 1948-1949

I

The Truman administration viewed the Czechoslovak communist coup in February 1948 and the blockade of Berlin in June as hard evidence that the Soviet Union was aggressively consolidating its control over the entire bloc. It seemed that the Soviets were even willing to risk military confrontation with the West to do it. The administration now adopted a policy of readiness for the possibility of war; strategic objectives began to dominate U.S. foreign economic policy.[1] The embargo of the Soviet bloc was primarily intended to reduce the military potential of the Soviet Union and its satellites.[2] The administration no longer made the democratization of Eastern Europe its primary concern; after Tito's break with the Soviets in 1948, the administration's minimum political objective was to use the embargo to pull the other socialist countries out of the Soviet orbit.

The idea of an embargo of American and European exports to the Soviet bloc emerged in conjunction with the Truman administration's containment policy and plans for the ERP. The Marshall Plan gave priority to Western Europe for the export of items in short supply in the United States. These commodities were to be controlled to ensure a ready supply to countries involved directly in the ERP. In reality, as the embargo policy evolved in 1948 administration officials defined national security so broadly that for all practical purposes they adopted an almost total embargo of exports to the Soviet bloc countries. Ultimately the administration hoped to retard the growth of the socialist economies and cause their complete collapse.

By 1949, a few officials in the State Department represented the only significant opposition left in the U.S. government to a drastic reduction in economic relations with the Soviet bloc. The American public was convinced of the real threat of communism to American security, and Congress and the Truman administration reflected (and to a certain extent created) these fears. The Commerce Department, the Joint Chiefs, and the National Security Council (NSC) were all in favor of a tighter embargo of exports to the Soviet bloc and called for increased efforts to bring Western Europe into line with the licensing program.

On the other hand, the consolidation of the Workers' Party and the Socialist Party in December 1948, and the formation of the Council for Mutual Economic Assistance (Comecon) in 1949, did not signal an immediate change in Polish trade policy toward the West. Although many in the State Department had predicted that the Soviet bloc would try to sabotage the Marshall Plan,[3] even after Marshall aid began to pour into Western Europe Poland continued to be an important trading partner for the countries participating in the ERP. The Polish government sought ways to expand intra-European trade despite some opposition from other Comecon members.

II

The Truman administration began to discuss the use of an economic embargo on the Soviet bloc in the summer of 1947. Bernard Baruch, the U.S. representative to the U.N. Atomic Energy Commission, argued for using "all possible economic measures in our relations with Russia." Baruch even suggested that the United States buy scarce commodities such as surplus Cuban sugar and raw materials from Third World countries to prevent their shipment to the Soviet bloc.[4] In the fall, the NSC also recommended the termination of shipments to the Soviet bloc of scarce resources or any product that could contribute to the bloc's military potential. Although Commerce Secretary Averell Harriman agreed with the strategic objectives of the embargo, he was concerned that an embargo would contradict the Open Door principles that were a foundation of U.S. postwar foreign economic policy. Harriman argued that the objective of reducing Soviet military capabilities "should be achieved if possible without any overt act of arbitrary discrimination against the U.S.S.R. and its satellites."[5]

The State Department also had reservations that economic warfare violated the charters of the IMF and the IBRD. In November, the State Department proposed an embargo that would differentiate between the Eastern European governments according to the department's perception of their independence from the Soviet Union and their domination by communist parties. The State Department singled out Yugoslavia, Albania, Rumania, Bulgaria and the Soviet Union for "rigorous" treatment, recommended giving Poland, Hungary, Czechoslovakia, and the Soviet occupation zone of Germany "greater flexibility," and called for an even less restrictive embargo on Finland and Austria. The State Department opposed the export of military equipment to any of these countries, however, and in order to control these sales the department proposed a new Munitions Control Act to succeed the president's Neutrality Proclamation that was due to expire at the end of June 1948. The State Department stipulated that "semi-military equipment," such as explosives or specialized tools, could be exported to countries in the last two groups for "civilian use." Capital equipment for "war-supporting industries" could be shipped to Finland and Austria only. Finally, the department called for the free trade of other raw materials, consumer goods, and items not in short supply in the United States and Europe.[6] Administration officials hotly debated what constituted a "war-supporting industry," and the administration eventually adopted a broad interpretation of the embargo that included most industrial and manufactured goods.

The department viewed a more limited embargo as a precaution against a Soviet bloc counter-embargo of essential coal, food, and timber exports to Western Europe. The State Department called on U.S. representatives to the IBRD to "support loans to countries in the Soviet sphere which will contribute to the success of a positive economic recovery program in which the U.S. and other powers are jointly associated." In addition, the department still thought that certain American objectives could be achieved through loans "to countries which we consider still open to influence."[7]

Poland was a prime candidate for such loans, and some officials in the State Department lobbied for a more flexible trade and loan policy and a selective embargo of exports to Poland. On the other hand, the State Department's newly created Policy Planning Staff, headed by Kennan, pushed for a stricter economic embargo of the entire Soviet bloc. In late November 1947, Kennan's group recommended that the United States embargo anything that could increase the war potential of the Soviet Union, including technology and items in short supply. The Policy Planning Staff favored issuing export licenses for all goods going to Europe, and although it understood that this was incompatible with U.S. free trade policies, Kennan's group argued that the Soviet bloc was disregarding them anyway. The Policy Planning Staff recognized the possibility of a counter-embargo by the Soviet bloc, but warned that "in present circumstances any increase in the economic strength of the Soviet Union and the satellite countries will be used to oppose, rather that to promote, the interests of real European recovery."[8]

Nonetheless, the Policy Planning Staff recognized the significant contribution of Polish coal to the ERP; Kennan's group supported efforts to foster Eastern Europe's trade with Western Europe in return for the Soviet bloc's "making concessions to European recovery." The Polish coal trade was one of these desired concessions, but the Policy Planning Staff did not clearly state how the United States intended to gain economic concessions from Poland while the United States was conducting an economic embargo. The Policy Planning Staff was also optimistic that the United States could control Western European trade with the Soviet bloc.[9] The most obvious failure of the policy was the fact that Poland was able to circumvent the embargo by selling coal to Western Europe for strategic goods.

President Truman and others in the State Department still opposed a stricter embargo program at the end of 1947, although by that time about 20 percent of American exports required export licenses.[10] Truman told the press that there was no reason to restrict machinery exports to the Soviet Union at the present time. The State Department's Economic Affairs Division criticized the Policy Planning Staff's recommendation to issue licenses for all exports to Europe, because this policy would make the Marshall Plan susceptible to criticism as an anti-communist measure that would divide Europe. Acting Secretary of State Robert Lovett also thought that an expanded licensing program would place a heavy burden of red tape on the Commerce and State Departments.[11] At first Truman supported a limited embargo that would not jeopardize such essential Soviet exports as manganese, chrome, and platinum,[12] but the NSC eventually adopted a tighter embargo that reflected the Policy Planning Staff's recommendations.

At the end of 1947 the Commerce Department terminated shipments to the Soviet bloc of items that were either in short supply in the United States or were of possible military use. The Commerce Department screened all exports to Europe and granted export licenses on the basis of three criteria; a country had to show that there was "adequate justification for its requirements" of a particular item, that export of the item would contribute to European and world economic recovery, and that through the export of any product the "position of the U.S. [would] not [be] adversely affected."[13]

The Commerce Department announced in January 1948 that after 1 March all exports to Europe would require a license from the department's Office of International Trade (OIT). According to the Commerce Department, the licenses were not intended to embargo exports to any one country, but rather to control the export of scarce commodities.[14] After the Czechoslovak communist coup in February, however, there was a growing consensus in the State Department for a stricter licensing program and an embargo of an increasing number of exports to the Soviet bloc. Secretary of State Marshall and State Department counselor Charles Bohlen supported East-West trade in non-strategic items, but at a meeting of State and Commerce Department officials in March, they decided that the objective of U.S. economic policy would be to "inflict the greatest economic injury to the USSR and its satellites." Marshall still favored a selective embargo of exports to Eastern Europe,[15] but by then even he had expanded his definition of a strategic item. At the end of March Truman's cabinet approved Marshall's recommendation that "the commodities should be those the denial of which would affect the production in key segments of the Soviet and satellite economies."[16]

No one in the administration seriously thought that Poland could afford to stop its shipments of coal to Western Europe, but in order to ensure these deliveries the Commerce Department recommended conducting trade with Poland and the Soviet bloc on a quid pro quo basis. The Commerce Department thought that export licenses could be used to bargain for economic and political concessions, something that most officials in the State Department now considered fruitless.[17]

An ad hoc committee of representatives from the State Department, the Agriculture Department, the Atomic Energy Commission, the Interior Department, the National Security Resources Board, and the Munitions Board of the National Military Establishment first met in March to develop an embargo list. The problem of the re-export of Marshall Plan goods to the Soviet bloc was raised at these meetings, and the committee recommended that each export to Europe carry with it a "navicert" which would specify the commodity's intermediate and final destinations.[18] The navicert was not very effective, and the re-shipment of American goods from Western to Eastern Europe, as well as the direct export by allied countries of goods that appeared on the

American embargo list seriously undermined the administration's embargo program.[19]

The Commerce Department eventually categorized exports into four classes: 1) those of military significance, 2) those of indirect military significance or vital to economic development, 3) those important to maintaining the basic economy of Eastern Europe, and 4) those commodities of no particular economic significance.[20] The export of items in the first category were strictly prohibited, and the Commerce Department wanted to negotiate for essential imports from the Soviet bloc in return for exports in the second and third categories. By the time Charles Sawyer succeeded Harriman as commerce secretary in May 1948, however, the licensing program had become a virtual embargo of any export that could in any way contribute to the industrial and military capacities of the Soviet bloc. Sawyer adopted a broad interpretation of items that were to be included in the first three categories. Harriman, now head of the ECA and the U.S. special representative to the OEEC, better understood the importance of Eastern European trade to Western Europe; he argued for a reduction in the items included in the first category and a more liberal interpretation of the licensing program generally. Furthermore, Harriman did not think that the Western European countries could or would agree to embargo all of the items included in the first category.[21]

Shortly after assuming office Sawyer ordered a halt of industrial exports to Eastern Europe. He even rejected export licenses for coal cars, locomotives, and other equipment that Poland had asked to buy in 1947 with the $40 million Export-Import Bank loan. At the beginning of June 1948, the State Department, the NSC, and the National Security Resources Board wanted to review this strict licensing policy, fearing the possible loss of strategic imports from Eastern Europe and the Soviet Union.[22] Marshall recognized the folly of such a complete embargo. He wrote Sawyer that he was opposed to "linking specific export licenses with specific imports from the U.S.S.R." Marshall thought this would favor certain American industries and might encourage the Soviets to barter all trade agreements. Furthermore, Marshall cited the vast administrative problems of the licensing program that had already surfaced. Marshall advocated embargoing items for security reasons only, and called for the immediate formulation of a shortened list.[23]

State Department officials also recognized that without the cooperation of Western Europe a stricter embargo policy would only hurt American exporters. At the end of 1948 a State Department report concluded that

> our economic policy in Poland seems to continue to be a negative approach to isolate ourselves from her trade. . . . Other Western powers . . . are leaving no stones unturned in expanding their trade with Poland.

In addition, the State Department warned that the United States could be blamed for the impasse in trade relations. In reference to the cotton that Poland had been unable to purchase in the United States, the department predicted that "if negotiations become too difficult Poland will look elsewhere for a source of [cotton] supply and will have made a reasonable good record that trade with the U.S. is virtually impossible if not absolutely impossible."[24]

III

After the United States began to restrict most exports to Poland in 1948, there was no longer any real chance that the Export-Import Bank or the IBRD would grant loans for that country. The embargo and the shortfall in foreign loans dealt a severe blow to Minc's reconstruction plans; there was little investment capital left for the consumer and agricultural industries. Minc stifled his critics within the government by purging those officials who favored a more balanced growth plan of heavy and consumer industry. In February, Minc accused Central Planning Office chief Czesław Bobrowski of favoring a non-Marxist economic plan and removed him from office.[25] This consolidation of the PPR's control over the economy foreshadowed the formal political elimination of the PPS when the two parties united into the Polish United Workers' Party (PZRP) in December.

But the elimination of Minc's critics within the economic ministries did not correspond with a change in Poland's policy of economic cooperation with the United States and Western Europe. Poland still needed to trade with the West and maintained slim hopes for reconstruction loans and other American economic assistance. For example, in March a top official in the Polish National Science Institute of Rural Economy recommended extending an invitation to a group of "competent" American agricultural economists to act as consultants for the Polish agricultural industry.[26] Although nothing came of this proposal, in early April Poland signed an international wheat agreement to "assure supplies of wheat to importing countries and to assure markets to exporting countries at equitable and stable prices."[27]

At this point the Soviets were still not pressuring Poland to cut economic ties to the West. In fact, the Soviets themselves were trying to circumvent and undermine the Marshall Plan and the emerging American embargo by changing their tactics in the ECE. Although Poland had been a cooperative member of the ECE since 1945, according to Polish ECE representatives the Soviets participated mainly as observers. But in May 1948, the Soviets proposed to expand the competency of the ECE by creating new committees to promote the unity of the European economy. Polish economic officials thought that one of the main conditions for the expansion of East-West trade was the flow of Western investments into Eastern Europe. In spite of the tense state of Soviet-American relations in 1948, they also expressed optimism about the many opportunities for commercial exchanges with the West.[28]

In the fall, the Soviet bloc countries also turned to the U.N. General Assembly to complain about the unfair American trade and loan practices. Poland, Czechoslovakia, and the Soviet Union submitted a resolution condemning "international trade discrimination" by the United States. Polish Foreign Minister Zygmunt Modzelewski criticized the political nature of the export licensing criteria, citing items on the American embargo list such as synthetic resin, radio lamps, and tubing for condensers, goods that he claimed could not possibly used as tools of war. Modzelewski also charged the United States with discrimination against Poland in the IBRD.[29]

The State Department denied these charges. The assistant secretary in the Economic Affairs Division, Willard Thorp, claimed that the licensing policy was formulated "to achieve equitable distribution of commodities in short supply, to make effective our efforts to assist [the] ERP, and in the interest of national security." Thorp criticized Poland's practice of bilateralism in commercial relations, and said that

> if the United States . . . wished to practice discrimination, whether for political or other

> purposes, then the clearly indicated course would be for it to base all its trade relations on bilateralism, for by that means trade pressures can be most easily applied.[30]

In reality, the Truman administration *was* leaning toward a policy of trading with the Soviet bloc on a quid pro quo basis.

On 9 April Winiewicz told Thorp that Minc was exasperated about not getting an American cotton loan, the abrupt end to American relief for Poland, and Poland's inability to make needed purchases with the $50 million U.S. Army surplus credit. Before these surplus supplies were exhausted in 1948, Poland was able to use only about $30 million of the credit. The Polish government had requested bulldozers and shovels to remove rubble from Warsaw, but the United States denied these requests on the basis that this equipment could be used to build military fortifications. Truly astounded by such reasoning, Winiewicz and his colleagues sometimes wondered whether American officials had "lost touch with reality."[31]

Winiewicz also complained about the delay in receiving export licenses for some $12 million in goods purchased with the $40 million Export-Import Bank loan. Winiewicz said that the embargo of certain goods to Poland contributed to the impasse on a nationalization compensation or Lend-Lease accord, and he asked the State Department for a clarification of the embargo policy. Thorp refused to link these issues and told the Polish ambassador that the embargo policy was still being formulated. Thorp said that the embargo was originally motivated by the administration's fear that war with the Soviet Union was "inevitable." Thorp added that the United States would not export materials that contributed to the Soviet bloc's military potential. Nonetheless, he maintained that the United States wanted to continue to trade with the Eastern European countries.[32]

The Polish government still thought that it had several bargaining chips to negotiate limits on the export controls. Ambassador Griffis told Marshall in March 1948 that the Polish government had given Winiewicz permission to reopen the nationalization compensation issue, presumably with new Polish concessions.[33] The Polish government also hinted that payment of Lend-Lease debts was possible. In a conversation with East European Division chief Llewellyn Thompson, Polish embassy counselor Litynski again tried to link a compensation agreement to export licenses for commodities such as a blooming and slabbing mill for the Polish steel industry. Although it would have meant disaster for the Polish economy, Litynski also hinted that Polish coal exports to Western Europe might be suspended if the United States did not lift the export controls.[34]

The Poles persisted in their efforts to gain an export license for this blooming and slabbing mill throughout 1948. At the end of March the Polish government asked Ambassador Griffis to send U.S. embassy officials to the steel plant where the blooming and slabbing mill was to be used, in order to assure the Americans that the plant was not a military industry.[35] Polish economic official Grosfeld told Griffis that Minc was very irritated about the denial of an export license for the blooming and slabbing mill; Grosfeld warned that a continuation of the American embargo "may cause [a] reversal [of the] present Polish foreign trade policy and pattern." This obvious reference to Polish coal exports did not cause Griffis any alarm because he knew that Poland could not afford to stop these exports. But Griffis, like Lane before him, was becoming more and more frustrated with his futile attempts to protect American interests in Poland. Citing press attacks and the refusal of the Polish government to allow U.S. diplomats to visit prisoners claiming American citizenship, Griffis wrote Marshall in April that "I greatly hope and urge that no favorable action will be taken on the export licenses except in constant consultation with this Embassy."[36]

Based on a visit to the steel mill, the U.S. embassy's new chargé d'affaires, Edward Crocker, reported that unless Poland received capital goods from the West such as the blooming and slabbing mill, the Polish steel industry could not significantly increase its annual production of 1.6 million tons of raw steel for at least four to six years. Crocker reported that "the Polish Government attaches tremendous importance to obtaining the blooming and slabbing mill now on order in the United States." He doubted that the Soviet Union could provide such a sophisticated mill, or that Great Britain would be able to deliver one for several years.[37]

Polish officials tried to convince the Americans that the Soviet Union might be able to supply a blooming and slabbing mill if the United States held up the license. Lucjan Horowitz, Grosfeld's deputy in the Ministry of Foreign Trade, maintained that Minc was losing some of his independence from Moscow as a result of the many setbacks in Polish-American economic relations. But Horowitz also revealed to Crocker that it was unlikely that Poland would get a steel mill from the Soviet Union. According to Crocker, Horowitz said that "the Soviets will promise anything to reduce US prestige." Although Crocker thought that Horowitz, a moderate socialist, was trustworthy, Crocker also recommended that the United States should not relax its export controls. Furthermore, Crocker said that the embassy thought that the mill "would certainly add to Poland's war potential . . . and that it would supply the keystone without which Polish steel production may not be noticeably increased within the immediate future."[38] Even without the American mill Crocker's assessment proved to be wrong. As a result of Minc's investment priorities in heavy industry and steel mills obtained from the Soviet Union, Polish production of crude steel rose over 37 percent from 1948 to 1952.[39]

At the end of July 1948, Thompson told Winiewicz that the Commerce Department would not restrict all exports to Poland and would expedite licenses for some goods. Thompson said that the steel mill license would be delayed until there was evidence that it would be used for civilian purposes. He admitted that the denial of this license was related to the international situation, which was extremely tense following the imposition of the Soviet blockade on West Berlin in June. In a departure from the State Department's earlier separation of these issues, Thompson linked a more liberal U.S. licensing policy and an IBRD loan to an agreement on compensation for nationalized American property and the payment of Poland's outstanding Lend-Lease debts.[40]

The Polish leadership hoped to establish a better economic relationship through the new U.S. ambassador to Poland, Waldemar Gallman, who succeeded Griffis in the summer of 1948. President Bierut told Gallman that the "Polish Government would support every attempt to further trade with the U.S,"[41] and Modzelewski informed Gallman that there were still many items, from raw materials to machinery, that Poland wanted to buy in the United States. Modzelewski expressed his bewilderment over the State Department's contention that embargoed tin-can making machinery for the preserving industry could contribute to Poland's military potential. He hoped that the United States would clarify its licensing program in the near future. Modzelewski even raised the possibility of signing a new commercial treaty with the United States. In a cable to his superiors in Washington, Gallman recommended that the administration explore the possibilities of expanding trade with Poland.[42]

By the end of 1948, however, the emerging consensus in Washington was for stricter, not looser export controls. The administration expanded its definition of a strategic export; even ball bearing sales to Poland were rejected. Late in the year the Poles requested two export licenses totalling $79,000 for ball bearings for conveyor belts for the coal mining industry. The Poles had already purchased over $152,000 worth of American-made ball bearings in 1947. Even Sawyer favored the sale, but U.S. military leaders lobbied against it, arguing that all ball bearings should fall into the first category of non-exportable items. At that time 80 percent of all types of ball bearings were in the second category.[43] The administration eventually canceled the ball bearing sales, and the Poles had to turn to Western Europe to fill its orders.

Frustrated in its efforts to buy goods in the United States, in August the Polish government eliminated almost four fifths of the personnel in the Polish-American Reconstruction and Supply Commission in New York. Grosfeld informed the U.S. embassy in Warsaw that the remaining staff would concentrate its efforts on finding markets for Polish goods, rather than trying in vain to gain export licenses from the Commerce Department.[44]

In part as a reaction to the American export licensing policy, the Polish government began to classify information about its economy in 1948. In early January, the U.S. consulate in Gdansk reported to the State Department that Minc had instructed Polish officials not to provide any consular representative or any foreigner with information relating to Polish commerce, industrial planning, or budgets.[45] The Polish press and representatives in the Polish Diet also began a heated campaign against U.S. economic policy. The former Polish ambassador to the United States, Oskar Lange, spoke of "a new offensive of American imperialism,"[46] and a PPR deputy in the diet asserted that "the peoples of the entire world continue to struggle against American capital for their economic independence." Polish officials even characterized the people of Great Britain, France, Italy, and other countries participating in the Marshall Plan (with the notable exception of Germany) as victims of aggressive American attempts to dominate the European economy.[47] For example, another PPR deputy criticized the French government's decision to join the Bizone and hoped that the traditions and the patriotism of the French working class, peasantry, and intellectuals would be strong enough to keep France out of grasp of the imperialists.[48]

IV

The American embargo on virtually all exports to Poland in 1948 sent the Poles shopping elsewhere. Much to the chagrin of the Truman administration, Western Europe provided many of these goods and even the credits to buy them.[49] The Polish government tried to establish its financial credibility and increase its volume of trade with Western Europe by signing nationalization compensation agreements with France in 1948, and with Denmark, Switzerland, and Sweden in 1949.[50] Western European exporters shipped many embargoed goods to Eastern Europe, while their American counterparts were cut off from this potentially lucrative trade.

Even after Marshall Plan funds began to flow into Western Europe in 1948, the dollar shortage dictated that the ERP countries import essential goods from Eastern Europe. In the fall of that year, the Polish Ministry of Industry and Trade estimated that if trade between Eastern and Western Europe returned to prewar levels, Western Europe could reduce its dollar deficit by one third. Because of this persistent dollar shortage, Polish economists thought that Western Europe would try to obtain bilateral agreements to import coal, other raw materials, and grain from Eastern Europe; they hoped that Poland would continue as one of Western Europe's leading trade partners in Eastern Europe.[51] The *New York Herald Tribune* reported that "since its decision not to have anything to do with ERP was made last July the Warsaw Government has renewed or concluded commercial agreements with 15 countries, including Sweden, Italy, Switzerland, Denmark, France, Great Britain, and the American Zone of Germany."[52]

Sweden was one of Poland's most important trading partners throughout the early postwar period. At the same time that the Polish government was attacking the United States for its discriminatory economic policies, it praised Sweden as "one of the first European countries besides the Soviet Union that entered into normal economic relations with us, and these relations have been expanded and strengthened."[53]

Rather than restricting Poland's trade with Western Europe, the Soviets agreed to reduce their imports of reparations coal to 6.5 million tons in 1948 so that Poland could increase its hard currency earnings from coal exports, and then use that money to buy capital goods in the

West.[54] It is also significant that Poland continued to do a brisk trade with Yugoslavia even after Tito fell out of favor with Stalin. In November, Horowitz told Ambassador Gallman that trade relations with Yugoslavia had deteriorated somewhat in the fall, but that now they were improving.[55] It was not until July 1949 that Poland ended its commercial cooperation with Yugoslavia.

The Polish government was careful not to alienate the West after Comecon was formed in January 1949. Early in the year Horowitz informed Gallman that Polish trade with the Soviet bloc was growing not because of Soviet pressure or a change in Minc's trade policy, but rather as a result of U.S. export controls and Poland's shortage of hard currency. Lychowski told Gallman that Comecon was formed in part to meet the challenge of the Marshall Plan and the discriminatory export licensing program. On the other hand, he assured Gallman that the Comecon countries understood the importance of Western European trade to their individual industrialization programs, and added that the Comecon countries were not making plans for "bloc trading" with the West. In another conversation with Gallman, Horowitz implied that Comecon had been formed for political rather than economic reasons. He said that the Soviet Union would ask Eastern Europe for consumer goods that Poland was trying to export anyway.[56]

The Polish government persisted in its efforts to expand commercial contacts with the United States in 1949. Ambassador Winiewicz frequently inquired about the operation of the export licensing program and the chances of obtaining the blooming and slabbing mill and ball bearings from American firms. The Poles thought that because of the U.S. government's renewed interest in a nationalization compensation agreement, they might be able to negotiate a reduction in the number of embargoed goods. But once again the State Department refused to link the two issues.[57] The Polish government was able to renew a $13 million loan from Bankers Trust of New York, however. The State Department had no objection to this loan, even though this money could be used to buy embargoed items in Western Europe.[58]

Poland's membership in Comecon did not preclude its cooperative behavior in the ECE either. After a meeting of the ECE Committee on Trade and Development in Geneva in February, Lychowski told U.S. embassy officials that he was very optimistic about the prospects for more East-West trade, especially because the dollar shortage was preventing Western Europe from meeting all of its import requirements. Lychowski identified one the fundamental dilemmas of the American economic embargo on Poland and the rest of the Soviet bloc:

> The political policy of the U.S. is aimed at preventing the development of Eastern Europe, with the result that Eastern Europe does not form as large a market as it might for Western European products and cannot, in turn, supply Western Europe with those imports which Western Europe must ultimately find outside the dollar area.[59]

The Polish delegation introduced two resolutions to the ECE in March, one calling for a study of ways to expand intra-European trade, and another to examine the impact of "existing restrictive measures applied by some countries for the purpose of influencing the internal affairs and foreign policy of other countries."[60]

Only the State Department fully understood the importance of intra-European trade for the success of the Marshall Plan, however. A State Department report in April contended that "measures involving substantial reduction of this trade would raise political as well as economic difficulties in several ERP countries." The State Department recommended that U.S. trade policy "be designed to assure continuance of Eastern Bloc exports critical to Western economic recovery and defense potential, including strategic materials needed by [the] U.S."[61]

The challenge for the Truman administration's foreign economic policy was to balance this need for East-West trade with national security considerations. The threat of war dominated the thinking of more and more U.S. government officials in 1949, and by then Congress was in no mood to accept any trade with the Soviet bloc. By having lobbied Congress for the Marshall Plan as an anti-communist measure, the Truman administration had difficulty defending any significant commercial relations between the ERP countries and the Soviet bloc, including Poland. Even Western European trade with Eastern Europe in non-strategic items came under attack in Congress. During the Senate debate on Marshall Plan appropriations in 1949, Senator William Langer of North Dakota questioned raising taxes to pay for the Marshall Plan while the British were signing trade agreements with Poland to import such commodities a eggs, bacon and lumber products.[62] Bohlen had to explain to Congress that the expansion of intra-European trade was essential for the success of the recovery program.[63]

The Senate confirmation hearing of secretary of state nominee Dean Acheson in January 1949 did not help the State Department's case. Once again Acheson was forced to defend the $90 million loan package that the United States had granted Poland in 1946 (when he was acting secretary of state). The Senate Foreign Relations Committee reexamined Acheson's involvement in the law firm that had represented the Polish government in the loan negotiations. Acheson repeated that he had no longer been a partner in the firm in 1946. He told the committee that the administration had granted the loan in 1946 to ensure free elections in Poland, but he admitted that the loan agreement itself did not include a direct promise from the Polish government to hold free elections. Acheson went over old territory in pointing out that the loan was intended to benefit of the Polish coal industry, which in turn aided Western European economic recovery through increased Polish coal exports. When committee Chairman Arthur Vandenberg reminded Acheson that Ambassador Lane had counseled against the loan at the time, Acheson responded that "the unanimous opinion of the officers of the State Department was on one side and the Ambassador took a different view."[64] Lane himself lobbied against Acheson's confirmation in the press, telling the *New York Times* that "[Acheson] has been noted for his appeasement of the Soviet Union during his former career in the State Department."[65]

V

After the Soviets tested the atomic bomb and the Chinese communists won the civil war in 1949, the State Department was on the defensive and could not effectively lobby for a more liberal policy toward Western European trade with the Soviet bloc. But this trade continued despite American efforts to force the ERP countries to comply with the export control program. Poland was still able to purchase in Western Europe many of the goods embargoed by the United States.

NOTES

1. Gardner, "Will the Real Mr. 'X' Please Stand Up," 84.

2. Robert H. Ferrell, ed., *The American Secretaries of State and Their Diplomacy* (New York: Cooper Square Publishers, Inc., 1972), vol. 16, *Dean Acheson*, by Gaddis Smith, 379.

3. See Hogan, *The Marshall Plan: America, Britain, and the Reconstruction of Western Europe, 1947-1952*, 55.

4. James Forrestal, *The Forrestal Diaries*, Walter Millis, ed. (New York, Viking Press, 1951), 291.

5. Harriman to the NSC, 14 November 1947, *FRUS, 1948* 4:506-507.

6. State Department Eastern European Working Party report, "Immediate U.S. Economic Policy Toward Soviet Sphere," 19 November 1947, *FRUS, 1948* 4:499, 500-503.

7. State Department Eastern European Working Party report, "Immediate U.S. Economic Policy Toward Soviet Sphere," 19 November 1947, *FRUS, 1948* 4:504-505.

8. Policy Planning Staff report, "United States Policy on Trade with the Soviet Union and Eastern Europe," 26 November 1947, *FRUS, 1948* 4:489-498.

9. Policy Planning Staff report on "United States Policy on Trade with the Soviet Union and Eastern Europe," 26 November 1947, *FRUS, 1948* 4:489-498.

10. Paterson, *Soviet-American Confrontation: Postwar Reconstruction and the Origins of the Cold War*, 69.

11. Willis Armstrong to Edwin Martin (deputy director, OIT), 10 December 1947, *FRUS, 1948* 4:509-511; and Lovett to Harriman, 8 December 1947, ibid., 508-509.

12. Pollard, *Economic Security and the Origins of the Cold War*, 201. The Soviet Union reduced sales of these materials to the United States at the end of 1948.

13. Paper by Harriman to the NSC, 14 November 1947, ibid., 506-507.

14. Department of Commerce press release, 15 January 1948, *FRUS, 1948* 4:514.

15. Memorandum of conversation by Henry Koch (acting director of the Occupied Areas Division of the Economic Affairs Division), 16 March 1948, *FRUS, 1948* 4:524-526.

16. Memorandum by Marshall, 26 March 1948, *FRUS, 1948* 4:527.

17. Memorandum by Marshall, 26 March 1948, *FRUS, 1948* 4:527-528; Report by the Ad Hoc Subcommittee of the Advisory Committee of the Secretary of Commerce, 4 May 1948, ibid., 536-542; and "U.S. Objectives with Respect to Russia," NSC 20/1, August 1948, in Etzold and Gaddis, eds. *Containment: Documents on American Policy and Strategy, 1945-1950*, 176-190. Later in 1948 the NSC pinpointed the objectives of the administration's economic policy toward Eastern Europe: "the aim of U.S. policy in time of peace is to place the greatest possible strain on the structure of relationships by which Soviet domination of this area is maintained . . . to maneuver the Russians out their position of primacy and to enable the respective governments to regain their freedom of action." The objective that democratic or capitalist countries emerge in Eastern Europe was now remote; a first step toward that goal was Eastern Europe's gaining a modicum of independence from the Soviet Union, as Tito had done.

18. Memorandum from the Department of Commerce, 9 March 1948, *FRUS, 1948* 4:523-524.

19. Charles Sawyer to Marshall, 20 May 1948, *FRUS, 1948* 4:544.

20. Report by the Ad Hoc Committee of the Advisory Committee of the secretary of commerce, 4 May 1948, *FRUS, 1948* 4:539-540.

21. Memorandum of conversation, Edward G. Posniak (Division of Investment and Economic Development), Martin (Office of International Trade Policy), and Armstrong (Commercial Policy), 1 June 1948, *FRUS, 1948* 4:545-549.

22. Memorandum of conversation, Posniak, Martin, and Armstrong, 1 June 1948, *FRUS, 1948* 4:545-549.

23. Marshall to Sawyer, 9 July 1948, *FRUS, 1948* 4:550-551.

24. "Poland," undated document, Truman Papers, PSF, Subject File, box 186.

25. Bobrowski, *Wspomnienia ze stulecia*, 191; Różański, *Śladem wspomnien i dokumentów, 1943-1948*, 521; see also Torańska, *Oni*, 318. Berman claimed that the Cold War climate forced the PPR to eliminate the government's economic experts in favor of politically reliable persons.

26. Memorandum by Dr. St. Antoniewski, 23 March 1948, Ministry of Industry and Trade Records, File 3004.

27. Department of State *Bulletin*, 11 April 1948, 474.

28. Notes on the present matter of the ECE, 4 September 1948, Ministry of Industry and Trade Records, File 3004.

29. Modzelewski, *Polityka Zagraniczna Polski: Artykuły i Przemówienia*, 171-173. The General Assembly defeated the resolution on 26 November.

30. Department of State *Bulletin* 19 (28 November 1948): 666; and United Nations, *Yearbook of the United Nations, 1948-1949* (New York: Columbia University Press, 1950), 482-485.

31. Winiewicz, *Co pamiętam z długiej drogi życia*, 394.

32. Memorandum of conversation, Thorp, Elbrick, etal., and Winiewicz and Litynski, 9 April 1948, *FRUS, 1948* 4:531-534.

33. Griffis to Marshall, 19 March 1948, RG 59, 711.60c, box 3426.

34. Memorandum of conversation, Thompson and Litynski, 25 March 1948, RG 84, General Records, box 60. Litynski did not name a figure for the amount of compensation, however, and the Poles considered the American claim of $100 million to be too high.

35. Griffis to Marshall, 31 March 1948, RG 84, General Records, box 60.

36. Griffis to Marshall, 3 April 1948, *FRUS 1948* 4:528-530.

37. Crocker to Marshall, 20 May 1948, RG 59, 611.60c31, box 2847.

38. Crocker to Marshall, 31 May 1948, RG 84, General Records, box 60.

39. Alton, *Polish Postwar Economy*, 179.

40. Memorandum of conversation, Thompson and Winiewicz, 30 July 1948, *FRUS, 1948* 4:555-556.

41. Gallman to Marshall, 16 October 1948, *FRUS, 1948* 4:572-574.

42. Gallman to Marshall, 10 November 1948, RG 59, 711.60c, box 3426.

43. Marshall to Warsaw, 10 December 1948, RG 84, General Records, box 60.

44. Crocker to Marshall, 13 August 1948, RG 59, 611.60C5, box 2847.

45. Parker W. Buhrman (American consul general in Gdansk) to Marshall, 7 January 1948, RG 59, 860c.501, box 6382.

46. *New York Times*, 20 January 1948, 3.

47. Polish Diet Records, 24 February 1948, 100.

48. Polish Diet Records, 25 February 1948, 121.

49. Gallman to Marshall, 23 December 1948, RG 59, 611.60c31, box 2847.

50. Dudek, *Międzynarodowe aspekty nacjonalizacji w Polsce*, 107-111; and Gillian White, *Nationalization of Foreign Property* (New York: Frederick Praeger, 1961), 193-196.

51. Notes on the present matter of the ECE, 4 September 1948, Ministry of Industry and Trade Records, File 3004.

52. *New York Herald Tribune*, 2 May 1948, in *Congressional Record*, 80th Cong., 2nd sess., 94:A3173-3174.

53. Polish Diet Records, 26 June 1948, 53.

54. Dewar, *Soviet Trade with Eastern Europe 1945-1949*, 43.

55. Gallman to Marshall, 16 November 1948, RG 84, General Records, box 60.

56. Memorandum of conversation, Thorp, etal., and Winiewicz, 13 January 1949, RG 84, General Records, box 96; Gallman to Acheson, 13 January 1949, RG 59, 860c. 50, box 6382; Gallman to Acheson, 27 January 1949, RG 84, General Records, box 96; memorandum to Gallman from James F. Hodgson (commercial attaché), 3 February 1949, ibid.; and Gallman to Acheson, 2 February 1949, ibid.

57. Memorandum of conversation, Thorp, etal., and Winiewicz, 13 January 1949, RG 84, General Records, box 96.

58. Memorandum by Fred K. Salter (East European Division), 25 February 1949, RG 59, 860c.51, box 6385.

59. Memorandum of conversation, Lychowski and Henry Ramsey, 2 March 1949, RG 84, General Records, box 98.

60. ECE: Interim Report, Polish Draft Resolution, ECE Economic and Social Council, 8th sess., 10 March 1949.

61. "Understandings on Export Control in East-West Trade," 28 April 1949, RG 59, General Records of the Office of the Executive Secretariat, box 2, National Archives.

62. *Congressional Record*, 81st Cong., 1st sess., 17 February 1949, 95:1348.

63. Pollard, *Economic Security and the Origins of the Cold War*, 163.

64. United States Senate, Hearings of the Committee on Foreign Relations on the nomination of Dean Acheson for secretary of state, 13 January 1949, 81st Cong., 1st sess., 1949, National Archives,

Washington. This was not entirely correct, because the East European Division also had reservations about the loan.

65. *New York Times*, 8 January 1949, 3.

Chapter Eight

Polish Foreign Economic Policy, 1949-1950

I

Secretary of State Dean Acheson and the State Department were well aware that the success of the embargo of strategic exports to the Soviet bloc depended upon the cooperation of Western Europe. This cooperation was not immediately forthcoming, however. Despite the pressure exerted by Washington on the ERP countries in 1949, there were serious breaches in the export control program, and the Polish government frequently publicized its trade with Western Europe to show the U.S. government that the embargo was not working.[1] The haphazard implementation of the embargo and Western Europe's lack of cooperation with it until the Korean War seriously undermined the embargo's effectiveness.

Furthermore, most American policymakers failed to recognize the strength and resiliency of the Soviet bloc economies, and how American policy was helping the Soviet Union to consolidate its control over Eastern Europe.[2] More than one historian of U.S. foreign economic policy has observed that the denial of trade, financial aid, and technology to the Eastern European countries probably hastened their integration into the Soviet political and economic sphere.[3]

On the other hand, the capitalist-country portion of Polish imports actually increased in 1948 and 1949.[4] Until the Korean War, Poland was able to purchase many embargoed goods from non-aligned countries such as Sweden and Switzerland, NATO members Denmark and Great Britain, and the western zones of Austria and Germany. The frequency of Polish attacks on U.S. economic policy increased dramatically in the last half of 1949, however. The Polish government withdrew from the IBRD, the IMF, and the FAO in 1950, and only then did Poland begin to reduce its volume of trade with capitalist countries.

II

Acheson understood that there were unfortunate but necessary compromises that had to be made to achieve the embargo's main objective of reducing the Soviet bloc's capacity to make war. In a telegram to the U.S. embassy in Warsaw in April 1949, Acheson mentioned the disadvantages of the licensing program for American exporters and the possibility of alienating some Western European countries that did not choose to follow the export control guidelines.[5] There were certain European countries (most notably Switzerland and Sweden) that had economic and political objections to the embargo. Unless Congress and the American public accepted a relaxation in the export control policy, however, Acheson did not think that the administration could change its policy.[6]

Meanwhile, Polish officials were becoming more and more exasperated with the inconsistencies in the American licensing program. In July 1949, Polish Acting Foreign Minister Stefan Wierblowski complained to U.S. Ambassador Waldemar Gallman that sixty-four products that Poland wanted to buy in the United States were still pending licenses. Wierblowski said that Poland had already paid in part or in full for twenty-two of them; one of these was the blooming and slabbing mill for the Polish steel industry. Wierblowski pointed out that Poland had imported U.S. goods valued at $55 million in 1948, but only $5 million in the first quarter of 1949. Gallman simply replied that the OEEC countries had first priority for American exports.[7]

The problems experienced by the Poles with the licensing program were caused in part by the haphazard way in which the embargo was implemented, but it was also a conscious strategy of the State Department to delay licensing exports to Poland. Acheson wrote the U.S. representatives to the ECE in Geneva in April that "we desire to keep [the] Pol [sic] government somewhat confused re our export policy." At this point Acheson thought that as long as Poland continued to ship coal to Western Europe there was no point in trying to increase East-West trade. Acheson was willing to hold talks with the Poles for "tactical reasons," however.[8]

Although most administration officials agreed with the strategic objectives of the embargo program, they often debated the embargo's unfortunate side effects. The consensus in the State Department was that Poland's dependence on the Soviet economy would have happened even without the American embargo of loans and exports, but the State Department had to admit that the embargo had "resulted in stimulating indigenous production and eastern economic integration, which in the long run will reduce Poland's dependence on the West."[9] Ambassador Gallman conceded that U.S. policy may have accelerated this development, but he thought that the embargo policy was successful in reducing Soviet war potential and that a "more liberal [American] economic policy would merely have reduced the tempo of [Poland's] Sovietization." Nonetheless, Gallman was told by some "friendly Poles" in March that the embargo policy was hurting pro-Western elements in the Polish government, such as Grosfeld and Horowitz. Therefore Gallman still advocated a "highly flexible approach in application of our export license policy to Poland." He added that the Great Britain had signed a trade agreement with Poland in January to supply raw materials and capital equipment in exchange for agricultural goods. Gallman thought that this trade pact would help slow the process of collectivisation in Poland. By severing virtually all significant economic ties to Poland, Gallman recognized that the United States was forfeiting whatever small influence that it might have on domestic economic developments in Poland.[10]

On the other hand, Gallman thought that American loans and economic assistance to Poland a few years earlier had had little impact on preventing the Sovietization of Poland anyway. By now he thought that it was too late to stop this development. All that the United States could expect from a more liberal trade policy toward Poland, Gallman argued, was to encourage "passive resistance" in the way Tito had broken from the Kremlin. Gallman said that there was potential for Polish-American trade in tires, cotton, dyes, textile equipment and even petroleum, but he favored the embargo of equipment for heavy industry (such as the blooming and slabbing mill). He did not think that the Soviets could supply a steel mill until 1955. In his opinion the benefits of the strategic embargo far outweighed the disadvantages because it was slowing the military buildup in Poland.[11]

On 9 April 1949, Acheson cabled Gallman that he had a "reliable source" who maintained that Poland was trading with Western Europe only because some goods could not be purchased in the Soviet Union. According to Acheson's source, Minc and Berman were deceiving the West by claiming that trade with Western Europe would help Poland achieve independence from the Soviet Union. Supposedly the Soviets Union disapproved of most of this trade, when in fact they were actually encouraging it. Acheson wrote that the "Department considers this in accord with Commie [sic] methods and well calculated to assist attainment [of] their objectives."[12] If for whatever reason the Soviets were actually encouraging East-West trade in certain goods, then the U.S. embargo policy was certainly responsible in part for the Poland's greater reliance on Soviet bloc trade.

Although Acheson thought that the primary Soviet objective in Eastern Europe was the rapid development of the bloc's military capacity, he still agreed with Gallman's call for a flexible embargo policy for Poland. He told Gallman that the State Department was lobbying for licenses for coal mining equipment, for example, but that the American military establishment was worried about the strategic ramifications of such trade. Acheson mentioned that the American public was swayed by the "deadly parallel" made to the sale of iron to Japan before Pearl Harbor, an argument that made a flexible embargo policy even more difficult to sell to Congress.[13]

The State Department issued a policy statement in late June that was similar to the strict but selective embargo policy that was endorsed by its diplomats in Warsaw. Some commercial exchanges would be allowed. For example, the State Department raised no objections to a proposed IBRD timber loan to Poland, although the Polish government rejected it in protest over its inability to acquire a loan for the coal industry. The department also said that it would not block private American loans to finance Polish purchases of American cotton; Poland would have to make promises to export certain goods to Western Europe in order to qualify for a U.S. government loan, however. Finally, the State Department repeated its opposition to linking a nationalization compensation agreement to a loosening of the licensing program.[14]

By this time the embassy's views were in full harmony with Washington's. Ambassador Gallman echoed the sentiments of his predecessor Stanton Griffis by arguing for a bare minimum in essential trade between Poland and the West: "Anything additional which is done to assist Poland at this time works to the benefit of the Soviet Union."[15] Another embassy diplomat, Henry C. Ramsey, even hoped that the embargo of the Soviet bloc would force the Soviet Union to allow an independent Polish government: "If the USSR is to be dislodged from Eastern Europe short of war, it will be accomplished, in my opinion, by maintaining our present momentum, to which our restrictive trade policy has contributed because it has augmented Soviet difficulties."[16]

Poland's coal exports and relatively rapid economic recovery put the Polish government in a good position to overcome the embargo in 1949. Ambassador Gallman told the State Department that Poland had some leverage in its trade relations with Western Europe because of a recent surplus in agricultural and coal production. Gallman thought that Poland was in a better position than Western Europe to conduct a trade war and that Poland could try to sabotage the ERP. Gallman wrote Acheson that "these considerations lead us to believe that the West is by no means in the driver's seat in respect of East-West trade with Poland and that we shall not be entirely successful in denying to Poland goods which will add to the Soviet war potential." Gallman continued to support the flexible embargo of exports to Poland to ensure the shipment of Polish coal to Western Europe.[17]

Outside of a few State Department officials who argued for a less comprehensive embargo, the administration was now unified behind the embargo's strategic objectives. The consensus of the Commerce Department, the Joint Chiefs, the Policy Planning Staff, and the NSC was that Soviet control over Eastern Europe was complete and that the Eastern European countries were mere economic and political adjuncts of the Soviet Union. In August, the Policy Planning Staff defined the minimum political objectives of American foreign policy in Eastern Europe as the "reduction of Soviet influence there to something like normal dimension," or to "foster communist heresy" such as Tito's break with Stalin. The Policy Planning Staff still thought that economic diplomacy could best achieve this objective by "jolting the CMEA structure."[18]

Much of this Policy Planning Staff report was adopted by the NSC in September 1949; NSC-58 considered Poland and the rest of the Soviet bloc to be part of the Soviet "monolith." The NSC directive blamed the Soviet Union for the economic integration of the bloc:

> The satellites states have under Soviet compulsion reoriented their economies from the West to the East. The Kremlin forced this readjustment with the purpose of exploiting the satellites for the aggrandizement of Soviet economic-military might and preventing their contact with the West.[19]

This policy left little leeway for relaxation of the export controls on Poland even if trade with that country was essential for the rapid recovery of the Western European economies.

Reports that U.S. foreign economic policy was inadvertently helping the Soviets to consolidate their control over Poland now fell on deaf ears. Chargé d'affaires Cecil Lyon wrote the State Department that the "restrictive policy has helped to disrupt the immediate plans of Polish Communists, but it has also stimulated their efforts toward indigenous production and Eastern European economic integration, which are included in long-range plans of the Communists."[20] The second secretary of the embassy, Thomas Bowie, thought that the lack of the blooming and slabbing mill had seriously retarded the growth of the Polish economy, but admitted that a substitute mill near Cracow would soon begin operating.[21] The OIT agreed that "it must be recognized that drastic measures of Western economic warfare against the satellites may, under present conditions, result not in Titoism but only in accelerating the present rate of their integration into a Soviet bloc country."[22] Gallman also conceded that

> propaganda-wise, we are not in strong position [to] attack Soviet economic hegemony over Poland for [the] reason that friendly Poles, and even certain astute western diplomatic representatives, believe U.S. economic policy has accelerated [the] Sovietization of Poland.[23]

At a meeting in London in late October, however, the U.S. ambassadors in Eastern Europe endorsed the strict embargo policy recommended in NSC-58. There was general agreement among the ambassadors that the economic sanctions were hindering the industrial output of the bloc countries and that the Soviet inability to supply some of these goods was causing economic disagreements within Comecon. The ambassadors viewed economic pressure as the best means by which American strategic objectives could be achieved, and recommended that the United States should "bring fully to bear on the Soviet-satellite relationship the economic forces which we control or influence."[24] They cited Washington's economic policy toward Yugoslavia as a model for future economic policy toward any other countries in Eastern Europe that showed real independence from Moscow. As a result of Yugoslavia's break with the Soviet Union in 1949, the United States rewarded that country with a loosening of export controls, an Export-Import Bank loan, relief aid, and other grants and loans.[25]

When the State Department issued its first progress report on the implementation of NSC-58 in early February 1950, the department was still studying the economic vulnerabilities of each satellite and the various means that the United States could use to weaken Soviet control over them.[26] In the spring of 1950, however, the East European Division admitted that the severing of economic ties to Eastern Europe left the United States with few diplomatic means to further its interests in the area. In order to maintain some contacts in Eastern Europe and to ensure Western European recovery, the East European Division lobbied for "a certain volume of East-West trade in non-security items."[27]

Another State Department review of the embargo policy in 1950 found that although the effects of the controls had not been "spectacular," they had seriously retarded the growth of some Eastern European industries. The State Department also recognized that mainly American exports were being controlled, but warned that a similar Western European embargo would reduce trade with Eastern Europe by approximately 25 percent and could jeopardize Western Europe's import of strategic raw materials from Eastern Europe.[28]

III

One of the Polish government's biggest frustrations with the U.S. export embargo was the government's inability to obtain a set list of embargoed items. Often the Polish authorities wasted much time and effort in contracting for goods that the United States denied or delayed export licenses. Litynski, the economic counselor in the Polish embassy in Washington, complained to the Economic Affairs Division about the length of time it took to receive a definite reply on export licenses, and said that he would rather get a quick rejection so that Poland could purchase the goods elsewhere. Litynski pointed out that although the Commerce Department eventually approved licenses for brass condenser tubes and tractor tires, Poland had already purchased the condenser tubes from Belgium and the tractor tires from Great Britain. Although Poland had been able to find alternative supplies, Litynski said that the Europeans often raised the prices of some goods, knowing that Poland had no other source of supply. Economic affairs officials told Litynski that they hoped that the licensing procedure would be expedited, but in reality the Truman administration was in no hurry to help the Poles overcome these purchasing problems.[29]

After Polish officials realized the extent of the American embargo, however, they were able to use coal to bargain with Western Europe for most of these strategic items. The Joint Chiefs lobbied for an increase of American coal exports to Europe in order to plug this hole in the embargo, but this solution was unrealistic because of the dollar shortage in Europe, the lack of shipping, and the high cost of transport. It was actually cheaper for the United States to buy Polish coal for Western Europe. In 1948 the ECA authorized $11.2 million in ERP funds to purchase Polish coal, and authorized several million more by mid-1949.[30] No other Soviet bloc country received direct benefits of the Marshall Plan in this way.

Naturally Polish officials were very concerned with any American proposals to increase U.S. coal exports. In May 1948, Grosfeld, told U.S. embassy officials that there would be no surplus of coal in Europe for the next five years even if Great Britain, Germany, and Poland could meet their production targets. But he noted that if American coal were shipped to Europe in larger amounts, there could be a surplus and a big drop in prices, which would make both American and Polish coal exports unprofitable.[31] At that time Polish coal could not be replaced by an increase in German production, American coal, or petroleum from the Middle East.

Direct exports of American goods to the Soviet bloc declined significantly in 1948, but Poland continued to conduct a lively trade with the recipients of Marshall Plan assistance. Poland even traded with the western zones of Germany until the spring of 1949, when the U.S. government attempted to subject all Trizonal trade with Poland to the export control program. When General Lucius Clay decided to delay shipments of some $10 million in goods to Poland pending export licenses, the Polish government accused the United States of abrogating their trade agreement. The Polish authorities criticized Clay's action as "shortsighted" and claimed that "Poland was now importing capital goods from most Western European countries, from the UK, and even in small quantities from the US" anyway. The Poles informed the U.S. embassy in Warsaw that if they acquired the export licenses for these goods, the present volume of Polish trade with the Trizone (about $13 million annually) could be tripled. This would have meant a major

Polish concession to Germany's role in the ERP and to the economic reconstruction of Europe as a whole. Polish officials even said that Poland could increase trade with Germany without becoming economically dependent on that former enemy country.[32]

Poland was able to obtain most of the goods on the second and third categories of the American embargo list from Western Europe. For example, Horowitz told Gallman that Poland was purchasing ball bearings in Sweden and Austria. Horowitz said that "Pol [sic] purchases in the U.S. were now confined to cotton and absolutely essential products unobtainable elsewhere."[33] Great Britain continued to do a brisk trade with Poland as well. British officials argued that East-West trade was an "essential part" of the ERP, and that Great Britain would pursue this trade if it made economic sense. Future Labour Party Prime Minister Harold Wilson, then president of the British Board of Trade, said that "politics do not enter into the United Kingdom's East-West trade relations either negatively or positively." In contrast to the United States, Wilson claimed that "the Foreign Office has not retarded the development of important trade negotiations with Eastern Europe," and that Great Britain would only control exports of "direct military or strategic value."[34] Consequently the British control list was much shorter than the U.S. list of embargoed items.

Stanisław Rączkowski, now a Bank of Poland official, told American diplomats in Warsaw that Poland was able to purchase coal mining equipment in Western Europe. He claimed that even though the IBRD had rejected the Polish loan requests, coal production had increased "enormously." Rączkowski said that Poland's urgent needs were no longer for coal mining equipment, but rather for a variety of capital goods related to the agricultural industry, especially refrigerated railroad cars.[35]

Although Poland's need for new coal mining equipment may not have been as urgent in 1949, Poland was still trying to purchase it in the United States. In September, the ECA's Agency for International Development urged the Commerce Department to grant the licenses, arguing that Western Europe needed more Polish coal.[36] The OIT agreed that Polish coal production still needed to be expanded in 1949, reasoning that an

> expansion of Polish coal output will in the long run be reflected in decreased prices to Western Europe and therefore decreased industrial production costs. To the extent that Western Europe's costs are lowered, their dependence upon U.S. aid will be decreased.[37]

As long as Polish coal continued to flow into Western Europe at acceptable levels, however, the Truman administration saw no need to grant the licenses.

As the United States began to move away from close cooperation with the ECE after Marshall Plan agencies began to operate in 1948, Poland tried to use the ECE to defend itself against economic isolation from the United States and its allies. The Polish government took great interest in maintaining multilateral cooperation within the ECE's Coal Committee, especially to set quotas for German coal production. During meetings of the Coal Committee in August 1949, the United States and Great Britain refused to represent their occupation zones in Germany, and told the French and Polish delegations to discuss West German coal production with representatives of the newly created Federal Republic of Germany. Although the Polish, French, and Norwegian delegations were unhappy with this development, the Poles continued to support the work of the Coal Committee and used it as a forum to lobby for a reduction in U.S. coal shipments to Europe.[38]

Throughout 1949 the Polish government tried to improve its commercial connections with Western Europe through the ECE. The U.S. deputy representative to the ECE in Geneva, Paul Porter, reported to Washington in May that the "Czechs and particularly [the] Poles have shown considerable desire [to] expand trade with [the] West." Porter said that the head of the British delegation was convinced of the sincerity of Poland's desire to maintain trade contacts and to act independently of the Soviet Union in economic affairs.[39] Porter added later that the OEEC countries received Polish proposals for increased trade with Western Europe "openmindedly," but that the proposals were rejected by the Soviet Union and "received no support whatever from the other EE [Eastern European] delegations."[40] Porter added that the United States should exploit this Soviet bloc disunity by discouraging Western European exports of heavy industrial goods, and by encouraging an increase in Western European trade with Eastern Europe in consumer goods, some raw materials, and equipment for light industry.[41] The U.S. embassy in Warsaw opposed this strategy, arguing that the United States should not try to increase trade with Poland beyond the needs of the ERP countries. The State Department supported Western Europe's trade with Poland only if it somehow benefitted the Western European countries more than Poland, but of course there was no objective measure of the relative advantages of this trade to each side.[42]

Poland persisted in its efforts to circumvent the licensing program in 1950.[43] Early in the year Litynski again inquired about the ball bearings for coal industry machinery that Poland had purchased in the United States before the licensing program went into effect in 1948. The State Department now told him that licensing decisions were linked to U.S. relations with Poland as a whole. Although State Department officials were concerned that the export controls were hurting American exporters, and that it would be difficult to coerce Western Europe to cooperate, they could give Litynski no assurance that the administration would loosen the export licensing program in the near future. The Commerce Department finally notified the Polish government in April that the department had rejected the licenses.[44]

In part as a result of the embargo, the American share of Poland's total foreign trade plummeted to 2.1 percent in 1949, down from approximately 10 percent in 1947, and 5 percent in 1948.[45] Poland's efforts to increase trade with Western Europe, especially with Scandinavia, Great Britain, France, Italy, and even the Trizone of Germany proved fruitful, however. Poland's imports from capitalist countries increased until 1950. Capitalist countries supplied 52.5 percent of Poland's imports in 1948, and 57.4 percent in 1949. Investment goods accounted for over 60 percent of these imports.[46]

If the State Department had actively pursued an increase in trade with Poland in 1950, by that time Congress would not have allowed it anyway. Congress even attacked U.S. imports of Polish ham. Polish ham constituted approximately half of the value of Poland's exports to the United States before the Second World War, and Poland succeeded in reviving these exports after the war. After the Department of Agriculture approved Polish meat packing regulations in 1950, this trade increased significantly.[47]

Herbert B. Moeller of the Atalanta Trading Corporation of New York City conducted most of the Polish ham trade, and in January 1950, Moeller consulted with the Economic Affairs Division before going to Poland to extend a ham contract. Moeller wanted to check with the State Department about some new stipulations that the Polish government had made in the contract, such as the employment of a Polish "national" in Moeller's firm. Moeller said that at first he had given in to this demand, but that later he changed his mind. The Economic Affairs Division raised no objections to the trip, however. On the other hand, Ambassador Gallman recommended against it, because Moeller might be in danger of violating Poland's State Secrets Act and could be subject to arrest. At first Moeller canceled the trip, but at another meeting the East European Division officials told him again that he could go ahead with the trip. Gallman wrote Acheson that Moeller was quite pleased with the results of his visit with Polish officials, especially because the Poles had agreed to an automatic annual extension of the agreement. He also reported that Moeller told Polish officials that the ham agreement was dependent on reciprocal imports of American surplus lard and tallow. Acheson informed Gallman later that Moeller had no official status to barter these items.[48]

Congress criticized this ham trade on the basis that the Polish government could use the hard currency from these sales to purchase strategic items on the European market. One Pennsylvania congressman argued that "in light of our enormous expenditures designed on the one hand to stop communism in Europe I cannot detect the logic in a policy which on the other hand acts to build up the economy of a country which is definitely Leftist."[49] In addition, the National Independent Meat Packers Association wrote a letter to Georgia Senator Walter George in December 1949 protesting the Polish ham imports. The meat packers claimed that there was no shortage of pork in the United States, and added that "we should not encourage competitive importations from Communist nations."[50] Subsequently George requested that the State Department ban Polish canned ham imports, but the State Department replied that the administration could not disrupt the free market by telling a business where to purchase imports.[51] Of course, this rationale was not entirely consistent with the administration's licensing policy that was penalizing some American exporters.

Despite opposition from the State Department, the Senate introduced a bill to restrict the import of Polish ham under a blanket embargo of any pork imports from countries that were not participating in the ERP.[52] During the Senate hearings on the bill in May 1950, the bill's supporters could not prove that Polish canned hams, which were of superior quality and commanded a higher price, competed with

American canned hams. Representatives of the Agriculture Department argued that Polish imports from April 1949 to March 1950 amounted to only one twenty fifth of one percent of the annual U.S. production of pork. Moeller submitted letters from retailers attesting to their satisfaction with the Polish hams, and he himself testified that

> depriving Poland of the privilege of exporting its pork products to the United States can be considered as discriminatory and would probably force Poland, on account of lack of dollars, to discontinue purchasing from us such surplus commodities as lard, tallow and cotton, to the detriment of our meat producers and cotton growers.

On the other hand, supporters of the bill pointed out that there was nothing to prevent Poland from using the money earned from ham sales in the United States to buy armaments or capital equipment for Polish arms industries.[53] Although there was a growing anti-communist mood in Washington in 1950, a complete embargo on trade with Poland lacked support from the State Department, the Agriculture Department, or other importers in addition to Moeller. The bill failed to pass.

IV

When the Soviets began to exert more political pressure on the PZRP to conform to Stalinist economic and political policies in 1949, the Polish government gradually reassessed its policy of economic cooperation with the West. Gomułka was purged from the party in early 1949, and the ongoing purges of the other communist parties in Eastern Europe necessitated caution on the part of Polish officials in any dealings with Western Europe or the United States, lest Moscow accuse them of Titoism. For example, Gallman reported that in reference to the State Department's idea of an American cotton for Polish coal exchange,

> the reduced influence of Western-oriented officials in shaping Polish foreign trade policy due to reorganization [in the] Ministry [of] Industry and Commerce would . . . be a deterrent to successful consummation of cotton in lieu of dollar transactions with ECA countries.[54]

Economic discussions between American diplomats and Polish officials, which prior to 1949 had been relatively free of political pressures from Moscow, were now more strained. During a conversation with Minc in July about this cotton for coal exchange, one American diplomat in Warsaw noted that Minc "froze" and ended any frank discussions when hard-liners Berman, Wierblowski, and two high-ranking Polish army officers entered the room.[55]

The vigorous, Marxist attacks on American foreign economic policy also appeared more frequently in the Polish press in 1949. In October, *Rzeczpospolita* wrote that "the steadily growing economic strength of the Soviet Union and the people's democratic countries is the greatest obstacle hindering American imperialists in the realization of their war plans."[56] The press repeatedly contrasted the allegedly thriving socialist economies with the crises-ridden U.S. and Western European economies. The press called the Marshall Plan a failure, citing Western European budget and dollar deficits, unemployment, and reduced production in key industries. *Życie Gospodarcze* contended that

> the United States, the stronghold of imperialist capitalism, has found itself in the chains of an economic crisis since the end of 1948. . . . The Marshall Plan has not succeeded in its endeavor to monopolize the market for American surplus goods. Instead of trade, the United States offers the Marshall Plan countries the 'export' of unemployment and economic crisis.[57]

In April 1950, the same journal republished an article from a Soviet economic journal in which Truman's financial policy was equated with Hitler's attempt to make the German mark the world currency in the 1930s.[58] The propaganda now extolled the benefits of Soviet economic assistance, which allegedly had no strings attached.[59]

Judging from the vitriolic propaganda campaign leveled at the United States in 1949, it became obvious that Minc would not seek any more economic assistance or significant imports from the United States. American diplomats in Warsaw reported that Polish officials often borrowed Soviet attacks on the United States, but used them with even more "venom." Minc declared that in order to realize the targets set in the new Six-Year Plan that was to begin in 1950, "our task calls for an inexorable fight against the defeated [Polish] reactionaries who, on orders from the American imperialists, are endeavoring to organize sabotage and diversion in Poland."[60] During a meeting of the PZRP Central Committee in May, Bierut predicted that the United States was headed for another depression and labeled American leaders "fascists, warmongers, and monopolists." He criticized the United States as "culturally barbarous and money-mad,"[61] and accused the U.S. government of employing "totalitarian domestic and foreign policies."[62] American diplomats in Warsaw now understood that in the frigid atmosphere of superpower relations, the Polish leadership had little room to maneuver, and that a change in Polish-American relations now depended solely upon reducing Cold War tensions.[63]

Minc no longer claimed publicly that his government could gain independence from the Soviet Union by trading with the West. Now he argued that Poland had to be strengthened as a socialist state, independent as much as possible from the capitalist economies.[64] By then administration officials were rejecting any arguments that a more liberal licensing program would increase Poland's independence from the Soviet Union anyway. When Lychowski tried using this tactic to lobby again for the blooming and slabbing mill, the State Department said that this reasoning was "invalid because Pol [sic] has no political independence in any basic respect."[65]

A recurring theme of Polish propaganda in 1949 was that Western Europe, like Poland, was being economically coerced by the United States. Minc knew that some trade with Western Europe was indispensable to the growth of the Polish economy, and with this line of thinking his government could justify some trade with capitalist countries. One PZPR deputy in the Polish Diet criticized American attacks on Great Britain's trade agreement with Poland, characterizing Great Britain and France as victims of "dollar diplomacy." He added that "if the Americans behave so unceremoniously with the British and French, it is easy to guess the real prospects for the independence of other important yet smaller 'partners' of such clever 'cooperation' with the United States."[66]

The Polish government also began to criticize the IBRD for withholding reconstruction loans on political grounds, and finally withdrew from the bank in March 1950. Oskar Lange chastised the United States for discrimination in its licensing program and loan policy, adding that "even the International Bank for Reconstruction and Development, which is formally an organization working under the jurisdiction of the United Nations, has conformed to such policy."[67] The State Department interpreted Poland's withdrawal from the bank as another example of Moscow's effort to "isolate the countries of the Soviet orbit from the free world."[68] In reality, the Polish government had little to lose by leaving the bank, because it was obvious that Polish reconstruction loans had been rejected on political, not economic grounds.[69]

One month later Poland also left the FAO, citing once again the discriminatory policies of the United States. The State Department called these charges "ridiculous." The move came as no surprise because the Polish government had been criticizing American proposals in the FAO for over a year. Before a FAO meeting in November 1949, S. Królikowski, an economic official in the Polish government, told Lychowski that the United States intended to pressure the OEEC countries into creating a Western European agricultural organization that would support American agricultural exports and discourage imports from Eastern Europe. Królikowski recommended that Poland lobby the FAO for an agricultural policy for Europe similar to the coal policy adopted in the ECE. That policy called for European self-sufficiency and for the purchase of American exports as a last resort. He added that Poland should argue that American attempts to restrict East-West trade would result in widespread unemployment. After the FAO rejected the Polish proposals, Poland quit the organization and relied on bilateral agreements to facilitate exports of its agricultural products.[70] Ironically, one of those agreements was to sell canned hams in the United States.

Despite its official anti-capitalist propaganda campaign, in reality the Polish government regarded mutually beneficial trade with Western Europe as essential to Poland's economic growth. *Życie Gospodarcze* freely reported the many trade agreements that Poland signed with almost all of the ERP countries. The press also listed the goods that were exchanged, items that were often on the American embargo list. Even into 1950, when Polish attacks on U.S. foreign policy became even more frequent and more stinging, the Polish press continued to praise trade with Western Europe. *Życie Gospodarcze* even wrote that there were good prospects for an expansion of trade with Western Europe beyond present levels.[71]

V

The decline in direct commercial relations with the United States in 1948 and 1949 was still not accompanied by a new Polish policy of economic isolation from the West. The formation of Comecon did not preclude Polish economic cooperation with Western Europe either. Polish coal shipments to Western Europe continued uninterrupted. By the end of 1950, however, a combination of increased American coal exports to Europe, increased coal production in Germany, the U.S. embargo, and Soviet demands for the economic integration of the Comecon countries forced Poland to shift its trade pattern. The total value of Poland's trade in 1948 amounted to $1.053 million; only one third of that ($358,000,000) was with the Soviet bloc. By 1952 the total value of Poland's trade increased to $1.589 million, but now two thirds of its trade was with the Comecon countries ($1.065 million).[72] This trend would continue until 1956.

NOTES

1. Annual economic report by James F. Hodgson (commercial attaché) to Acheson, 15 February 1949, RG 84, General Records, box 96.

2. Wolf, *U.S. East-West Trade Policy: Economic Warfare Versus Economic Welfare*, 128.

3. Pollard and Wells, "1945-1960: The Era of American Economic Hegemony," 341; and Gajda, *Polska Polityka Zagraniczna, 1944-1971*, 99.

4. Janusz Kalinski, *Polityka Gospodarcza Polski w latach 1948-1956* [The economic policy of Poland in the years 1948-1956] (Warsaw: Książka i Wiedza, 1987), 188.

5. See for example, the letter from Thomas Bowie (second secretary of the embassy) to F.H. Jusenius (vice-president, Diamond Iron Works, Minneapolis), 8 September 1949, in *Congressional Record*, 81st Cong., 1st sess., 17 February 1949, 95:1348. Bowie replied favorably to Jusenius's inquiry about the possibility of exporting farm equipment to Poland, but by the end of 1949 it was difficult to receive an export license for any type of equipment destined for the Soviet bloc countries.

6. Acheson to Warsaw, 9 April 1949, RG 84, General Records, box 98.

7. Gallman to Acheson, 21 July 1949, RG 59, 711.60c, box 3426.

8. Acheson to Geneva, 21 April 1949, RG 84, General Records, box 98.

9. Department of State Policy Statement: Poland, 25 June 1949, *FRUS, 1949* 5:502-516; and minutes of NAC meeting, 26 October 1948, *FRUS, 1948* 4:575-578.

10. Gallman to Acheson, 19 March 1949, RG 84, General Records, box 98.

11. Gallman to Acheson, 27 April 1949, 611.60c31, box 2847.

12. Acheson to Warsaw, 9 April 1949, RG 84, General Records, box 98.

13. Acheson to Warsaw, 9 April 1949, RG 84, General Records, box 98.

14. Department of State Policy Statement: Poland, 25 June 1949, *FRUS, 1949* 5:502-516; and minutes of NAC meeting, 26 October 1948, *FRUS, 1948* 4:575-578.

15. Gallman to Acheson, 14 July 1949, RG 59, 611.60c31, box 2847.

16. Ramsey to Gallman, 23 June 1949, RG 84, General Records, box 98.

17. Gallman to Acheson, 14 July 1949, RG 59, 611.60c31, box 2847.

18. Policy Planning Staff Paper 59, 25 August 1949, *FRUS, 1949* 5:21-26; and James Webb (acting secretary of state) to James Lay (executive secretary of the NSC), 2 February 1950, *FRUS, 1950* 4:7-8. In February, the Treasury and Commerce Departments, the National Security Resources board, and the ECA were asked to contribute to these studies.

19. NSC draft report on NSC-58, 29 August 1949, RG 59, Office of the Executive Secretariat, E396.2, box 2; NSC 58/2, "A Report to the President on United States Policy Toward the Soviet Satellite States in Eastern Europe," 8 December 1949, National Security Council Reports, Records Group 273, National Archives; and memorandum from Webb to Lay, 12 December 1949, Truman Papers, PSF, National Security Council Meetings, box 207.

20. Cecil Lyon, (chargé d'affaires) to Acheson, 19 September 1949, RG 59, 711.60c, box 3426.

21. Memorandum by Bowie, 8 December 1949, RG 84, General Records, box 98.

22. Memorandum prepared in the Department of State in the OIT, 4 April 1950, *FRUS, 1950* 4:107-114.

23. Gallman to Acheson, 19 March 1949, RG 59, 611.60c31, box 2847.

24. Conclusions and recommendations of the London Conference of United States Chiefs of Mission to the Satellite States (October 24-26), undated, *FRUS, 1949* 5:28-35.

25. Campbell, "American Policy Towards the Satellites and National Communism," 305.

26. National Security Council report on NSC 58/2 by Webb, 3 February 1950, Truman Papers, PSF, NSC Memoranda.

27. Paper prepared in the Eastern European Affairs Division, undated (used in the Foreign Ministers' Conference in London in May 1950), *FRUS, 1950* 4:14-17.

28. Paper prepared in the Department of State, undated, *FRUS, 1950* 4:150-152.

29. Memorandum of conversation, Litynski and Armstrong (Commercial Division), 8 June 1949, RG 84, General Records, box 99.

30. Wexler, *The Marshall Plan Revisited: The European Recovery Program in Economic Perspective*, 79.

31. Memorandum of conversation, Grosfeld, Hodgson, and Henry Ramsey (second secretary of the U.S. embassy), 20 May 1948, RG 84, General Records, box 60.

32. Gallman to Acheson, 28 February 1949, RG 59, 860c.6362, box 6389; and memorandum of conversation, Lychowski and Ramsey, 2 March 1949, RG 84, General Records, box 98.

33. Gallman to Marshall, 17 November 1948, RG 84, General Records, box 60.

34. Report on trade with Eastern Europe, F.P. Bartlett (counselor in the U.S. embassy in London), 15 February 1949, RG 84, General Records, box 98.

35. Memorandum of conversation, Rączkowski and Cecil Lyon, 16 February 1949, RG 84, General Records, box 98.

36. Memorandum to Richard Bissell, Jr., (assistant administrator for Program in AID) from James McCullough (director, AID-ECA Fiscal and Trade Policy Division), undated (ca. September 1949), RG 286, Commodity Subject Files, box 1.

37. Office of International Trade to the Licensing Committee of the Commerce Department, 20 September 1949, RG 286, Country Subject Files, box 3.

38. United States delegation to ECE Coal Committee in Geneva to Acheson, 22 September 1949, RG 84, General Records, box 96.

39. Porter to the State Department, 27 May 1949, RG 84, General Records, box 98.

40. Porter to Acheson, 31 May 1949, *FRUS, 1949* 5:120-122.

41. Editorial note on Porter telegram to Acheson, 8 June 1949, *FRUS, 1949* 5:124.

42. Editorial note on telegram from the U.S. embassy in Warsaw to Acheson, 14 July 1949, *FRUS, 1949* 5:135-136.

43. United States embassy in Warsaw to Acheson, 20 January 1950, RG 59, 748.00, box 3605; and Trizonial Trade Agreement with Poland, 28 July 1949, RG 84, General Records, box 98.

44. Memorandum of conversation, Litynski and R. B. Wright, 1 February 1950, RG 59, 448.118, box 1992; memorandum prepared in the Department of State in the OIT, 4 April 1950, *FRUS, 1950* 4:107-114; and letter from Thomas Blaisdell (assistant secretary of commerce) to Modzelewski, 10 April 1950, Department of Commerce, Central Correspondence File of the Office of the Secretary of Commerce, 1950-1955, box 143, National Archives.

45. Annual economic report from the U.S. embassy in Warsaw to the State Department, RG 59, 15 May 1950, 848.00, box 4931.

46. Kalinski, *Polityka Gospodarcza Polski w latach 1948-1956*, 188.

47. Gallman to Acheson, 1 February 1949, RG 59, 860c.50, box 6382.

48. Memorandum of conversation, Herbert Moeller and Posniak, etal., 10 January 1950, RG 59, 411.46E31-41.489, box 1836; Gallman to Acheson, 25 January 1950, ibid.; Gallman to Acheson, 21 March 1950, ibid.; Acheson to Gallman, 25 March 1950, ibid.; Charles F. Brannan (secretary of agriculture) to Senator Elmer Thomas (chairman of the Agriculture and Forestry Committee), 25 April 1950, United States Senate, 81st Cong., 1st sess., Hearings of the Committee of Agriculture and Forestry, File S.3055; Gallman to Acheson, 5 April 1950, ibid. This was not much of a bargaining chip anyway. Although Poland imported eight million pounds of tallow in 1949, the Polish authorities told Gallman in April that they would soon have their own domestic supply.

49. Paul B. Dague (congressman from Pennsylvania) to Acheson, 6 December 1949, RG 59, 611.60c5, box 2847.

50. R.D. Stearns (regional vice-president of the Central Division of National Independent Meat Packers Association) to Senator Walter F. George (Georgia), December 1949, RG 59, 611.60c5, box 2847.

51. Jack K. McFall (assistant secretary in the State Department) to Senator George, etal., 10 January 1950, RG 59, 411.46E31-411.489, box 1836.

52. United States Senate, 81st Cong., 1st sess., Hearings of the Committee on Agriculture and Forestry, 17 February 1950, File S.3055.

53. United States Senate, 81st Cong., 1st sess., Hearings of the Committee on Agriculture and Forestry, 26 May 1950, File S.3055.

54. Gallman to Acheson, 21 March 1949, RG 59, 611.60c31, box 2847.

55. Gallman to Acheson, 7 July 1949, RG 59, 611.60c31, box 2847.

56. From *Rzeczpospolita*, 1 October 1949, in Gallman to Acheson, 10 October 1949, RG 59, 860c.50, box 6382.

57. *Życie Gospodarcze* 4 (1 November 1949): 924.

58. *Życie Gospodarcze* 5 (1 April 1950): 329-335.

59. Polish Diet Records, 3 February 1950, 30-33, 59; ibid., 7 March 1950, 135; ibid., 4 April 1950, 138; and ibid., 19 April 1950, 140.

60. Article by Minc in *Pravda*, reported in *Trybuna Ludu*, in Lyon (U.S. embassy counselor) to Acheson, 20 September 1949, RG 59, 860c.50, box 6382.

61. Report on 4th Plenum of the PZPR Central Committee in Warsaw to Department of State, 26 May 1950, RG 59, 748.00, box 3605.

62. *New York Times*, 14 May 1950, 29.

63. United States embassy in Warsaw to the Department of State, 24 March 1950, RG 59, 748.00, box 3605.

64. From *Cominform Journal*, 18 November 1949, in Schoefeld (U.S. embassy counselor) to Acheson, 18 November 1949, RG 84, General Records, box 98.

65. Webb to the U.S. consulate in Geneva, 14 June 1949, *FRUS, 1949*, 5:126-127.

66. Polish Diet Records, 3 March 1949, 83-84.

67. Polish Diet Records 11 January 1949, 74.

68. Department of State *Bulletin*, 27 March 1950, 497.

69. Sekular, "Stosunki gospodarcze między Polska i Stanami Zjednoczonymy Ameryki po II wojnie światowej," 21. The Poles withdrew their contribution of $1,875,000 from the bank.

70. Department of State *Bulletin*, 15 May 1950, 777; memorandum from S. Królikowski (economic counselor) to Lychowski, January 1949, Ministry of Industry and Trade Records, File 3004; and Królikowski to Lychowski, 30 August 1949, ibid.

71. *Życie Gospodarcze* 5 (1 May 1950): 429-430.

72. Spulber, *The Economics of Communist Eastern Europe*, 412. Similar dramatic shifts in the direction of trade occurred in Czechoslovakia and Hungary.

Chapter Nine

The Impact of Economic Warfare on the Polish Economy, 1949-1952

I

When Secretary of State Dean Acheson proposed a militarization of American containment policy in the spring of 1950 (in NSC-68), and when the Korean War broke out in June, significant economic relations between the United States and Poland had already ended. The economic battle of the Cold War was on, and the Truman administration now concentrated its efforts on forcing Western Europe to fall into line with the embargo of strategic exports to the Soviet bloc. Administration officials foresaw a long-term struggle with the forces of socialism, whether directly in Europe or in the Third World.[1] In NSC-68, the National Security Council again called for a "restriction of E-W [sic] trade in items of military importance to the East."[2] Poland was a special concern for the NSC as a conduit for Western military hardware to the rest of the Soviet bloc. Joseph Flack, the new U.S. ambassador in Warsaw, put it simply that the strategic goods acquired by Poland from Western Europe went for "eventual Soviet military use."[3] In addition, Senator Joseph McCarthy of Wisconsin began his crusade against communist influence in the State Department in 1950, and once again he raised the question of Acheson's role in granting the $90 million loan package to Poland in 1946. McCarthy charged that "it was Acheson who placed the guns, the whips, the blacksnakes, and the clubs in the hands of those Communists . . . to keep a Christian population under Soviet discipline."[4] The issue was raised yet again in the *New York Times* over a year later.[5]

In this Cold War atmosphere it was barely feasible for the Truman administration to balance the various objectives of U.S. foreign economic policy toward the Soviet bloc. On the one hand economic warfare was expected to reduce the military potential of the Soviet bloc, while on the other the economic sanctions were intended to foster

Titoism and divisions within the bloc. Another policy goal was to maintain support for the welfare of the people of Eastern Europe. In fact, the economic embargo tended to make Poland and the other Eastern European countries more economically dependent on the Soviet Union. Furthermore, the embargo failed to reduce to any great degree the military capacity of the Soviet bloc, because Moscow forced the Eastern European governments to spare no expense to build their militaries. But as a result of the Polish government's increased military spending, the Polish people ultimately suffered a decline in their standard of living.

II

Before the summer of 1950, there was considerable debate within the U.S. government over Western Europe's compliance with the strategic embargo of the Soviet bloc. The State Department and the ECA recognized the need for some essential intra-European trade, while Congress and the Defense Department called for a tighter embargo and for sanctions against the ERP countries that did not comply with it. After Korean War began in June 1950, the State Department and the ECA agreed with a stricter licensing program, but they still argued that certain countries of Western Europe needed to trade with Eastern Europe, especially with Poland. The State Department and the ECA also questioned the wisdom of U.S. sanctions against Western European countries that defied the embargo.

The NSC began to use the term "economic warfare" to describe various U.S. foreign economic policies, such as the commercial embargo on the Soviet bloc, the use of economic assistance to reward those countries who sided with the United States in the Cold War, and the preemptory buying of scarce raw materials.[6] The NSC eventually decided to rule out a total trade embargo, however, reporting to Truman in early 1951 that "a complete embargo might well serve to orient the European satellites, particularly Poland and Czechoslovakia, even more rapidly and more deeply toward the USSR."[7]

The State Department's and the ECA's strongest argument for a limited embargo was Western Europe's need for Polish coal. Western Europe had a shortage of coal again in late 1950 and early 1951 in part because of the Truman administration's decision to rearm Western

Europe; military industries there now had added energy needs. Replacing Polish coal with American coal was too costly, and Western Europe was unable to produce enough coal to meet the new demand.[8] It was risky policy to embargo strategic exports to Poland without jeopardizing these essential Polish coal exports, however.[9] The ECA reported to the NSC in February 1951 that Sweden and Denmark would be "crippled" without imports of Polish coal.[10] State Department counselor Willard Thorp testified at Congressional hearings on the embargo that Poland was the chief source of coal for Austria and Italy as well. Thorp reflected the State Department's efforts to use trade as a diplomatic tool by arguing that perhaps a modicum of Soviet bloc economic dependence on the West would give the United States more leverage if a real crisis arose.[11] Even Commerce Department officials, who had consistently supported a stricter embargo, told Congress that the present licensing system was adequate.[12]

Of course, the coal exports were vital to Poland because they used coal to bargain for investment goods from the ERP countries.[13] Ambassador Flack admitted that for Poland "the effect of the coal shortage [in early 1951] has been to reduce somewhat the pinch of restrictive export licensing policies."[14] According to the ECA, Poland received between 35 to 40 percent of its imports of industrial and transportation equipment from the sale of coal. When Poland increased its coal exports to Western Europe after the outbreak of the Korean War, the ECA observed that "this would not seem to be compatible with a thesis that Poland is using coal exports as an instrument of economic warfare, though it does use them for hard bargaining."[15]

Congress began to exert more pressure on the administration's foreign economic policy in 1950. In the fall, Congress restricted American economic assistance to countries that exported strategic goods to the Soviet bloc.[16] Congress adopted a very broad definition of a strategic good. A year later Congress passed the Mutual Defense Assistance Control Act (Battle Act), which was intended to coordinate all aspects of U.S. foreign economic policy and to bring stiffer sanctions against ERP countries that exported strategic items to Eastern Europe.[17] The next Mutual Defense Assistance Control Act of 1952 included even tougher punishment for ERP countries engaging in this trade.

For the first time since the end of the war, the Polish government actively sought to trade more with the Soviet bloc than with the West. On the other hand, Polish officials continued to call for an expansion of East-West trade and a reduction in the number of embargoed goods. Tough bargaining with its coal exports enabled Poland, better than the other Soviet bloc countries, to acquire necessary goods for the Six-Year Plan (1950-1955). American intelligence reports found that the Polish industrialization plan would be seriously retarded without these imports of equipment from Western Europe,[18] and in February 1951, the ECA discussed the idea of creating a special fund to subsidize the high cost of American coal. The Economic Defense Staff (EDS) of the ECA thought that the costs of this fund would be too high, however, and suggested that a better way to cause a drop in the high cost of Polish coal was to ship more American coal to Western Europe. A lack of shipping caused the EDS to lament that "at present we cannot even satisfy the need for U.S. coal apart from the displacement of Polish coal." The ECA finally recommended that the administration ask Congress to create a special coal fund. Until that was done the ECA suggested using all available shipping to increase American coal exports.[19]

Because Poland could trade coal for strategic goods, U.S. diplomats in Warsaw thought that Poland was a source of supply of these items for the entire Soviet bloc.[20] One controversy that emerged in the fall of 1951 concerned the trans-shipment of General Motors and Ford automobile parts from Denmark to Poland. The ECA and the State Department recommended approval of the sale, because Denmark had no other way to acquire Polish coal.[21] Truman accepted their recommendations at the NSC meeting of 29 August,[22] but the Defense Department protested the sale on the grounds that American coal could cover Danish needs if only Congress would finance it.[23] This was not entirely true because shipping was still in shortage at that time.[24]

Some members of Congress immediately questioned the deal. Senator James P. Kem of Missouri criticized the action as detrimental to U.S. security:

> The equipment is such as could be used in military transport units as large as 6x6 trucks. . . . It has been reported that Polish trucks are being used by Communist forces in Korea. Certainly they would be used by the Reds in the event of trouble in Europe.[25]

Minnesota Senator Hubert Humphrey sent a letter to the State Department from a constituent who also criticized the auto parts sale to the communists.[26] When Congressman Edward Rees of Kansas also raised objections to the sale, the State Department told him that Denmark and Western Europe needed Polish coal, and that some trade with Poland was the only way for the Danes to get it. The State Department admitted that coal was in short supply in part because of the rearmament program in Western Europe.[27] Based on the State Department's arguments, the Danish auto parts deal went through.

In an effort to stop these leaks in the embargo, Senator Kem proposed an amendment to the Battle Act in 1952 that denied any more aid to ERP countries that defied the embargo program. Acheson sent a note to the chairman of the Senate Foreign Relations Committee, Tom Connally, arguing against the amendment on the grounds that Great Britain, France, Italy, and Germany would be "unable to meet the conditions of our aid."[28] The amendment passed, but Congress gave the White House the power to make exceptions. And the administration did just that. For example, the administration approved of deliveries of Dutch oil drilling equipment and a Danish tanker to Poland, deals that had been signed several years before. The administration argued that cutting aid to these countries would merely undermine the Western European defense buildup.[29]

Until 1952, the administration searched in vain for ways to plug the hole in the embargo caused by Poland's trade with Western Europe. The administration tried to ship more American coal to Europe, but as one official in the ECA put it, "the real problem, particularly as far as Sweden is concerned, is one of payment [in hard currency]."[30] In November 1951, when Austria agreed to ship ball bearings to Poland in exchange for approximately 160,000 tons of coal that Austria needed for the winter months, the State Department approved the transaction because of the prohibitively high cost of shipping American coal to Austria.[31] In February 1952, William Welk, now chairman of the EDS,[32] concluded that the "United States could not afford to replace Polish coal deliveries to Western Europe."[33] On the other hand, he recommended that the administration study ways to alleviate the shipping shortage, such as determining the cost of putting "mothball" ships into service.[34] Two weeks later the EDS issued a report estimating the costs of replacing Polish coal for 1952-1953 at approximately $180 million. The EDS concluded that "in the longer run the solution of the problem of Western Europe's dependence upon both

Soviet bloc coal and U.S. coal lies in increased Western European production."[35] When Western European coal production rose in the first four months of 1952, Welk contended that only in "exceptional circumstances" could Poland exert pressure to obtain strategic imports.[36]

Welk was right. The combination of a mild winter of 1951-1952, U.S. coal deliveries to Western Europe of 28 million tons in 1951, and a unified and tougher trading position adopted by the Scandinavian countries forced Poland to reduce its coal prices by up to 20 percent in the summer of 1952. The coal glut significantly reduced Poland's ability to bargain for strategic items.[37] For example, in early 1953 the administration was able to reject a shipment of $172 million in ball bearings from Austria to Poland.[38]

III

It is impossible to calculate accurately the overall impact of the U.S. embargo on the Polish economy, but undoubtedly it caused serious disruptions in Minc's reconstruction plans. The Polish economy continued to grow in the early fifties, but at the end of 1949 the Polish press began to report shortages of raw materials and equipment for the agricultural sector, and a need for new machines for the textile and steel industries.[39] United States embassy officials in Warsaw reported that in a speech on the futility of the embargo President Cyrankiewicz "may have unconsciously revealed how much the Moscow one-way concept of Soviet-satellite trade is pinching the Polish economy, and how much it feels the lack of strategic materials procurable only in America."[40] In 1953, the embassy reported that for the first time the coal industry had failed to achieve its plan for 1952, and that Poland was behind on some coal deliveries to Western Europe.[41]

Although the Polish government publicly claimed that no "credit blockade, as a political pressure, will be able to paralyze or check to any serious extent the Polish plan of economic reconstruction,"[42] in reality the Polish leadership was extremely worried about its economic isolation from the West. The U.S. embassy in Warsaw observed that Polish officials had "the fear that our export licensing policy will gravely handicap Poland's rehabilitation and industrialization as planned in her Three- and Six-Year Plans."[43] The strategic embargo and the lack of investment loans from the West had a significant impact on the fulfillment of several segments of the Three-Year Plan that ended in 1949. The investment priority that Minc gave to the coal industry can be seen in the rise in coal production coal from 59.1 million tons in 1947 to 74.1 million tons in 1949,[44] but this figure fell short of the 77.5 million tons called for in the plan.[45] The profits from these coal exports also did not meet expectations. Although the absolute value of coal exports rose in this period, profits fell short by about one third of the plan in 1947, nearly hit the target in 1948, but then fell short of the plan by one fifth in 1949.[46]

Poland nearly reached most of the principle objectives of the Three-Year Plan by the end of 1949,[47] but some of the production targets that were not reached were a direct result of American loan and trade policy. Investment goals for Polish industry fell far short of the original plan of 1946,[48] partially as a result of the lack of foreign investment loans. Poland also imported much more in 1948 and 1949 than had been planned. The Three-Year Plan called for an increase of only 9.8 percent in imports for these two years, but in fact imports increased 39 percent.[49] The shortfall in the agricultural sector was evident in the cost overruns in purchases of non-investment agricultural goods. The revised plan of 1948 called for spending only 2 percent of the value of all imports on non-investment agricultural imports in 1949, but that figure actually rose to 68 percent; the costs of those imports caused a serious depletion in Poland's already meager hard currency reserves. As a result, the Poland's expenditures on investment imports in 1949 were only half of the plan.[50] Investment imports for 1946-1949 amounted to only about one third of the targets set in the Three-Year Plan.[51] Although Polish exports were 18 percent higher in 1949 than originally planned, only 80 percent of the import plan was achieved, mainly due to the lack of foreign loans.[52] One noted Polish economic historian has claimed that this lack of foreign investment forced Poland into greater economic self-sufficiency, caused serious retardation in the growth of consumer industries, and resulted in the inefficient use of labor, materials and investments.[53]

Although the embargo prevented Poland from acquiring some technology and equipment that was unavailable in the Soviet bloc or in the Third World, until the summer of 1951 Poland was quite successful in obtaining some of these goods from Western Europe.[54] In November 1950, the State Department admitted that although Poland was being deprived of some American goods that were not "readily available elsewhere," Poland was getting some items on the embargo list from Western Europe, primarily from Sweden and Switzerland.[55] As for modernizing the coal industry with equipment from the West, in early 1951 the Office of Intelligence Research in the State Department found that Poland was meeting most of its import requirements through trade with Great Britain, France, Italy, and Sweden.[56] Sweden and Great Britain supplied about one half of the European machinery exported to the Soviet Union and Poland in 1950.[57] Sweden was Poland's main trading partner in Western Europe, and still supplied more than 20 percent of Western European machinery exports to the Soviet bloc in 1951. In 1952, this percentage declined when Swedish machinery exports to Poland dropped by about 14 percent.[58]

When Norway, West Germany, and Austria began to switch to other sources of coal in 1950, Polish coal exports to Western Europe dropped from 11.8 million tons in 1949 to 10.5 million tons in 1950, and declined again to 9.9 million tons in 1951. The drop in coal exports obviously affected Poland's bargaining position for needed industrial materials.[59] In June 1951, Cyrankiewicz asked the Polish people to support a $300 million loan fund to increase production in the raw materials industries.[60] Eugeniusz Szyr, the deputy chairman of the Polish State Economic Planning Commission, stated later in the year that "we must, without delay, develop our own raw material base for those areas in which imports are threatened."[61] The Ministry of Industry and Trade had already predicted in 1949 that if Poland did not receive any more foreign loans, the balance of payments would hinder the import of investment goods and slow the tempo of Polish economic growth.[62] Indeed, the importation of essential investment goods became even more difficult in the next few years; in 1952 the Poles were forced to sell over $1 million in gold to cover raw materials purchases and to repay credits.[63] In early 1953, the Swedish, Danish and Finnish diplomatic missions in Warsaw told Ambassador Flack that Poland was in great need of investment goods for the Six-Year Plan and that the decline in coal imports was causing serious payment problems.[64]

Publicly the Polish leadership stated that they did not need trade with the West, but the U.S. embassy in Warsaw reported in 1952 that "as regards trade relations with non-Soviet countries, Poland continued to talk out of both sides of her mouth." Western European diplomats in Warsaw told their American counterparts that "Poland was becoming increasingly embarrassed economically as a result of the lack of needed items which she could obtain only from the West."[65]

There was a marked change in Poland's attitude toward trade with the West after 1950. Since the inception of the ECE in 1947, Polish representatives to the ECE had cooperated with the West in facilitating and increasing intra-European trade. But in June 1950, for the first time the American delegation reported that Polish representative Juliusz Katz-Suchy was now "the most offensive EE [Eastern European] representative," while his predecessor, Tadeusz Lychowski, had been "the most moderate of the EE group." The American representatives added that Katz-Suchy's "consistently obnoxious behavior did more to unite [the] West and embarrass [the] East than any other single factor."[66] They even described the Soviet delegate as more compromising.[67]

That summer the U.S. embassy in Warsaw also reported that the Polish government was actively restricting trade with the West. According to a reliable source, Berman had instructed the heads of the economic departments to reduce trade with West as much as possible.[68] The ECA reported that Poland intended to double its trade with the Soviet Union during the period of the Six-Year Plan, and wanted to reduce its trade with the rest of the non-socialist countries by about one third.[69] Now Minc publicly stated that Poland would actively seek socialist economic connections, and that he would defend the Polish economy against dependence on the capitalist West.[70] But according to Władisław Landesberg, a defector from the Polish Ministry of Foreign Trade, until August 1950 "the rate at which Polish foreign trade has shifted from West to East has not been dictated by Polish or Soviet preference but by the impact of the strategic materials control exercised by the West." He contended that the Minc's arguments about maintaining Poland's economic independence from the capitalist countries was mere propaganda.[71] The remaining interest the Polish leadership had in trade with the West was dictated by the fact that Poland could not get some of its import needs from the socialist countries or from the Third World.

The countries of Western Europe that were dependent on Polish coal were the first to feel the effects of the tougher Polish trade policy in 1951. Austria, for example, had difficulty acquiring coal from Poland because the Poles insisted on steel, bearings and other machinery in return, and then raised the price of the coal 100 percent in March.[72] Poland warned Denmark that coal would be put on its own "strategic list" if the embargo continued.[73] When Norway, Sweden and Switzerland encountered similar difficulties in bargaining for Polish coal, the ECA recommended confronting Poland on a common front to force a drop in prices. When Poland began to export more of its coal to the Comecon countries, the share of Poland's exports to the developed capitalist countries dropped steadily from a high of 52.4 percent in 1948 to only 31.4 percent in 1952.[74]

There was a dramatic change in the direction of Polish trade after 1950. The Soviet share of Poland's trade increased 52 percent from 1948 to 1953, while in those same years trade with the capitalist countries dropped from 54 percent of Poland's trade to only 30 percent.[75] This shift in trade toward the Comecon countries was most dramatic in Poland's imports of investment goods. In 1948, imports of investment goods from the Soviet Union amounted to only 2 percent of Poland's investment imports, but during the period of the Six-year Plan the Soviet bloc share increased to 80 percent.[76] Polish imports of machines and transportation equipment from the Soviet Union and other socialist countries (including China) nearly doubled from 1950 to 1952.[77] They increased slightly with the developed capitalist countries as well from 1950 to 1951, but only because of the increased bargaining power of Polish coal in early 1951. These imports of machines and transportation equipment from the West declined from 1952 to 1956.[78]

In 1951, the Polish press also stepped up its criticism of the U.S. program for rearming Europe and restricting East-West trade. In February, *Życie Gospodarcze* called the Marshall Plan and the rearmament program "two parts of the same American enterprise, bringing economic ruin and political subjugation to the people of Western Europe."[79] The press chastised the West for the reconstruction of Germany, and equated the nazification of German society in the thirties with the renazification and remilitarization of West Germany under Chancellor Konrad Adenauer and American monopoly capitalists.[80] The press singled out American, German, and to a lesser extent British economic policies for the harshest criticism, but still called for international efforts to reduce trade barriers.[81]

A big propaganda opportunity for Poland came at the international trade conference held in Moscow in the spring of 1952. The Truman administration refused to attend the conference, but most of the Western European countries sent delegations, and several American businessmen attended unofficially.[82] The Polish press quoted one American, Arthur Deutsch, as stating that "assuring the American people full employment is possible only on the condition that United States trade is developed with all the countries of the world." According to Polish reporters, Deutsch also declared his opposition to any U.S. trade barriers against the socialist world.[83] The Polish press wrote that another American businessman at the conference, Oliver Vickery, had argued that the only way to avoid a third world war was through peaceful economic and cultural exchanges.[84]

The Polish delegation expressed interest in reviving trade all of the countries of Western Europe, even West Germany. The Poles maintained that the embargo was hurting Western Europe more than Poland. The Poles promised that if the West eliminated trade barriers, Poland would export more coal westward.[85] Undoubtedly this was an attempt to acquire Western technology, but in the frigid Cold War atmosphere of 1952, and because of the reduced demand for Polish coal in Western Europe, there was little Poland that could do or say to increase its trade the West.

IV

The primary objective of the Truman administration's strategic embargo of the Soviet bloc was to reduce the bloc's war-making potential. The United States hoped to create bottlenecks in the Eastern European economies that would retard the bloc's military buildup. Except for the lack of Western technology, however, Poland's armaments industries grew at a fast pace.[86] Minc had always given investment priority to heavy industries that could be converted for military use, while agriculture and other consumer industries suffered from a lack of modernization. As a result, Poland's standard of living rose very slowly in the first half of the fifties.

The embargo failed to reduce to any great extent the Polish contribution to Soviet bloc's defenses.[87] The CIA found that 7.2 percent of the Polish government's expenditures went to the military in 1948, and 9.9 percent in 1949.[88] The CIA also claimed that since the end of the war, a much greater proportion of the Soviet bloc GNP went to the military than in the West.[89] An American journalist reported in the spring of 1950 that Polish defense expenditures amounted to about 10 percent of the national budget.[90]

In fact, Polish defense spending was even higher than that. According to Politburo member Edward Ochab, the Soviets summoned representatives of the Comecon states to Moscow in 1950 to discuss an increase in defense spending. Ochab told the Soviets that a rapid arms buildup would exacerbate an already difficult economic situation in Poland, and warned the Soviets that "a worsening of the people's standard of living may threaten an outbreak of strikes." Nonetheless, the Polish government had to increase its defense spending, which Ochab said caused "disproportions and deformations in the Six-Year Plan."[91] Poland's revised economic plan called for five times more spending on the military in 1953 than in 1949, with the biggest increase of 74 percent coming in 1951 and 1952.[92] Berman admitted later that defense spending was closer to 15 percent of the budget in the early fifties, and maybe more.[93]

The Polish leadership claimed that Poland's defense expenditures were falling while criticizing the United States for increasing its military spending. In March 1950, a deputy in the Polish Diet contended that only 7.9 percent of the Polish budget was earmarked for defense that year, down from 8.4 percent in 1949.[94] He maintained that the United States was spending 60 percent of its federal budget on defense, and only 1 percent on cultural activities.[95] A year later another deputy claimed that Polish defense spending was only 7.2 percent of the budget for 1951, and alleged that U.S. defense spending amounted to 75 percent of the federal budget.[96] In the fall of 1951, the Poles conceded that defense spending had increased to 8 percent of the national budget, but only in reaction to the arms buildup in the West.[97] Polish propaganda became even more ludicrous in 1952. Polish Diet Deputy Dorota Kluszynska claimed that the United States was spending 85 percent of its federal budget on the military. She said that as a result the building of schools in the United States had been postponed and that instead of going to school, "eight-year old children were being worked to exhaustion" in American factories.[98]

Poland's military spending was a enormous drain on the economy, however. Henryk Różański, a Polish representative to Comecon, recalled later that defense spending really slowed Polish economic reconstruction in the early fifties, not the embargo.[99] An economist from the Secretariat of the Central Committee of the PZRP estimated that 80 percent of the machine-building industry served the needs of the military, leaving little investment for agriculture, consumer goods industries, and fuels industries.[100]

American economic policy toward Poland was primarily designed to stunt Poland's economic and military growth, but the Truman administration also hoped that the economic hardships caused by the embargo would promote Titoism. Furthermore, the administration searched in vain for a way to show its concern for the welfare of the Polish people.[101] There was no way to reconcile these aims, however, for aside from the moral support that the United States gave the Polish people through Radio Free Europe and the Voice of America, the economic sanctions had the effect of lowering the Polish people's standard of living.[102] American economic warfare did not push the Polish economy into any serious crisis in the early fifties, and the regime's political control was never threatened. In addition, an NSC report on U.S. policy toward Eastern Europe in 1951 admitted that "no fundamental change in the Soviet-satellite relation has become discernable."[103]

Although Polish economic performance lagged behind the West after the war, until the middle fifties life was getting relatively better. In certain sectors of the Polish economy relative growth far surpassed that of Western Europe. Electrical energy production jumped six times in Poland from 1937 to 1955, while approximately doubling in France, West Germany, and Italy. Steel production for these same years rose almost four times in Poland, dropped slightly in West Germany, doubled in Italy, and increased by approximately 50 percent in France. Per capita meat consumption in Poland in 1955 was 168 percent of the average meat consumption for 1933-1937. In contrast, West Germany's meat consumption in 1955 was only 87 percent of the average meat consumption for 1933-1937, Italy's 95 percent, and France's 118 percent.[104]

But by most measures Poland's standard of living could not compare to Western Europe's. In the fall of 1952, Poland was forced to ration meat, fats, soap, and sugar. Katz-Suchy, the Polish representative to the ECE, admitted that his government had to take this measure because of the slow growth in the agricultural industry.[105] The ECE estimated that the cost-of-living index in Poland increased 132 percent from 1949 to 1953.[106]

Another unavoidable impact of the embargo was the faster integration of the Comecon countries. The State Department had already guessed in the fall of 1949 that the embargo may "result not in

Titoism but only in accelerating the present rate of their integration into a Soviet bloc country."[107] Surprisingly, the Soviet Union's own economic recovery enabled it to provide at least a minimum of the needs for the Polish Six-Year Plan.[108] The Polish-Soviet trade agreement of June 1950 called for Poland to receive steel mills, an oil factory, and a total five-year credit of 400 million rubles (about $100 million) at 2 percent interest. The agreement also called for an increase of 34 percent in total trade between the two countries in 1950.[109]

Some of these items directly replaced American goods. For example, Poland never acquired the blooming and slabbing mill from the United States, and in 1949 the U.S. embassy in Warsaw reported that the biggest bottleneck to the "full functioning" of the Polish economy was the lack of the steel mill. On the other hand, the embassy admitted that a substitute Soviet mill would soon begin operating.[110] The giant steel works of Nova Huta near Cracow was the eventual result, and the mills were geared to use Soviet iron ore.[111] By the end of 1950, the State Department admitted that "our [embargo] policy has also resulted in stimulating indigenous production and eastern European integration, which in the long run will reduce Poland's dependence on the West."[112] Józef Winiewicz recalled later that this was indeed the case.[113]

V

A leading authority on U.S. economic sanctions contends that in few cases did an embargo result in a change in the political behavior of the target state: "There has been a striking consensus in the literature dealing with the economic sanctions suggesting that sanctions have often failed to achieve their avowed political purposes."[114] The economic embargo of Poland was no exception; the policy was not very successful in reducing the military potential of the Soviet bloc, in encouraging Titoism, or in somehow showing the Polish people that the United States still cared about their welfare. On the other hand, there is much evidence that American economic pressure on Poland assisted Soviet efforts to integrate the Polish economy into Comecon.

NOTES

1. See Gaddis, *Strategies of Containment: A Critical Appraisal of Postwar American National Security Policy*, 83-85, for a discussion of Acheson's militarization of containment and the policy of no negotiation; see Lloyd C. Gardner, *Architects of Illusion: Men and Ideas in American Foreign Policy* (Chicago: Quadrangle Books, 1970), 205; see Paterson, *On Every Front: The Making of the Cold War*, 171; and Graebner, *America as a World Power*, 154-155.

2. NSC-68, 14 April 1950, in Etzold and Gaddis, eds. *Containment: Documents on American Policy and Strategy, 1945-1950*, 401.

3. Flack to Acheson, 19 March 1951, *FRUS, 1951: Europe: Political and Economic Developments* (Washington: U.S. Government Printing Office, 1985), 4:1494. Waldemar Gallman resigned in June 1950, and Flack replaced him on 30 November 1950.

4. "Analysis of Senator McCarthy's Public Statements," Department of State *Bulletin*, 17 July 1950, 106; see also *Congressional Record*, 81st Cong., 2nd sess., 96:9183.

5. *New York Times*, 20 August 1951, 3.

6. CIA report, "Vulnerability of the Soviet Bloc to Economic Warfare," 19 February 1951, Truman Papers, PSF, NSC Meetings File, box 211.

7. Report by Lay to the NSC, 21 August 1950, *FRUS, 1950* 4:163-172; Department of State Policy Statement, 27 November 1950, ibid., 4:1040-1051; memorandum from Secretary of Commerce Sawyer to the NSC, 17 January 1951, *FRUS, 1951: National Security Affairs and Foreign Economic Policy* (Washington: U.S. Government Printing Office, 1979), 1:1001-1005; memorandum from Thorp) to Henry R. Labouisse (director of the Planning Staff of the European Affairs Division), 25 January 1951, ibid., 1:1009-1012; and "Report to the President on United States Policies and Programs Which May Affect the War Potential of the Soviet Bloc," 9 February 1951, ibid., 1:1028.

8. Testimony of Willard L. Thorp, 23 January 1951, U.S. Senate, 82nd Congress, 1st sess., Hearings of the Committee on Interstate and Foreign Trade, Senate Resolution 365, National Archives; Ambassador Joseph Flack to Acheson, 9 January 1951, RG 84, General Records, box 11; and Department of State Division of Research for USSR and

Eastern Europe report, "Poland Exploits European Coal Shortage," 16 March 1951, RG 286, Country Subject Files, box 3.

9. See Webb to the U.S. embassy in London, 10 March 1951, *FRUS, 1951* 4:1490-1492.

10. ECA report, "Trade of the Free World with the Soviet Bloc," February 1951, 14, Truman Papers, PSF, NSC Meetings File, box 211. Sweden received 40 percent of its coal from Poland in 1951, Denmark 28 percent, and Norway 26 percent.

11. United States House of Representatives, Hearings on the Mutual Defense Assistance Control Act of 1951, 3 April 1951, Committee on Foreign Affairs, *U.S. Foreign Policy and the East-West Confrontation*, Vol. 14: *Committee and Subcommittee Hearings and Briefings*, 13-20; see also U.S. House of Representatives, Hearings on the Mutual Defense Assistance Control Act of 1951, 5 April 1951, ibid., 182-186.

12. United States House of Representatives, Hearings on the Mutual Defense Assistance Control Act of 1951, 9 March 1951, *U.S. Foreign Policy and the East-West Confrontation*, 90-91; and ibid., 3 April 1951, 151-152.

13. See State Department Division of Research for USSR and Eastern Europe report, "Poland Exploits European Coal Shortage," 16 March 1951, RG 286, Country Subject Files, box 3. For example, the Netherlands exported rubber, tin, and diesel motors to Poland, and Sweden supplied Poland with the iron ore, pulp, and ball bearings that Poland could not get from the United States.

14. Flack to the Department of State, 1 April 1951, RG 59, 748.00, box 3606.

15. ECA report, "Trade of the Free World with the Soviet Bloc," February 1951, 69, 104, Truman Papers, PSF, NSC Meetings File, box 211.

16. Lay to the NSC, 21 August 1950, *FRUS, 1950* 4:163-172. This law was called the Cannon amendment.

17. This was also known as the Battle Act after its sponsor, Representative Laurie Battle of Michigan. See Adler-Karlsson, *Western Economic Warfare, 1947-1967: A Case Study in Foreign Economic Policy*, for a more detailed examination of the embargo.

18. CIA report, "Vulnerability of the Soviet Bloc to Economic Warfare," 19 February 1951, Truman Papers, PSF, NSC Meetings File, box 211.

19. "Polish Profiteering in Coal Exports to W. Europe," 27 February 1951, RG 286, Country Subject Files, box 3.

20. Flack to Acheson, 1 October 1951, RG 59, 748.00, box 3607; see also the annual economic report for 1951, in U.S. embassy in Warsaw to the Department of State, 31 March 1952, RG 59, 848.00, box 4931. The embassy reported that ball bearings, ships, iron ore, copper and cobalt from France, Finland, Austria, Sweden, Iceland, and a few other countries outside of Europe were being shipped to Poland.

21. Report prepared by the Department of State and the ECA, "Export of Automotive Parts via Denmark for Poland," 24 August 1951, *FRUS, 1951* 1:1169-1174; and memorandum by Linder (deputy assistant secretary of state for economic affairs) to Acheson, 28 August 1951, ibid., 1:1174-1176.

22. Memorandum of NSC meeting, 29 August 1951, Truman Papers, PSF, NSC Meeting Files, box 214.

23. Lovett (acting secretary of defense) to Foster (administrator of the ECA), 6 September 1951, *FRUS, 1951* 1:1177-1178.

24. Memorandum from Linder (deputy assistant for economic affairs) to Webb, 11 September 1951, *FRUS, 1951* 1:1180-1182.

25. State Department memorandum, unsigned, 10 October 1951, RG 59, 448.118-448.49B9, box 1992.

26. Letter by Al Borgen of Minneapolis, Minnesota, to Senator Hubert Humphrey (Minnesota), 25 October 1951, relayed to the Department of State, 9 November 1951, RG 59, 448.118-448.49B9, box 1992. Borgen wrote that the transaction "stinks."

27. Letter from Jack K. McFall (assistant secretary of state) to Representative Edward H. Rees (Kansas), 18 January 1952, RG 59, 448.118-448.49B9, box 1992. Poland supplied about 40 percent of Denmark's coal needs in 1950, but this figure dropped in 1951 when the Poles demanded auto parts for these exports.

28. Acheson to Senator Tom Connally (Texas), 9 June 1952, *FRUS, 1952-1954: General Economic and Political Matters* (Washington: U.S. Government Printing Office, 1983), 1:848.

29. Truman letter to Richard B. Russell, (chairman of the Senate Committee on Armed Services, 22 April 1952, Truman Papers, White House Central Files, Confidential File (Mutual Defense), box 26; and memorandum by Acheson and Harriman to Lay, 23 April 1952, *FRUS, 1952-1954* 1:837.

30. Memorandum from K. Mathiason to H.R. Rogers on the ECA Coal Program, 2 November 1951, RG 286, Commodity Subject Files, box 1, Coal File.

31. Webb to Vienna, 26 November 1951, RG 84, Classified General Records, box 11.

32. The ECA ended its operation when the first Battle Act passed in October 1951, and the Economic Defense Staff became part of the Mutual Security Administration headed by Averell Harriman. That agency was in the Agency for International Development, which replaced the ECA in 1952.

33. Welk to H.R. Rogers, 27 February 1952, RG 286, Commodity Files, box 1, Coal File.

34. H.R. Rogers to Arthur Syran, 6 March 1952, RG 286, Commodity Files, box 1, Coal File.

35. East-West Trade Studies No. 10, "The Problem of Replacing Coal Currently Imported from the Soviet Bloc with Free World Coal," 12 March 1952, RG 286, Commodity Files, box 1, Coal File.

36. Minutes of the Mutual Security Act Ad Hoc Coal Action Program Working Group, 8 April 1952, RG 286, Commodity Files, box 1, Coal File.

37. Memorandum by Acheson and Harriman to Lay, "Fifth Progress Report on NSC 104/2," 22 September 1952, *FRUS, 1952-1954* 1:876-896.

38. Memorandum by Acheson and Harriman to Lay, "Sixth Progress Report on NSC 104/2," 19 January 1953, *FRUS, 1952-1954* 1:913.

39. Memorandum by Thomas Bowie (second secretary of the U.S. embassy in Warsaw), 8 December 1949, RG 84, General Records, box 98.

40. U.S. embassy in Warsaw to the Department of State, 10 February 1950, RG 59, 748.00, box 3605.

41. Roy L. Lowry (second secretary of the U.S. embassy in Warsaw) to the Department of State, 11 March 1953, RG 59, 848.00-848.002, box 4931.

42. Edward S. Crocker to Marshall, 2 January 1948, RG 59, 860c.51, box 6385.

43. Henry C. Ramsey (second secretary of the U.S. embassy in Warsaw) to Marshall, 26 October 1948, RG 59, 711.60c, box 3426.

44. Alton, *Polish Postwar Economy*, 171.

45. J. Taylor, *The Economic Development of Poland, 1919-1950* (Ithaca: Cornell University Press, 1952), 202.

46. Alton, *Polish Postwar Economy*, 275; Kalinski, *Plan Odbudowy Gospodarczej, 1947-1949*, 267-268.

47. John Michael Montias, *Central Planning in Poland* (New Haven: Yale University Press, 1962), 53.

48. According to Alton, *Polish Postwar Economy*, 271, investment amounted to only 69 percent of the original draft targets of the Three-Year Plan, but in the revised versions overall investment amounted to 95 percent of the plan.

49. Stanisław Polaczek, *Integracja gospodarcza krajów socjalistycznych a handel zagraniczy Polski* [The economic integration of the socialist countries and the foreign trade of Poland] (Warsaw: Państwowe Wydawnictwo Ekonomiczne, 1971), 34.

50. Plan of non-investment agricultural imports, 1948, Central Planning Office Records, File 2393; and Alton, *Polish Postwar Economy*, 274.

51. Alton, *Polish Postwar Economy*, 273.

52. Wojciechowski, "Handel Zagraniczny Polski," 375.

53. Kalinski, *Plan Odbudowy Gospodarczej, 1947-1949*, 98.

54. See Adler-Karlsson, *Western Economic Warfare, 1947-1967: A Case Study in Foreign Economic Policy*, 73, 199. Until May 1950, one of the leaks in the embargo program was trade between West and East Germany. One West German Social Democrat estimated that trade in embargoed items amounted to 70 percent of all trade.

55. Department of State Policy Statement, 27 November 1950, *FRUS, 1950* 4:1051.

56. State Department Office of Intelligence Research report, "Vulnerability of the Soviet Bloc to Existing and Tightened Western Economic Controls," 26 January 1951, Truman Papers, PSF, NSC Meetings File, box 211.

57. ECE *Economic Bulletin for Europe* 3:2 (1951): 53.

58. ECE *Economic Bulletin for Europe* 4:3 (1952): 38-39; and ECE *Economic Bulletin for Europe* 5:2 (1953): 46.

59. ECE *Economic Bulletin for Europe* 4:3 (1952): 42.

60. *New York Times*, 20 June 1951, 11.

61. Szyr speech in *Nowe Drogi*, December 1951, reported by Roy Lowry (second secretary of the U.S. embassy in Warsaw) to the Department of State, 3 June 1952, RG 59, 848.00, box 4931; see also

Saheen Ayubi, etal., *Economic Sanctions in U.S. Foreign Policy* (Philadelphia: Foreign Policy Research Institute, 1982), 79, for a discussion of how self-reliance often develops in a embargoed country.

62. Notes on the matter of foreign investment credits, undated (ca. June 1949), Ministry of Industry and Trade Records, File 3004.

63. Kalinski, *Polityka Gospodarcza Polski w latach 1948-1956*, 192.

64. Flack to the secretary of state, 13 January 1953, RG 84, Classified General Records, box 20.

65. Annual economic report for 1952, in U.S. embassy in Warsaw to the Department of State, 11 March 1953, RG 59, 848.00, box 4931.

66. The U.S. Resident Delegation to the ECE to Acheson, 16 June 1950, *FRUS, 1950* 4:35.

67. Department of State Policy Statement, 27 November 1950, *FRUS, 1950* 4:1049.

68. Warsaw to Acheson, 31 August 1950, RG 59, 848.00, box 4931.

69. Statement by Robert N. Golding (special assistant to the deputy administrator, ECA) during House Committee on Foreign Affairs hearings on the Battle Act, 5 April 1951, U.S. House of Representatives, *U.S. Foreign Policy and the East-West Confrontation*, 177.

70. Annual economic report for 1950, in U.S. embassy in Warsaw to the Department of State, 18 June 1951, RG 59, 848.00, box 4931; and *Życie Gospodarcze* 6 (16 October 1951): 1100.

71. Walter J. Stoessel (acting chief, Peripheral Report Unit, HICOG, Frankfurt) to the Department of State, 8 May 1952, RG 59, 400.46E9-400.516, box 1782. Landesberg defected in December 1951.

72. National Security Council Determination 2, 14 June 1951, Truman Papers, Records of the National Security Council, box 5, Truman Library, Independence, Missouri.

73. Mr. Spofford (U.S deputy representative on the North Atlantic Council) to Acheson, 24 April 1951, *FRUS, 1951* 4:1501-1503.

74. United States embassy in Norway to the ECA mission in Paris, 1 August 1951, RG 286, Country Subject Files, box 8; Office of the U.S. Special Representative to the OEEC to Acheson, 2 August 1951, ibid.

75. Bruno Kiesewetter, *Der Ostblock: Aussenhandel des östlichen Wirtschaftsblockes einschliesslich China* [The eastern bloc: the foreign trade of the eastern economic bloc including China] (Berlin: Safari Verlag, 1960), 36-37; see also Spulber, "Problems of East-West Trade and Economic Trends in the European Satellites of Soviet Russia," 398. Poland's total trade increased 51 percent from 1948 to 1952, and trade with the Soviet bloc increased
197 percent.

76. Kalinski, *Polityka Gospodarcza Polski w latach 1948-1956*, 191.

77. Ciepielewski, "Współpraca Gospodarcza Polski z Europejskim Krajami Socjalistycznymi," 413, 420; see also Gajda, *Polska Polityka Zagraniczna, 1944-1971*, 101. The socialist countries' share of total Polish trade increased from 44 percent in 1949 to 70 percent in 1953.

78. Długosz and Szczepaniec, *Stosunki handlowe Polski z rozwiniętymi krajami kapitalistycznymi*, 142; see also Janusz Kalinski, "Planowanie Gospodarcze." [Economic planning], in *Gospodarka Polski Ludowej, 1944-1955*, eds. Janusz Kalinski and Zbigniew Landau (Warsaw: Książka i Wiedza, 1986), 397. From 1951 to 1955 Poland received 23 percent of its imports of machines and equipment from capitalist countries.

79. *Życie Gospodarcze* 6 (1 February 1951): 129.

80. See for example *Życie Gospodarcze* 6 (16 October 1951): 1144-1147; *Życie Warszawy*, 1 January 1952, 1; and *Życie Warszawy*, 18 January 1952, 2.

81. See for example *Życie Gospodarcze* 7 (14 January 1952): 74-77; *Życie Gospodarcze* 7 (26 January 1952): 145-146; *Życie Gospodarcze* 7 (25 February 1952): 255-266; *Życie Gospodarcze* 7 (24 March 1952): 346-348; and Polish Diet Records, 29 February 1952, 26.

82. *Życie Warszawy*, 2 April 1952, 1; *Życie Warszawy*, 3 April 1952, 1-2; and *Życie Warszawy*, 5 April 1952, 1.

83. *Życie Warszawy*, 10 April 1952, 1.

84. *Życie Gospodarcze* 7 (21 April 1952): 489-493.

85. United States embassy in Warsaw to the Department of State, 21 April 1952, Records Group 166, Forest and Agricultural Service, Narrative Reports, 1950-1954, box 356, Poland-Foreign Trade File, National Archives; see Winiewicz, *Co pamiętam z długiej drogi życia*, 442; and *Życie Gospodarcze* 7 (5 May 1952): 554-555.

86. See Montias, *Central Planning in Poland*, 64-65.

87. See Hogan, *The Marshall Plan: America, Britain, and the Reconstruction of Western Europe, 1947-1952*, 393. The increase in defense spending by the European NATO countries from 1949 to 1951 was more successful in achieving this objective. According to Hogan, defense expenditures increased from $4.4 billion in 1949 to $8 billion in 1951.

88. CIA report 59-49, 2 August 1949, Truman Papers, PSF, Intelligence File, box 256.

89. CIA report 64-66, 12 November 1952, Truman Papers, PSF, Intelligence File, box 256. Part of the increased defense spending was due to the introduction of military conscription in Poland in 1949.

90. *Washington Evening Star*, 30 May 1950, cited in *Congressional Record*, 81st Congress, 2nd sess., 96:A429.

91. Ochab interview in Torańska, *Oni*, 37-38; see also Sokolowski, *Obroty zagraniczne Polski w okresie 1945-1958*, 10; and Eugeniusz Szyr quoted from *Nowe Drogi*, December 1951, in Lowry to the Department of State, 3 June 1952, RG 59, 848.00, box 4931.

92. Alton, *Polish Postwar Economy*, 222-223.

93. Berman interview in Torańska, *Oni*, 309.

94. Polish Diet Records, 6 March 1950, 41.

95. Polish Diet Records, 6 March 1950, 47; and ibid., 23 March 1950, 119.

96. Polish Diet Records, 27 April 1951, 8.

97. Speech by Stefan Wierblowski at the U.N. General Assembly, 26 September 1951, *Zbiór Dokumentów* 1 (September 1951): 28-54.

98. Polish Diet Records, 28 March 1952, 107-112; see also ibid., 1 August 1952, 46. The Polish communists portrayed women and children as the victims of the capitalist monopoly economies in the United States and Western Europe. In this session one deputy alleged that wages and salaries for women in the West were about 20 percent less than those for men, which in this case was probably true.

99. Interview by author with Henryk Różański, 22 March, 1988, Warsaw.

100. Montias, *Central Planning in Poland*, 62-64.

101. Department of State Policy Statement, 27 November 1950, *FRUS, 1950* 4:1040-1051.

102. See Donald L. Losman, *International Economic Sanctions* (Albuquerque: University of New Mexico Press, 1979), 127. Losman quotes another authority on economic sanctions, John Galtung, who says that "the collective nature of economic sanctions makes them hit the innocent along with the guilty." The Polish people suffered more from the sanctions than those Poles who actively supported the regime.

103. NSC progress report on the implementation of NSC 58/2, 22 May 1951, Truman Papers, PSF, NSC Meetings File, box 212.

104. From the *Yearbook of the Food and Agricultural Association, 1956*, and *Rocznik Statystyczny, 1956*, in Józef Krynicki, *Problemy Handlu Zagranicznego Polski, 1918-1939, 1945-1955* [Problems of Polish foreign trade, 1918-1939, 1945-1955] (Warsaw: Państwowe Wydawnictwo Naukowe, 1958), 200-201.

105. *New York Times*, 12 November 1952, 10.

106. Montias, *Central Planning in Poland*, 70.

107. Memorandum prepared in the Department of State by the OIT, 4 April 1950, *FRUS, 1950* 4:108.

108. See Losman, *International Economic Sanctions*, 17, 128, who argues that sanctions have more impact if the states are in geographical proximity and if the economic damage is sufficient to create "domestic political pressures." The Soviet Union would not allow the Polish economy to collapse, or domestic pressures to topple the regime.

109. Kalinski, *Polityka Gospodarcza Polski w latach 1948-1956*, 189-190; and Taylor, *The Economic Development of Poland, 1919-1950*, 198.

110. Memorandum by Bowie, 24 October 1949, RG 84, General Records, box 98.

111. Wandycz, *The United States and Poland*, 347.

112. Department of State Policy Statement, 27 November 1950, *FRUS, 1950* 4:1051; see Margaret P. Doxey, *Economic Sanctions and International Enforcement* (New York: Oxford University Press, 1980), 111-112; see also Pollard, *Economic Security and the Origins of the Cold War*, 356, who likewise states that Eastern Europe as a whole became more independent from the West because of the development of their own industries.

113. Winiewicz, *Co pamiętam z długiej drogi życia*, 440; see Sokolowski, *Obroty zagraniczne Polski w okresie 1945-1958*, 10; see Pollard, *Economic Security and the Origins of the Cold War*, 247; and see also Adler-Karlsson, *Western Economic Warfare, 1947-1967: A*

Case Study in Foreign Economic Policy, 89. Karlsson writes that "the Western policy up till 1953 may have actually contributed to Stalin's successfully realizing one of his policy aims. It is of interest to note that in some of the interviews for this book with East European politicians and economists this point was emphatically given as the most important effect of the embargo policy."

114. Ayubi, etal, *Economic Sanctions in U.S. Foreign Policy*, 3.

Conclusion

I

In the atmosphere of suspicion and distrust that existed between the communist countries and the United States after the Second World War, the development of a friendly economic relationship between the United States and Poland called for tactful, well-coordinated economic diplomacy on both sides. The inability of either government to devise a skillful strategy often resulted in the failure of both to attain their respective goals. By the end of the Truman presidency, Poland was squarely under Soviet dominance, and direct Polish-American economic links were limited to little more than Polish exports of ham and Christmas ornaments.

On a broad scale, the foreign policy of the Truman administration was founded on the principle of protecting the national security of the United States.[1] This security was most often promoted through the "peace and prosperity" theme. In other words, if the United States developed the political and economic welfare of all peoples, then the United States would also enjoy domestic tranquility and peaceful foreign relations. As a result, the Truman administration publicly promoted democratic governments and the free market economies,[2] thinking that the United States could best avoid another depression and another world war by ensuring the economic health of the world. One diplomatic historian of the period has contended that "Washington policymakers seldom lost sight of their long-term objective: the creation of a multilateral global economy which would bring economic harmony and political stability to the postwar world — and financial benefits to American workers and businessmen."[3]

These general principles of American foreign policy remained firm during the Truman years, but the administration was less sure about how to implement its foreign policy in the case of Poland. Controversy within the U.S. government over the priorities of its foreign economic policy, as well as disagreements over the implementation of the policy in Poland undermined the realization of some policy goals. Certainly the Truman administration wanted a democratic Poland that would have a modicum of independence from the Soviet Union.[4] Given the administration's fear of a postwar depression, however, one of the primary objectives of American economic policy in the immediate postwar period was to develop the Polish economy to ensure its cooperation with Western Europe. The Truman administration's primary interest in Poland was not to eliminate the influence of leftist parties or to develop a free market economy there.[5] The Open Door to Poland was important, but a socialist economy could also trade with the West. Washington was also genuinely interested in Polish economic recovery for humanitarian reasons, as is evidenced by the extensive American relief contributions to Poland through the United Nations.[6]

The Truman administration did not reap the desired political benefits from its economic assistance to Poland in the first two years after the war, however. American relief aid and loans to Poland did not result in a reduction of Soviet political influence in the country. The Polish communist government did not allow free elections or develop a free market economy. On the other hand, American economic assistance helped the remarkably swift Polish recovery and facilitated Polish coal shipments to Western Europe. In this sense the administration met the humanitarian and economic goals of its policy toward Poland in the immediate postwar period.

With Poland's economy on the rebound by 1947, and Poland's shipments of coal to Western Europe increasing, political objectives now took priority in the administration's economic policy toward Poland. Of course, the deterioration in Washington's relations with the Soviet Union were another important factor in the administration's new foreign economic policy.[7] The administration made further economic assistance contingent on an improvement of the political climate in Poland and on the degree to which the Polish government showed its independence from the Soviet Union. The denial of any economic assistance after 1947 also did not have an impact on the dominant position of the Moscow-loyal communists in the Polish government. Poland's rejection of the Marshall Plan confirmed the perception of many U.S. government officials that the Polish government was a Soviet satellite in the economic sense as well, and that most of the Polish economy was geared to serve the interests of the Soviet Union. This was not yet the case.

In 1948, when war with the Soviet bloc seemed a real possibility, the United States began an embargo of most industrial goods. But the haphazard way in which the embargo was implemented, the lack of cooperation from Western Europe, and the ability of Poland to bargain coal for strategic items in Western Europe undermined the strategic objectives of the export licensing program. In addition, the American embargo on Poland failed to encourage national communism in Tito's mold. Rather than punish the communists, the embargo hurt the economic well being of the people of Poland who opposed the Polish regime.

The punitive American economic aid policy and the economic embargo achieved no political results. The Polish leadership frequently warned American officials that they would not make any political concessions for American trade or aid, and they did not budge from this position.[8] On the other hand, American economic policy actually contributed to Poland's greater economic dependence on the Soviet Union and Eastern Europe. The embargo also failed to retard Poland's military buildup significantly.[9] The increase in military spending in the West after the outbreak of the Korean War was met with changes in the Polish Six-Year Plan that increased defense spending. That spending forced the Polish government to underinvest in agriculture and consumer industries. American officials misjudged the Polish communists' willingness and ability to compromise the average Pole's standard of living in order to increase military spending.[10]

Toward the end of the 1940s these economic sanctions, rather than the Polish government's economic trade policy or the Kremlin's orders to sever economic connections with the West, pushed Poland into a greater dependence on the Soviet Union for trade and loans.[11] It made economic sense for Poland to be linked to the more prosperous West, thus reducing the burden of reconstruction on the Soviet Union, which of course had its own monumental reconstruction problem.[12] But as Swedish economist Gunnar Myrdal has contended, the American export embargo of strategic goods to Eastern Europe actually "greatly helped Stalin, and his cadre of politicians throughout the bloc to consolidate his empire."[13] By 1948 the State Department recognized that this was a possible side effect of the embargo, but strategic considerations mitigated against revising the policy. And when the Polish government was unable to gain needed loans and goods from the United States, the Soviet Union was able to provide some of Poland's needs. Soviet economic assistance and trade agreements helped the Polish government to meet the minimum requirements of the Polish people. As a result, the government achieved a modicum of public support for the first few years after the war. On balance, the conclusion can be made that U.S. economic policy was as much responsible for the integration of the Polish economy into Comecon as were Soviet attempts to bring Poland into its economic sphere.

On the other hand, Polish economic diplomacy was little more successful than American policy in achieving some of its main objectives. At the same time that some Polish officials were pleading for economic assistance from the United States, communist propagandists proclaimed the superiority of the socialist system and the ills of American capitalism, and some even maintained that socialist Poland really did not need economic assistance from the West. The Foreign economic assistance fell far short of the Polish government's official plans. Poland received only $90 million in loans from the United States during the Truman administration, and did not receive anything from the IBRD. Although the Polish communists had some success overcoming the embargo through the sale of coal to Western Europe, by the early fifties the Polish economy was really beginning to feel the effects of the lack of new technology and the reduction in trade with the West.

II

The Truman administration hoped that its economic embargo of the Soviet bloc would cause the socialist regimes to fall from economic stagnation and unfavorable comparisons to the more prosperous West. During the presidential campaign of 1952, General Dwight D. Eisenhower attacked the passive and reactive nature of Truman's containment policy. Eisenhower argued that the United States was not doing enough to liberate Eastern Europe from the Soviet Union. The lack of a forceful U.S. response to the uprisings in Czechoslovakia and East Germany in 1953 and to the Hungarian revolt in 1956 proved that Eisenhower's "policy of liberation" was little more than campaign rhetoric, and even Churchill criticized it.[14]

President Eisenhower did reevaluate American economic policy toward Eastern Europe, however. Eisenhower recognized that except for preventing the Soviet bloc from acquiring Western military technology, the embargo policy was largely a failure. Eisenhower thought that the distinction between some strategic and non-strategic goods made little sense given the complex interdependence of an industrial economy. Shortly after taking office he ordered a review of the policy, and adopted a policy that allowed Western Europe to increase its trade with Eastern Europe. Eisenhower tried to eliminate the one lever that Poland had to bargain for genuine strategic items, however, by increasing Western European coal production to replace Polish coal imports.[15] By the end of 1953 Poland's bargaining power was significantly reduced.[16]

Political reality prevented Eisenhower from lobbying publicly for a more liberal trade policy toward Poland, however, and there was also considerable opposition within his own administration to any change in the strict embargo policy.[17] The public's anti-communism had reached such a fever pitch by 1953 that many Americans questioned any trade with the Soviet bloc. For example, a New Jersey woman wrote the president expressing dismay over finding the label "Made in Poland" on her daughter's doll, and asked if "there is anything that we can do as mothers and American citizens to protect our children?" She wanted to know if the U.S. government condoned such trade.[18]

Nonetheless, Eisenhower followed the recommendations of his Commission on Foreign Economic Policy and limited the embargo to items that were "genuinely strategic." The commission thought that some trade in non-strategic items was a means for the West to maintain contact with the people of Eastern Europe, as well as a way to reduce the amount of American aid needed by Western Europe.[19] The Eisenhower administration reduced the number of items on the embargo lists by almost one half in 1954.[20]

III

In his 1985 monograph on U.S. economic policy and origins of the Cold War, Robert Pollard observed that

> the fact that Washington was unable to win political concessions from the Soviet-bloc countries during the late 1940s, when American economic leverage was at its peak, should give pause to later generations of U.S. policymakers entertaining the thought of sanctions.[21]

Perhaps one of the most important reasons for placing economic sanctions on Poland and the Soviet bloc was moral and emotional. The United States was frustrated in its attempts to find direct methods of furthering democracy in Eastern Europe. Even if the sanctions did not always produce the desired results, they fulfilled an emotional need to do something concrete to express American displeasure with communist policies. The advantages of the economic embargo in political terms were small if any, but as one historian has observed, the embargo "served as a safety-valve for wounded feelings and the general sense of hopelessness."[22]

Although this policy may have appeased the passions of American government officials and the American people, Truman administration officials generally did not seriously evaluate the effects of American economic policy toward Poland, or make changes in the policy if some of its objectives were not being met. John L. Gaddis points out that "reconsiderations [of foreign policy] require time, energy, and intellectual effort, commodities always in short supply."[23] American economic policy toward Poland throughout the Cold War resulted in increased economic hardship for the Polish people, for whom the United States repeatedly expressed its sympathy. The people of Poland will feel the long-range effects of American economic policy toward Poland during the Cold War long after the fall of communism.

NOTES

1. Pollard, *Economic Security and the Origins of the Cold War*, 7, 57; Gaddis, *Strategies of Containment*, 1982), 27; and Gaddis, "The Emerging Post-Revisionist Synthesis on the Origins of the Cold War," 173.

2. Paterson, *Soviet-American Confrontation: Postwar Reconstruction and the Origins of the Cold War*, 19.

3. Robert Hathaway, "1933-1945: Economic Diplomacy in a Time of Crisis," in *Economics and World Power: An Assessment of American Diplomacy Since 1789*, eds. William H. Becker and Samuel F. Wells, Jr. (New York: Columbia University Press, 1984), 320.

4. See Eduard Mark, "American Policy toward Eastern Europe and the Origins of the Cold War, 1941-1946: An Alternative Interpretation," *Journal of American History* 68 (September 1981): 327-332; and Pollard, *Economic Security and the Origins of the Cold War, 1945-1950*, 41,49. The Truman administration recognized that Eastern Europe would become a Soviet sphere of influence, but as Mark argues, it was the extent to which Moscow dominated politics there that disturbed Washington.

5. See Kolkos, *The Limits of Power: The World and United States Foreign Policy, 1945-1954* for this view. Gaddis refutes this view in "The Emerging Post-Revisionist Synthesis on the Origins of the Cold War," 174; see also Pollard, *Economic Security and the Origins of the Cold War, 1945-1950*, 4.

6. See Ambrose, *Rise to Globalism: American Foreign Policy 1938-1976*, 17. Ambrose argues that in the first five years the Truman administration was concerned primarily with economic objectives. By the middle of 1946, the primary goals for American economic policy were political as well as economic; see also Witold Jurasz, *Wpływ zagranicznej polityki ekonomicznej USA na rozwój polskiego eksportu do Stanów Zjednoczonych w latach 1946-1947*, 41. Jurasz argues that political objectives were always foremost in the minds of American officials, even before 1946.

7. Pollard and Wells, Jr., "1945-1960: The Era of American Economic Hegemony," 387; and Pollard, *Economic Security and the Origins of the Cold War, 1945-1950*, 23.

8. Several historians have criticized the absence of debate within the U.S. government over the effectiveness of the embargo. See Adler-Karlsson, *Western Economic Warfare, 1947-1967: A Case Study in Foreign Economic Policy*, 8, 31, 36; and Pollard, *Economic Security and the Origins of the Cold War, 1945-1950*, 242.

9. See Adler-Karlsson, *Western Economic Warfare, 1947-1967: A Case Study in Foreign Economic Policy*, 86; and Kovrig, *The Myth of Liberation: East-Central Europe in U.S. Diplomacy and Politics since 1941*, 93.

10. Wolf, *U.S. East-West Trade Policy: Economic Warfare Versus Economic Welfare*, 82; see also Paterson, *Soviet-American Confrontation: Postwar Reconstruction and the Origins of the Cold War*, 45.

11. See Paterson, *Soviet-American Confrontation: Postwar Reconstruction and the Origins of the Cold War*, 136; see also Samuel Pisar, *Coexistence and Commerce: Guidelines for Transactions Between East and West* (New York: McGraw-Hill Book Co., 1970), 2, 16; and see also Mark, "American Policy toward Eastern Europe and the Origins of the Cold War, 332-3.

12. Thompson, "The New Poland," 236.

13. Paterson, *Soviet-American Confrontation: Postwar Reconstruction and the Origins of the Cold War*, 74.

14. See Kovrig, *The Myth of Liberation: East-Central Europe in U.S. Diplomacy and Politics since 1941*; and Graebner, *America as a World Power*, 193.

15. Memorandum of discussion at the NSC meeting of 18 March 1953, *FRUS, 1952-1954* 1:939-942.

16. Krynicki, *Problemy Handlu Zagranicznego Polski, 1918-1939, 1945-1955*, 271. France imported about one fourth of the amount of coal in 1953 that it had imported in 1949. Norway and Italy imported less than half, and Sweden imported about two thirds.

17. Memorandum of discussion at the NSC meeting of 18 March 1953, *FRUS, 1952-1954* 1:939-942; memorandum for the secretary of defense from Arthur Radford (chairman of the Joint Chiefs of Staff), 16 December 1953, Eisenhower Papers, White House Office, Office of the Special Assistant for National Security Affairs, box 2, Eisenhower Library, Abilene, Kansas.

18. Letter from Adelaide Krumm to Eisenhower, 1 November 1953, RG 59, 411.46E3-411.489, box 1836.

19. Lamar Fleming, Jr. memorandum to the members of the Commission on Foreign Economic Policy, 17 December 1953, Commission on Foreign Economic Policy Records, 1953-1954, Eisenhower Library, Abilene, Kansas; and ibid., 30 December 1953.

20. J. Wilczynski, *The Economics and Politics of East-West Trade: A Study of Trade Between Developed Market Economies and Centrally Planned Economies in a Changing World* (London: MacMillan, 1969), 271; and Spulber, "Problems of East-West Trade and Economic Trends

in the European Satellites of Soviet Russia," 416. Further reductions in the list were made in 1957 and 1958.

21. Pollard, *Economic Security and the Origins of the Cold War*, 250.

22. Robert F. Byrnes, "Containment? Liberation? Coexistence? American Policy Toward East Central Europe, 1947-1955," in Stephen Kertesz, ed. *The Fate of East Central Europe: Hope and Failures of American Foreign Policy* (South Bend: University of Notre Dame Press, 1956): 85.

23. Gaddis, *Strategies of Containment: A Critical Appraisal of Postwar American National Security Policy*, 87.

Bibliography

UNPUBLISHED DOCUMENTS

Archiwum Akt Nowych [Archive of new records]. Warsaw.

Polish Government. Centralny Urząd Planowania, Akty 1945-1947 [Central planning office, records 1945-1947].

Polish Government. Komitet Ekonomiczny Rady Ministrów. Podkomitet do Międzynarodowych Spraw Gospodarczych, Akty 1945-1946 [Economic committee of the council of ministers, subcommittee of international economic affairs, records 1945-1946].

Polish Government. Komitet Ekonomiczny Rady Ministrów. Protokoły Posiedzenia Prezydium i Plenum Komitetu Ekonomicznego, 1945-1946 [Economic committee of the council of ministers. Protocols of the meetings of the presidium and plenary session of the economic committee, 1945-1946].

Polish Government. Ministerstwo Przemyslu i Handlu, Akty 1945-1947, 1949 [Ministry of industry and trade, records 1945-1947, 1949].

Polish Government. Prezydium Rady Ministrów, Akty 1945-1947 [Presidium of the council of ministers, records 1945-1947].

National Archives. Washington, D.C.

United States Department of Commerce. Central Correspondence File of the Office of the Secretary of Commerce, 1950-1955.

United States Department of State. Records Group 59. General Records of the Department of State. Decimal File, 1945-1949, 1950-1954.

United States Department of State. Records Group 59. General Records of the Department of State. General Records of the Office of the Executive Secretariat. Position Papers and Reports on Undersecretary Meetings, 1945-1952.

United States Department of State. Records Group 273. National Security Council Reports, 1947-1952.

United States Government. Records Group 166. Forest and Agricultural Service. Narrative Reports, 1950-1954.

United States Government. Records Group 286. Agency for International Development. Economic Cooperation Administration. Economic Defense Staff Reports, 1948-1952.

United States Government. Records Group 275. Export-Import Bank. *Minutes of the Export-Import Bank.* Vol. 6, 1946.

United States. Senate. Committee of Agriculture and Forestry. Hearings. 81st Cong., 1st sess., 1949.

United States. Senate. Committee on Foreign Relations. Hearings. 81st Cong., 1st sess., 1949.

United States. Senate. Committee on Interstate and Foreign Trade. Hearings. 82nd Cong., 1st sess., 1951.

National Records Center. Suitland, Maryland.

United States Department of State. Records Group 84. Foreign Service Posts of the Department of State. U.S. Embassy. Warsaw, Poland, 1945-1952.

Eisenhower Library. Abilene, Kansas.

Commission on Foreign Economic Policy (Randall Commission), Records, 1953-1954.

Eisenhower, Dwight D. Papers.

Truman Library. Independence, Missouri.

Acheson, Dean Papers.

Blaisdell, Thomas C. Jr. Papers.

Griffis, Stanton Papers.

Sawyer, Charles Papers.

Truman, Harry S. Papers.

INTERVIEWS

Kolipinski, Juliusz, aide to Władysław Gomułka, 1945-1948. Interview by author, 15 March 1988, Warsaw.

Rączkowski, Stanisław, vice director of economic organization in the Central Planning Office, 1946-1948. Interview by author, 10 March, 1988, Warsaw.

Różański, Henryk, Polish representative to Comecon, 1949-1954. Interview by author, 22 March, 1988, Warsaw.

PUBLISHED DOCUMENTS

Compendium Statystyczne Polskiego Handlu Zagranicznego w latach 1929-1938, 1945-1960 [Statistical compendium of Polish foreign trade, 1929-1938, 1945-1960]. Warsaw: Polska Izba Handlu Zagranicznego, 1961.

Etzold, Thomas H. and John L. Gaddis, eds. *Containment: Documents on American Policy and Strategy, 1945-1950.* New York: Columbia University Press, 1978.

Kozlowski, Ryszard and Jan Sziling, eds. *Historia PRL 1944-1950: Wybór Zrodel* [History of the People's Republic of Poland 1944-1950: Selected sources]. Torun: University of Mikolaj Kopernika Press, 1978.

Polish Government. Centralny Urząd Planowania. *Sytuacja Gospodarcza Polski* [Central planning office. The economic situation of Poland]. Warsaw, 1947.

Polish Government. Krajowy Rada Narodowa. *Sprawozdanie Stenograficzne, 1944-1946* [Polish national council, stenographic records, 1944-1946].

Polish Government. Sejm Ustawodawczy. *Sprawozdanie Stenograficzne, 1947-1952* [Polish legislative diet, stenographic records, 1947-1949].

Polish Ministry of Foreign Affairs. *Documents on the Hostile Policy of the United States Government Towards Peoples' Poland.* Warsaw, 1953.

United Nations. Economic Committee for Europe. Coal Division. "United Nations Monthly Bulletin of Coal Statistics." December 1950.

United Nations. Economic Committee for Europe. *Economic Bulletin for Europe*, 1949-1953.

United Nations. Economic Committee for Europe. Economic and Social Council Reports, 1948-1949.

United Nations. Reconstruction and Relief Administration. Operational Analysis Paper 1: *Transport Rehabilitation in Poland*. London, 1946.

United Nations. Relief and Rehabilitation Administration. Operational Analysis Paper 7: *Foreign Trade in Poland*. London, 1946.

United Nations. *Yearbook of the United Nations, 1948-1949*. New York: Columbia University Press, 1950.

United States Department of State. *Bulletin*, 1947-1952.

United States Department of State. *Foreign Relations of the United States*. Vols. 1-2, 1945: *The Conference of Berlin*. Washington, D.C.: United States Government Printing Office, 1960.

United States Department of State. *Foreign Relations of the United States*. Vol. 5, 1945: *Europe*. Washington, D.C.: United States Government Printing Office, 1967.

United States Department of State. *Foreign Relations of the United States*. Vol. 6, 1946: *Eastern Europe; the Soviet Union*. Washington, D.C.: United States Government Printing Office, 1969.

United States Department of State. *Foreign Relations of the United States*. Vol. 7, 1946: *The Near East and Africa*. Washington, D.C.: United States Government Printing Office, 1969.

United States Department of State. *Foreign Relations of the United States*. Vol. 1, 1947: *General; The United Nations*. Washington, D.C.: United States Government Printing Office, 1973.

United States Department of State. *Foreign Relations of the United States*. Vol. 4, 1947: *Eastern Europe; the Soviet Union*. Washington, D.C.: United States Government Printing Office, 1972.

United States Department of State. *Foreign Relations of the United States*. Vol. 4, 1948: *Eastern Europe; the Soviet Union*. Washington, D.C.: United States Government Printing Office, 1974.

United States Department of State. *Foreign Relations of the United States*. Vol. 5, 1949: *Eastern Europe; the Soviet Union*. Washington, D.C.: United States Government Printing Office, 1976.

United States Department of State. *Foreign Relations of the United States*. Vol. 4, 1950: *Central and Eastern Europe; the Soviet Union*. Washington, D.C.: United States Government Printing Office, 1980.

United States Department of State. *Foreign Relations of the United States*. Vol. 1, 1951: *National Security Affairs; Foreign Economic Policy*. Washington, D.C.: United States Government Printing Office, 1979.

United States Department of State. *Foreign Relations of the United States*. Vol. 4, Pt. 2, 1951: *Europe: Political and Economic Developments*. Washington, D.C.: United States Government Printing Office, 1985.

United States Department of State. *Foreign Relations of the United States*. Vol. 1, Pt. 2, 1952-1954: *General: Economic and Political Matters*. Washington, D.C.: United States Government Printing Office, 1983.

United States. House of Representatives. Committee on Foreign Affairs. *U.S. Foreign Policy and the East-West Confrontation*, Vol. 14: Committee and Subcommittee Hearings and Briefings. Washington, D.C.: U.S. Government Printing Office, 1980.

MEMOIRS

Bobrowski, Czesław. *Wspomnienia ze stulecia* [Memoirs from a century]. Lublin: Wydawnictwo Lubelskie, 1985.

Forrestal, James. *The Forrestal Diaries*. Edited by Walter Millis. New York: Viking Press, 1951.

Griffis, Stanton. *Lying in State*. Garden City: Doubleday and Co., Inc., 1952.

Korbonski, Stefan. *Warsaw in Exile*. New York: Frederick Praeger, 1966.

Lane, Arthur Bliss. *I Saw Poland Betrayed*. Indianapolis: The Bobbs-Merrill Co., 1948.

Różański, Henryk. *Śladem wspomnień i dokumentów, 1943-1948* [Tracing remembrances and documents, 1943-1948]. Warsaw: Państwowe Wydawnictwo Naukowe, 1987.

Winiewicz, Józef. *Co pamiętam z długiej drogi życia* [What I remember from the long trail of life]. Poznan: Wydawnictwo Poznańskie, 1985.

BOOKS

Adler-Karlsson, Gunnar. *Western Economic Warfare, 1947-1967: A Case Study in Foreign Economic Policy*. Uppsala: Almquist and Wiksells, 1968.

Alton, Thad Paul. *Polish Postwar Economy*. New York: Columbia University Press, 1955.

Ambrose, Stephen E. *Rise to Globalism: American Foreign Policy 1938-1976*. New York: Penguin Books, 1976.

Arkes, Hadley. *Bureaucracy, the Marshall Plan, and the National Interest*. Princeton: Princeton University Press, 1972.

Ayubi, Saheen, etal. *Economic Sanctions in U.S. Foreign Policy*. Philadelphia: Foreign Policy Research Institute, 1982.

Baldwin, David A. *Economic Development and American Foreign Policy, 1943-1962*. Chicago: The University of Chicago Press, 1966.

Boll, Michael M. *The Cold War in the Balkans: American Foreign Policy and the Emergence of Communist Bulgaria 1943-1947*. Louisville: The University of Kentucky Press, 1984.

Campbell, John C. *American Policy Toward Communist Eastern Europe: The Choices Ahead*. Minneapolis, Minnesota: University of Minnesota, 1965.

Daniel, Ute. *Dollardiplomatie in Europa: Marshallplan, Kalter Krieg und U.S. Aussenwirtschaftspolitik, 1945-1952* [Dollar diplomacy in Europe: The marshall plan, the cold war and U.S. foreign economic policy]. Düsseldorf: Droste Verlag, 1982.

Davies, Norman. *God's Playground: A History of Poland*. Vol. 2, *1795 to the Present*. New York: Columbia University Press, 1982.

Davis, Lynn E. *The Cold War Begins: Soviet-American Conflict over Eastern Europe*. Princeton: Princeton University Press, 1974.

DeSantis, Hugh. *The Diplomacy of Silence: The American Foreign Service, the Soviet Union, and the Cold War, 1933-1947*. Chicago: The University of Chicago Press, 1980.

Długosz, Stanisław and Wiesław Szczepaniec. *Stosunki handlowe Polski z rozwiniętymi krajami kapitalistycznymi* [Poland's trade relations with developed capitalist countries]. Warsaw: Państwowe Wydawnictwo Ekonomiczne, 1974.

Doxey, Margaret P. *Economic Sanctions and International Enforcement*. New York: Oxford University Press, 1980.

Dudek, Wiesław. *Międzynarodowe aspekty nacjonalizacji w Polsce* [International aspects of nationalization in Poland]. Warsaw: Państwowe Wydawnictwo Narodowe, 1976.

Ferrell, Robert H., gen. ed. *The American Secretaries of State and Their Diplomacy*. Vol. 16, *Dean Acheson*, by Gaddis Smith. New York: Cooper Square Publishers, Inc., 1972.

Gaddis, John L. *Strategies of Containment: A Critical Appraisal of Postwar American National Security Policy*. Oxford: Oxford University Press, 1982.

Gajda, Eugeniusz. *Polska Polityka Zagraniczna, 1944-1971: Podstawowe Problemy* [Polish foreign policy, 1944-1971: basic problems]. Warsaw: Wydawnictwo Ministerstwa Obrony Narodowej, 1972.

Gardner, Lloyd C. *Economic Aspects of New Deal Diplomacy*. Madison: University of Wisconsin Press, 1964.

Graebner, Norman. *America as a World Power*. Wilmington, Delaware: Scholarly Resources, Inc., 1984.

Herring, George C. Jr. *Aid to Russia, 1941-1946: Strategy, Diplomacy, and the Origins of the Cold War*. New York: Columbia University Press, 1973.

Hiscocks, Richard. *Poland: Bridge for the Abyss? An Interpretation of Developments in Post-War Poland*. London: Oxford University Press, 1963.

Hogan, Michael J. *The Marshall Plan: America, Britain, and the Reconstruction of Western Europe, 1947-1952*. Cambridge: Cambridge University Press, 1987.

Horowitz, David. *The Free World Colossus: A Critique of American Foreign Policy in the Cold War*. New York: MacGibbon and Kee, 1965.

Jurasz, Witold. *Wpływ zagranicznej polityki ekonomicznej USA na rozwój polskiego eksportu do Stanów Zjednoczonych w latach 1946-1947* [The effect of U.S. foreign economic policy on the development of Polish export to the United States in the years 1946-1947]. Warsaw: Polish Institute of Foreign Affairs, 1971.

Kalinski, Janusz. *Plan Odbudowy Gospodarczej, 1947-1949* [The economic plan of reconstruction, 1947-1949]. Warsaw: Książka i Wiedza, 1975.

Kalinski, Janusz. *Polityka Gospodarcza Polski w latach 1948-1956* [The economic policy of Poland, 1948-1956]. Warsaw: Książka i Wiedza, 1987.

Kersten, Krystyna. *Narodziny Systemu Władzy Polska, 1943-1948* [The origins of the system of government in Poland, 1943-1948]. Warsaw: Wydawnictwo Krag, 1985.

Kiesewetter, Bruno. *Der Ostblock: Aussenhandel des östlichen Wirtschaftsblockes einschliesslich China* [The Eastern bloc: foreign trade of the eastern economic bloc including China]. Berlin: Safari Verlag, 1960.

Kolko, Joyce and Gabriel. *The Limits of Power: The World and United States Foreign Policy, 1945-1954*. New York: Harper and Row Publishers, 1972.

Kovrig, Bennett. *The Myth of Liberation: East-Central Europe in U.S. Diplomacy and Politics since 1941*. Baltimore: Johns Hopkins University Press, 1973.

Krynicki, Józef. *Problemy Handlu Zagranicznego Polski, 1918-1939, 1945-1955* [Problems of Polish foreign trade, 1918-1939, 1945-1955]. Warsaw: Państwowe Wydawnictwo Naukowe, 1958.

Losman, Donald L. *International Economic Sanctions*. Albuquerque: University of New Mexico Press, 1979.

Lukas, Richard C. *Bitter Legacy: Polish-American Relations in the Wake of World War II*. Lexington: The University of Kentucky Press, 1982.

Lundestad, Geir. *The American Non-Policy Towards Eastern Europe 1943-1947: Universalism in an Area not of Essential Interest to the United States*. Oslo: Universitetsforlaget, 1975.

Mee, Charles L. Jr. *The Marshall Plan: The Launching of Pax Americana*. New York: Simon and Schuster, 1984.

Messer, Robert L. *The End of an Alliance: James F. Byrnes, Roosevelt, Truman, and the Origins of the Cold War*. Chapel Hill, Maryland: University of North Carolina Press, 1982.

Milward, Alan. *The Reconstruction of Western Europe, 1945-1951*. Berkeley: University of California Press, 1987.

Modzelewski, Zygmunt. *Polityka Zagraniczna Polski: Artykuły i Przemówienia* [Polish foreign policy: articles and speeches]. Warsaw: Państwowe Wydawnictwo Naukowe, 1960.

Montias, John Michael. *Central Planning in Poland*. New Haven: Yale University Press, 1962.

Pastusiak, Longin. *Roosevelt i sprawa Polska* [Roosevelt and the Polish question]. Warsaw: Książka i Wiedza, 1980.

Paterson, Thomas G. *On Every Front: The Making of the Cold War*. New York: W.W. Norton and Co., 1979.

Paterson, Thomas G. *Soviet-American Confrontation: Postwar Reconstruction and the Origins of the Cold War*. Baltimore: Johns Hopkins University Press, 1973.

Pisar, Samuel. *Coexistence and Commerce: Guidelines for Transactions Between East and West*. New York: McGraw-Hill Book Co., 1970.

Polaczek, Stanisław. *Integracja gospodarcza krajów socjalistycznych a handel zagraniczy Polski* [The economic integration of the socialist countries and the foreign trade of Poland]. Warsaw: Państwowe Wydawnictwo Ekonomiczne, 1971.

Pollard, Robert A. *Economic Security and the Origins of the Cold War, 1945-1950*. New York: Columbia University Press, 1985.

Rakowski, Mieczysław. *The Foreign Policy of the Polish Peoples' Republic*. Warsaw: Interpress Publishers, 1975.

Ripka, Hubert. *Czechoslovakia Enslaved: The Story of the Communist Coup d'Etat*. London: Victor Gollancz, Ltd., 1950.

Rose, Lisle A. *After Yalta*. New York: Charles Schribner's Sons, 1973.

Sokolowski, Mieczysław. *Obroty zagraniczne Polski w okresie 1945-1958* [Foreign commerce of Poland in the period 1945 to 1958]. London: Szkoła Nauk Politycznych i Społecznych, 1960.

Spulber, Nicolas. *The Economics of Communist Eastern Europe*. Boston: MIT Press, 1957.

Taylor, J. *The Economic Development of Poland, 1919-1950*. Ithaca: Cornell University Press, 1952.

Torańska, Teresa. *Oni* [Them]. Cracow: Krakowskie Towarzystwo Wydawnicze, 1986.

Wandycz, Piotr. *The United States and Poland*. Cambridge: Harvard University Press, 1980.

Westerfield, H. Bradford. *The Instruments of America's Foreign Policy*. New York: Thomas Crowell Co., 1963.

Wexler, Imanuel. *The Marshall Plan Revisited: The European Recovery Program in Economic Perspective.* Westport, Connecticut: Greenwood Press, 1983.

White, Gillian. *Nationalization of Foreign Property.* New York: Frederick Praeger, 1961.

Wilczynski, J. *The Economics and Politics of East-West Trade: A Study of Trade Between Developed Market Economies and Centrally Planned Economies in a Changing World.* London: MacMillan, 1969.

Wolf, Thomas A. *U.S. East-West Trade Policy: Economic Warfare Versus Economic Welfare.* Lexington, Massachusetts: D.C. Heath and Co., 1973.

Zyblikiewicz, Lubomir. *Polityka Stanów Zjednoczonych i Wielkiej Brytanii wobec Polski, 1944-1949* [The policy of the United States and Great Britain toward Poland, 1944-1949]. Warsaw: Książka i Wiedza, 1984.

DOCTORAL DISSERTATIONS

Cable, John N. "The United States and the Polish Question, 1939-1948." Ph.D. dissertation. Vanderbilt University, 1972.

Glinka-Janczewski, George H. "American Policy Toward Poland Under the Truman Administration, 1945-1952." Ph.D. dissertation, Georgetown University, 1966.

Pryor, Frederick. "The Foreign Trade System of the European Communist Nations." Ph.D. dissertation, Yale University, 1961.

Sekular, Mark. "Stosunki gospodarcze między Polska i Stanami Zjednoczonymy Ameryki po II wojnie światowej" [Economic relations between Poland and the United States after the second world war]. Praca Magisterska. Central School of Planning and Statistics, Warsaw, 1977.

ARTICLES

Berman, Jakub. "In the Struggle for the Peaceful Development of Postwar Europe." *Nowe Drogi* [New paths] 2 (March 1948): 7-16.

Bernstein, Barton J. "Commentary." In *The Truman Period as a Research Field: A Reappraisal, 1972*, ed. Richard S. Kirkendall, 161-190. Columbia, Missouri: University of Missouri Press, 1974.

Brzezinski, Zbigniew. "How the Cold War Was Played." *Foreign Affairs* 51 (October 1972): 181-209.

Byrnes, Robert F. "Containment? Liberation? Coexistence? American Policy Toward East Central Europe, 1947-1955." In *The Fate of East Central Europe: Hope and Failures of American Foreign Policy*, ed. Stephen D. Kertesz, 75-102. South Bend: University of Notre Dame Press, 1956.

Cable, John N. "Arthur Bliss Lane: Cold Warrior in Warsaw, 1945-1947." *Polish American Studies* 30 (Autumn 1973): 66-82.

Campbell, John C. "American Policy Towards the Satellites and National Communism." In *American Diplomacy in a New Era*, ed. Stephen D. Kertesz, 297-323. South Bend, Indiana: University of Notre Dame Press, 1961.

Ciepielewski, Jerzy. "Współpraca Gospodarcza Polski z Europejskim Krajami Socjalistycznymi" [Economic cooperation of Poland with the socialist countries of Europe]. In *Gospodarka Polski Ludowej, 1944-1955* [The economy of Peoples' Poland, 1944-1955], eds. Janusz Kalinski and Zbigniew Landau, 420-428. Warsaw: Książka i Wiedza, 1986.

Daoudi, M.S. and M.S. Dajani. "Poland: The Politactics of Sanctions." *Polish Review* 30 (No. 2 1985): 149-166.

Gaddis, John L. "The Emerging Post-Revisionist Synthesis on the Origins of the Cold War." *Diplomatic History* 7 (Summer 1983): 171-190.

Gardner, Lloyd C. "Rejoinder." In *The Origins of the Cold War*, eds. Lloyd C. Gardner, Arthur M. Schlesinger, Jr., and Hans J. Morganthau, 108-111. Waltham, Massachusetts, 1970.

Gardner, Lloyd C. "Will the Real Mr.'X' Please Stand Up?" In *Containment and the Cold War: American Foreign Policy Since 1945*, ed. Thomas G. Paterson, 85-95. Reading, Massachusetts: Addison-Wesley Publishing Co., 1973.

Haberter, Gottfried. "Economic Consequences of a Divided World." In *The Fate of East Central Europe: Hope and Failures of American Foreign Policy*, ed. Stephen D. Kertesz, 377-395. South Bend: University of Notre Dame Press, 1956.

Hathaway, Robert M. "1933-1945: Economic Diplomacy in a Time of Crisis." In *Economics and World Power: An Assessment of American Diplomacy Since 1789*, eds. William H. Becker and Samuel F. Wells, Jr., 277-332. New York: Columbia University Press, 1984.

Kalinski, Janusz, "Planowanie Gospodarcze" [Economic planning]. In *Gospodarka Polski Ludowej, 1944-1955* [The economy of Peoples' Poland, 1944-1955], eds. Janusz Kalinski and Zbigniew Landau, 144-167. Warsaw: Książka i Wiedza, 1986.

Kalinski, Janusz. "Zmiana Dekoracji." *Przegląd Tygodniowy* [Weekly review] 7 (1988): 1.

Kowalski, Włodzimierz. "Poland and the Western Powers 1945-1947." *Polish Western Affairs* 8 (No. 1 1967): 33-62.

Lundestad, Geir. "The American Policy Towards Poland 1943-1946," *American Studies in Scandinavia* 8 (Winter 1972): 5-28.

Mark, Eduard. "American Policy toward Eastern Europe and the Origins of the Cold War, 1941-1946: An Alternative Interpretation." *Journal of American History* 68 (September 1981): 313-336.

Morganthau, Hans J. "The Containment Policy and the Rationale of the Alliance System." In *American Diplomacy in a New Era*, ed. Stephen D. Kertesz, 63-82. South Bend, Indiana: University of Notre Dame Press, 1961.

Pollard, Robert A. and Samuel F. Wells, Jr. "1945-1960: The Era of American Economic Hegemony." In *Economics and World Power: An Assessment of American Diplomacy since 1789*, eds. William H. Becker and Samuel F. Wells, Jr., 333-390. New York: Columbia University Press, 1984.

Rachwald, Arthur R. "Poland Between the Superpowers: Three Decades of Foreign Policy." *Orbis* 20 (Winter 1977): 1055-1083.

Skowronski, Andrzej. "Security and Cooperative Policy: The Origins." *Polish Perspectives* 21 (December 1978): 15-21.

Spulber, Nicholas. "Problems of East-West Trade and Economic Trends in the European Satellites of Soviet Russia." In *The Fate of East Central Europe: Hope and Failures of American Foreign Policy*, ed. Stephen D. Kertesz, 396-424. South Bend: University of Notre Dame Press, 1956.

Thackrah, J. R. "Poland: Internal Developments and Effects on Anglo-American Relations, 1945-1947." *East European Quarterly* 20 (September 1986): 273-283.

Thompson, S. Harrison. "The New Poland." *Foreign Policy Reports* 23 (1 December 1947): 226-236.

Vancura, Georg. "Die Entwicklung nach dem Ende des Weltkrieges," [The development after the end of the world war] *Schweizerische Zeitschrift für Geschichte* [Swiss journal of history] 29 (No. 2 1979): 446-453.

Wojciechowski, Bronisław. "Handel Zagraniczny Polski" [The foreign trade of Poland]. In *Gospodarka Polski Ludowej, 1944-1955* [The economy of Peoples' Poland], eds. Janusz Kalinski and Zbigniew Landau, 366-397. Warsaw: Książka i Wiedza, 1986.

NEWSPAPERS AND JOURNALS

Głos Ludu [Voice of the people].
New York Times.
Przegląd Socjalistyczny [Socialist review].
Rzeczpospolita [The republic].
Trybuna Ludu [Tribune of the people].
Tygodnik Warszawski [Warsaw weekly].
Zbiór Dokumentów [Collection of documents].
Życie Gospodarcze [Economic life].
Życie Warszawy [Warsaw life].

Index